THE MESSAGE OF THE BIBLE
An Orthodox Christian Perspective

The Message of the Bible

An Orthodox Christian Perspective

by

GEORGE CRONK

CULTURAL COMM. OF ST. MARY'S
UKRAINIAN ORTHODOX CHURCH
54 WINTER ST.
NEW BRITAIN, CT 06051

ST. VLADIMIR'S SEMINARY PRESS
CRESTWOOD, NEW YORK 10707
1982

ACC. # 100

Library of Congress Cataloging in Publication Data

Cronk, George, 1939-
   The message of the Bible.

   Bibliography: p.
   1. Bible—Introductions. 2. Bible—Criticism,
   interpretation, etc. 3. Orthodox Eastern Church—
   Doctrinal and controversial works. I. Title.
BS475.C76   1982   220.6'1   82-7355
ISBN 0-913836-94-X

© Copyright 1982

by

ST. VLADIMIR'S SEMINARY PRESS

ALL RIGHTS RESERVED

ISBN 0-913836-94-X

PRINTED IN THE UNITED STATES OF AMERICA
BY
ATHENS PRINTING COMPANY
NEW YORK, N. Y.

For my wife, Anita,
and for my daughters,
Amanda, Alexandra, and Anita Julianna.

Contents

Preface

This book constitutes an introduction to the study of the Holy Bible in the light of the teachings of the historic Orthodox Church. It is intended for those who are generally familiar with the content of the Bible, but it is not a work of original scholarship written for experts in the field of biblical studies. In my analysis of the major themes of the Old and New Testaments, I have attempted to present clearly the central insights of Orthodox biblical theology and to suggest ways in which the message of the Bible is relevant to the contemporary problems and concerns of Orthodox Christians and of humanity in general. I have also taken into account the research which has been done during the past two centuries by modern biblical scholars. My major purpose throughout has been to "translate" and summarize the work of the scholars and theologians for the benefit of non-expert readers and students of Holy Scripture.

I would like to thank Fr. Paul Kucynda, pastor of the Orthodox Church of the Holy Resurrection in Wayne, New Jersey; Fr. Thomas Hopko, Assistant Professor of Dogmatic Theology at St. Vladimir's Orthodox Theological Seminary in Crestwood, New York; and Fr. Ted Bobosh, of the Department of Religious Education of the Orthodox Church in America, for encouraging me to write this book. I also owe my thanks to Paul Kachur of St. Vladimir's Seminary Press, whose able editorial assistance in the preparation of the final manuscript was indispensable. And, above all, my gratitude goes to my wife, Anita Loretta Cronk, without whose patience and love this volume would never have seen the light of day.

List of Abbreviations

OLD TESTAMENT

Genesis	Gn	Proverbs	Pr
Exodus	Ex	Ecclesiastes	Ec
Leviticus	Lv	Song of Solomon	Sg
Numbers	Nb	Wisdom of Solomon	Ws
Deuteronomy	Dt	Ecclesiasticus	Si
Joshua	Jos	Isaiah	Is
Judges	Jg	Jeremiah	Jr
Ruth	Rt	Lamentations	Lm
1 Samuel	1 Sm	Letter of Jeremiah	Lt Jr
2 Samuel	2 Sm	Baruch	Ba
1 Kings	1 Kg	Ezekiel	Ezk
2 Kings	2 Kg	Daniel	Dn
1 Chronicles	1 Ch	Hosea	Ho
2 Chronicles	2 Ch	Joel	Jl
1 Esdras	1 Esd	Amos	Am
Ezra	Ezr	Obadiah	Ob
Nehemiah	Ne	Jonah	Jon
Esther	Est	Micah	Mi
Judith	Jdt	Nahum	Na
Tobit	Tb	Habakkuk	Hab
1 Maccabees	1 Mc	Zephaniah	Zp
2 Maccabees	2 Mc	Haggai	Hg
3 Maccabees	3 Mc	Zechariah	Zc
Job	Jb	Malachi	Ml
Psalms	Ps		

NEW TESTAMENT

Matthew	Mt	1 Timothy	1 Tm
Mark	Mk	2 Timothy	2 Tm
Luke	Lk	Titus	Tt
John	Jn	Philemon	Phm
Acts	Ac	Hebrews	Heb
Romans	Rm	James	Jm
1 Corinthians	1 Co	1 Peter	1 Pt
2 Corinthians	2 Co	2 Peter	2 Pt
Galatians	Ga	1 John	1 Jn
Ephesians	Eph	2 John	2 Jn
Philippians	Ph	3 John	3 Jn
Colossians	Col	Jude	Jude
1 Thessalonians	1 Th	Revelation	Rv
2 Thessalonians	2 Th		

*All biblical quotes, unless otherwise noted, are
from the Revised Standard Version.*

CHAPTER 1

An Orthodox Christian Approach to the Study of the Bible

There are at least five reasons why Orthodox Christians should read and study the Holy Bible. First, according to Christian tradition, the Bible is the divinely inspired and thus authentic record of God's revelation of himself and of his will to mankind. Correctly understood, it is a primary source of truth concerning the nature of God, the condition of man and the overall purpose of the universe. Those who seek such truth must therefore have recourse to the witness of Holy Scripture.

Second, as an inspired record of divine revelation, the Bible is God's Word to mankind concerning himself and his kingdom. And that Word is addressed especially to those who are members of the Church, who are called to listen to it, heed it, take it to heart and respond to it in faith and obedience.

Third, the Orthodox Church teaches that the Bible is a verbal icon of God himself. Just as the persons and events depicted in painted icons are "really present" in and through their physical representations, so God is "really present" in and through the physical representation of his written Word. Through reading and studying Holy Scripture, through praying over it and meditating upon it, it is possible to make contact with, and commune with, God himself. Through the diligent and prayerful study of and meditation upon the Bible one can both "touch" and "be touched by" the eternal, undivided and life-creating Trinity.

Fourth, the liturgical life of the Orthodox Church is grounded in and expressive of Holy Scripture. It has been estimated that in the Divine Liturgy alone, and without counting readings from the epistles and gospels or the recitation of the Lord's Prayer, there are "98 quotations from the Old Testament and 114 from the New."[1] And in all Orthodox services throughout the year, the Bible is read almost constantly. It follows that one's understanding of and participation in the liturgies and services of the Church will be both deepened and intensified to the extent that one makes himself familiar with the contents of God's written Word.

Fifth, and finally, the Bible is a major expression of the holy tradition of the Orthodox Church. According to Fr. Kallistos Ware, "the Orthodox Christian of today sees himself as heir and guardian to a great inheritance received from the past, and he believes that it is his duty to transmit that inheritance unimpaired to the future."[2] But in order to perform this duty, Orthodox Christians will have to overcome a number of rather formidable obstacles. Faced with the secularized culture of the contemporary world, Orthodox Christianity must learn to dwell in the presence of, and frequently in competition with, a multitude of non-Orthodox philosophical and religious movements and organizations. Many Orthodox Christians are, in fact, tempted to depart from the Orthodox Church in response to the often quite attractive and effective enticements of these philosophies and religions. For far too many of today's Orthodox Christians, holy tradition has ceased to be a *living* and *life-sustaining* tradition. Cut off from his theological roots by political forces, by radical cultural change and by his own failure to live in the light and truth of God, the modern Orthodox Christian must make every effort to comprehend the doctrinal and liturgical foundations of his tradition and to express that comprehension in a *living* faith. Only then will he be able to perform his duty of preserving and passing on "the whole system of doctrine, Church government, worship, and art which Orthodoxy has articulated over the ages."[3] In seeking to carry out this task, it will be necessary to construct a specifically Orthodox critique of the predominantly secular, non-Orthodox and even anti-Christian beliefs and values of the present age. And an important part of this overall project will be the serious study of the content and meaning of Holy Scripture and the development of a world perspective that is grounded in and expressive of what Fr. Georges Florovsky has called "the scriptural mind."[4]

For these (and other) reasons, then, Orthodox Christians should make the reading and study of Holy Scripture a central concern of their lives. The Bible is, of course, a very large and complex collection of documents; and it is possible for the beginning Bible reader to get lost in the details of the sacred texts. What is important, as one seeks to develop a "scriptural mind," is to strive for a sense of the overall message of God's written Word, "a grasp of the Scriptures in their totality."[5] It is, in fact, the major purpose of this book to present a coherent survey of the central themes of the Holy Bible, and to outline, from the standpoint of Orthodox biblical theology, the general message of God's scriptural revelation.

The Books of the Holy Bible

The Bible contains two major parts: the Old Testament and the New Testament. From the standpoint of historic Christianity, the Bible is the book of salvation, a primary revelation of the manner in which God has acted and is acting to deliver humankind from the forces of evil. Man was intended to live in eternal fellowship with God, but has instead rebelled against his Creator. Having alienated himself from God, man has cut himself off from that spiritual wisdom, that moral and spiritual perfection and that eternal life which God originally intended him to enjoy. As a result of this self-induced alienation from God, man is lost and in bondage to the world, the flesh and the devil. But God has acted, in and through the person and work of Jesus Christ, to save man from his alienated condition. And God has revealed himself, his will and his plan for the salvation of the human race to the patriarchs and prophets of ancient Israel and to the apostles of Jesus—not in writing, but by way of direct revelation. The Bible is the written record of that original and unwritten revelation. The Old Testament tells the story of God's dealings with ancient Israel from approximately 2000 B.C. until the time of Jesus; and it contains, as its central message, God's promise to save mankind and the world through the "anointed one" (Messiah, Christ) of

Israel. And the New Testament proclaims Jesus of Nazareth to be the promised Christ, who has, through his life and deeds, fulfilled the divine plan of salvation and made it possible for man to be reconciled to God.

The text of the Old Testament, which was originally composed in Hebrew (and partly in Aramaic), has been historically transmitted in both a Hebrew and a Greek version. (Ancient Latin versions have also survived, but these are translations from either the Greek or the Hebrew texts.) These two versions (the Hebrew and the Greek) reflect a dispute among the Jews of the late pre-Christian and early Christian periods concerning the precise content and meaning of their Sacred Scriptures. One major element in that dispute had to do with the total number of books that should be regarded as divinely inspired and thus authoritative. Some Jews held to a "longer" canon of forty-nine books (the Greek word *kanon* means "standard" and has come to be used in the sense of "authoritative text"), while others adhered to a "shorter" canon containing thirty-nine books. Those who favored the shorter canon also thought that some portions of a few of the thirty-nine books should be deleted from Sacred Scripture (for example, certain parts of the books of Esther and Daniel). By the end of the first century A.D., the advocates of the shorter canon had won out, and the Hebrew version of the Old Testament, which has been passed down to the present day, thus contains only thirty-nine books. Among the Jews, this version is known as the Hebrew Bible.

The longer canon of the Old Testament has been preserved in the Greek version, which was produced between the third and first centuries B.C., and which has survived mainly because of its importance in the formation and transmission of the Christian biblical heritage. According to an ancient tradition, the Greek version had its beginning in Egypt during the reign of Ptolemy II Philadelphus (285-246 B.C). King Ptolemy wanted a copy of the *Pentateuch* ("the five scrolls," the first five books of the Hebrew Bible) for the famous library in Alexandria; and, under his sponsorship, seventy-two Jewish scholars, working for seventy-two days, produced a Greek translation of the Pentateuch from ancient Hebrew manuscripts. On the basis of this traditional story, the number "seventy-two" was rounded to "seventy," and the Greek Old Testament became known as the *Septuagint* (or *LXX—septuaginta* means "seventy" in Latin). By the middle of the first century B.C., forty-four additional books had been appended to the Septuagint. The Greek Old Testament, therefore, contains the shorter canon of the Jewish scriptures as well as other texts not included in the Hebrew Bible.

The Septuagint was the text most often quoted by the writers of the New Testament, and it was the version of the Old Testament most widely used in the early Christian community. For these reasons, the Orthodox Church has always regarded the Septuagint, rather than the Hebrew Bible, as the authoritative version of the Old Testament. In those (many) places where the wording of the Septuagint differs from that of the Hebrew Bible, the Orthodox Church holds that the Greek rendering is to be accepted as divinely inspired.[6] The Church is here following the practice of the New Testament writers themselves. For example, the Hebrew text of Isaiah 7:14 reads, "a *young woman [almah]* shall conceive and bear a son," while the rendering of the Greek text is, "a *virgin [parthenos]* shall conceive and bear a son." This Old Testament verse refers, of course, to the birth of the Messiah. And faced with the significant contrast between the Hebrew and Greek renderings of this verse, the New Testament follows the phrasing of the Greek text (see Mt 1:23).

The Greek Old Testament, then, is a collection of forty-nine books. This collection is subdivided into four sections. First, there are the "books of the law," or Pentateuch: Genesis, Exodus, Leviticus, Numbers and Deuteronomy. These books describe God's creation of the world, the original rebellion and fall of man and the history of God's chosen people, Israel, from the time of Abraham (c. 2000 B.C.) to the time of Moses (c. 1290-1250 B.C.). This material was compiled in written form between the tenth and fifth centuries B.C. Because so much of the Pentateuch is concerned with the revelation of the divine law to God's people, the Jews called this section of Holy Scripture the *Torah,* which is Hebrew for "law."

The second part is the "books of history": Joshua, Judges, Ruth, 1 and 2 Samuel, 1 and 2 Kings, 1 and 2 Chronicles, 1 Esdras, Ezra, Nehemiah, Esther, Judith, Tobit and 1, 2 and 3 Maccabees. Two other works associated with the Old Testament historical books are 2 Esdras, which was never a part of the Greek Old Testament, and 4 Maccabees, which is included in some ancient copies of the Septuagint. Neither of these books, however, is regarded as canonical by the Orthodox Church. The Old Testament books of history, which were written between the twelfth century B.C. and the first century A.D., trace the life of ancient Israel from the thirteenth century B.C. to the time of Christ.

Third, we have the "books of wisdom": Job, Psalms, Proverbs, Ecclesiastes, the Song of Solomon, the Wisdom of Solomon and Ecclesiasticus (or the Wisdom of Jesus ben Sirach). The Old Testament wisdom literature contains poetic, philosophical and theological discourses which argue that happiness is possible only through faith in and obedience to God. The books of wisdom were composed between the eleventh and first centuries B.C.

Finally, there are the "books of the prophets": Isaiah, Jeremiah, Lamentations, the Letter of Jeremiah, Baruch, Ezekiel, Daniel, Hosea, Joel, Amos, Obadiah, Jonah, Micah, Nahum, Habakkuk, Zephaniah, Haggai, Zechariah and Malachi. Most of these nineteen books were written between the eighth and the fourth centuries B.C.; but the books of Daniel and Baruch may have been composed as late as the second century B.C. The central theme of Old Testament prophecy is the coming of the Messiah and of the kingdom of God.

The materials in the Septuagint which are not contained in the Hebrew Bible are as follows: 1 Esdras, Judith, Tobit, 1, 2 and 3 Maccabees, the Wisdom of Solomon, Ecclesiasticus, the Letter of Jeremiah; Baruch, Psalm 151, the Prayer of Manasseh (from 2 Chronicles) and certain portions of Esther and Daniel. The canonicity of these materials was sometimes doubted even in the early Church, and has been disputed by many later Christian scholars. It is noteworthy, for example, that while there are many quotations from the Septuagint in the New Testament, none of these quotations are taken from the disputed portions of the longer canon. But it must also be noted that many of the early Church fathers considered the entire Greek Old Testament to be divinely inspired. In the course of time, therefore, the Orthodox Church has come to accept the disputed texts of the Septuagint as "deuterocanonical," that is, canonical in a secondary sense and standing "on a lower footing than the rest of the Old Testament."[7]

The Roman Catholic Church is in basic agreement with the Orthodox point of view on this matter, but does not accept 1 Esdras, 3 Maccabees, Psalm 151 or the Prayer of Manasseh as possessing even "deuterocanonical" authority; these latter texts are therefore excluded from Roman Catholic editions of the Old Testament. The Protestant churches have accepted the Hebrew Bible as the authoritative version of the Old Testament. Among Protestants, the disputed materials of the Greek Old Testament are known as the Apocrypha, the term "apocryphal" being used in the sense of "noncanonical." In some Protestant editions of the Bible, the Apocrypha are placed in a separate section between the Old and New Testaments or at the end of the New Testament; and in many Protestant editions, the "apocryphal" texts are not included at all.

While differing on the exact content of the Old Testament, Protestant, Roman Catholic and Orthodox Christians are agreed on the number and sequence of the twenty-seven books that make up the New Testament. All of the books in the New Testament were written in Greek between 50 and 100 A.D., either by apostles of Christ (Matthew, John, Peter and Paul), or by close and faithful associates of the apostles (Mark, Luke, James and Jude), and they contain eyewitness testimonies and theological interpretations concerning the person and work of Jesus Christ. As indicated earlier, the overall message of the New Testament is that through faith in Christ man can be reconciled to God and thus saved from the powers of ignorance, sin and death.

By the middle of the second century A.D., a great deal of writing about Jesus had been done. Since some of this literature was fanciful and unreliable, the Church, seeking to preserve the apostolic message of salvation through Christ, found it necessary to distinguish clearly between those writings which did and those writings which did not possess apostolic authority. And, on this basis, the New Testament canon as it is known today came into being. There were debates in the early Church concerning the canonicity of the book of Revelation, the letter to the Hebrews and the epistles of James, Peter, John and Jude. But by the fifth century, all of these books—along with the four gospels, the book of Acts and the letters of St. Paul—had been accepted by the Church as apostolic in origin, divinely inspired and thus canonical.

The New Testament canon of twenty-seven books contains four types of documents. The New Testament begins with the four gospels of St. Matthew, St. Mark, St. Luke and St. John. The gospels recount the major events in the life of Christ and proclaim the "good news" of salvation through Christ. Scholars have dated the writing of the gospels as follows: St. Mark, c. 65 A.D.; St. Matthew and St. Luke, c. 70 A.D.; and St. John, c. 85-90 A.D. Secondly, the Acts of the Apostles (or the book of Acts), written c. 70 A.D. by St. Luke, is a history of the foundation and growth of the first-century Church. It surveys the development of the Church from the ascension of Christ (c. 30 A.D.), through the missionary travels of St. Paul (c. 47-56 A.D.), to the first imprisonment of St. Paul in Rome (c. 59-61 A.D.). The third group is the letters (or epistles). There are twenty-one letters contained in the New Testament. Fourteen of these have been traditionally attributed to St. Paul: Romans, 1 and 2 Corinthians, Galatians, Ephesians, Philippians, Colossians, 1 and 2 Thessalonians, 1 and 2 Timothy, Titus, Philemon and Hebrews. The remaining seven letters—James, 1 and 2 Peter, 1, 2 and 3 John and Jude—are known as the "catholic epistles" because they are addressed not to local churches (for example, the Roman or the Galatian) or to individuals (such as Timothy or Titus) but to the whole (that is, universal or "catholic") Christian community. The letters of St. Paul were written between 50 and 67 A.D., and the catholic epistles were composed between 60 and 100 A.D. The New Testament letters contain expositions of the moral and doctrinal implications of the Christian faith. The authors of these letters (Paul, James, Peter, John and Jude) were seeking to maintain good order and orthodoxy of belief in the many Christian communities which had sprung up in the Mediterranean world by the middle of the first century A.D. Finally, we have the book of Revelation (or the Apocalypse). The term "apocalyptic" is used to characterize prophecies which point toward the end of time; and the New Testament apocalypse is such an "end-time" prophecy. Written in highly symbolic language, the book describes a vision of the second coming of Christ, the last judgment and the final establishment of the kingdom of God. This visionary book was written during the last decade of the first century A.D., and has been traditionally viewed as the work of St. John the apostle.

Although the Bible, as we have seen, contains two "testaments," the historic Christian Church has always stressed the basic unity of the biblical revelation. The Old and New Testaments are unified in that they were both written under the inspiration of the Holy Spirit, they both contain the same central theme and message concerning God's plan for the salvation of the human race and they both point in the same direction—the coming of the kingdom of God. The Bible, then, contains one revelation in two dispensations. And the key to the unity of Holy Scripture is Jesus Christ. He is the central figure in the divine plan of salvation revealed in God's written Word. From the Christian point of view, the Old Testament is a promise of, and a preparation for, the coming of the Messiah, of the Christ through whom the salvation of mankind will be effected; and in its proclamation of Jesus of Nazareth as the Christ, the New Testament affirms the fulfilment of the Old Testament message of salvation: in and through Jesus Christ, God has saved mankind and the world.

The Inspiration and Infallibility of the Bible

The Bible, as we have seen, is a book of books, a collection or library of sacred writings. The books contained in Holy Scripture were written, edited and compiled at various times, in various places and by various authors; but the Orthodox Church regards this collection of writings as an authentic and authoritative (that is, "canonical") revelation of truth concerning the relationships between God, man and the universe. The Bible is the written Word of God, "the supreme expression of God's revelation to man."[8]

The books of the Bible were written by men—that is, by Old and New Testament saints—who were guided in their writing by divine inspiration. From the standpoint of the Orthodox Church, "the entire Bible is inspired by God," and this means that it "contains no formal errors or inner contradictions concerning the relationship between God and the world."[9] The overall message of the Bible, that mankind has fallen under satanic bondage and that God has graciously acted in and through Christ to save us from that bondage, is infallibly true. According to the Orthodox doctrine of infallibility, the Church as a whole is the guardian of "the eternal spiritual and doctrinal message of God"[10] and is protected from error by the Holy Spirit. The Bible, therefore, as a testimony and proclamation of the Church concerning God's revealed plan of salvation, is without error in its central theological themes and affirmations.

It is not necessary, however, for the Orthodox Christian to insist upon the literal truth of every statement contained in Holy Scripture. Many Orthodox scholars believe that the Bible may contain "incidental inaccuracies of a non-essential character."[11] For example, the author of the book of Daniel describes Belshazzar as the "king" of Babylon and as the son of Nebuchadnezzar (r. 605-562 B.C.); but, in fact, Belshazzar was the son of King Nabonidus (r. 556-539 B.C.), and never became king himself, although he did serve as viceroy during his father's absences (see Dn 5:1-31). For another example, many scholars think that the story of God's creation of the world in the first chapter of Genesis assumes that "the universe [is] enwrapped in waters held back by a solid bell-shaped barrier called the firmament"[12]—and such an assumption is certainly at odds with what modern science has to say about the cosmos. But these kinds of historical and scientific inaccuracies do not undermine the coherence and validity of the essential theological message of Holy Scripture. The Orthodox Church, in affirming the divine inspiration and infallibility of the Holy Bible, does not exclude the possibility that the Bible might contain some minor errors of fact, but she insists upon the absolute truth of scripture's overall message of salvation.

The Interpretation of the Bible: Scripture and Tradition

The Orthodox Church believes herself to be the "One, Holy, Catholic, and Apostolic Church" spoken of in the Nicene Creed, the community of faith founded by Christ through his apostles (see Mt 16:13-20 and 18:15-20; and 1 Pt 2:4-10), the new Israel. Under the administrative and spiritual leadership of her bishops, who stand in the "apostolic succession"—that is, whose office and

authority are derived historically from the apostles of Christ—
the Church regards her own historic life and experience, her "holy
tradition," as a faithful preservation, continuation and development of the apostolic tradition, the spiritual legacy imparted by
Christ to his apostles and handed on by them to later generations
of Christian believers. To be an Orthodox Christian is to accept
the holy tradition of the Orthodox Church as *the* Christian tradition, to see the Orthodox Church as the divinely appointed guardian and teacher of the Christian faith and to live under the
spiritual authority and guidance of the bishops of the Church, the
living successors and representatives of Christ and his apostles.

The Orthodox faith is a living and experiential faith. It is
grounded in the conviction that God has revealed himself and his
plan of salvation to his chosen people of the old and new covenants, to ancient Israel and to the Christian community. Orthodox
Christians believe that God has made himself present and known,
and that he continues to make himself present and known, within
the continuing life and experience of his people—that is, within
the holy tradition of the Church. Holy tradition, then, is the living
and developing expression of the Orthodox faith, of the Church's
ongoing experience of and response to the grace and love of God.
Holy tradition is not merely a collection of written documents,
or a body of doctrinal beliefs, or a set of customary practices. It
is, in the words of Fr. Thomas Hopko, "the total life and experience of the entire Church transferred from place to place and
from generation to generation . . . the very life of the Church as
it is inspired and guided by the Holy Spirit."[13] To live one's life
within the holy tradition of the Church is to experience the reality
and presence of God—Father, Son and Holy Spirit—in the midst
of his people.

Holy tradition has been articulated in a number of outward
forms. Its primary and normative articulation is to be found in
the Bible itself, "the main written source and inspiration of all
that developed in later ages."[14] Other outward elements of holy
tradition are the liturgies and liturgical texts of the Church; the
Nicene Creed; the doctrinal definitions of the seven ecumenical
councils which were held between the fourth and the eighth
centuries; the writings of the fathers of the Church (that is, those
great theologians and spiritual teachers who have explained and

defended the Christian faith through the ages); certain pronouncements of local councils and of individual bishops which
have been accepted by the Church as a whole; the canon laws of
the Church; and the icons and other art forms produced by the
Church in her ongoing effort to give expression to her faith in
God. Through these outward forms of holy tradition, the Orthodox Church has sought to preserve, defend and proclaim the
deposit of faith which has been entrusted to her by Christ and
his apostles.

The Bible, then, is a part of the holy tradition of the Church,
of the Church's living, experiential and faithful response to God.
Scripture and tradition are not two different expressions of the
Christian faith. Holy tradition is the *source* of Holy Scripture;
holy tradition is the faith of which Holy Scripture is an expression. Scripture exists, lives and reveals its meaning within the
tradition of the Church. To separate, isolate and contrast scripture
and tradition "is to impoverish the idea of both alike."[15] The full
meaning of God's written Word can be expounded, therefore, only
from within the historic unfolding and expression of the faith of
the Church, only from the standpoint of holy tradition in its
entirety.

Since scripture is "given" within the context of tradition, it
must also be read, interpreted and understood within that context.
And since, as we have seen, tradition is "the total life and experience" of the Church, it follows that the Church is the sole authoritative interpreter of the Bible. Christ is the founder and head of
the Church, and the Church is the body of Christ (see Eph 4:1-16
and 5:21-33). This means that Christ lives in, inspires and guides
his Church through the Holy Spirit. Christ, in and through the
Church, "provides the correct interpretation of the Bible" and of
other aspects of holy tradition. "It is only within the living Tradition of the Church and the direct inspiration of Christ's Spirit that
the proper interpretation of the Bible can be made."[16] Thus, the
Orthodox Christian must make every effort to read the Bible in the
light of the historic and living faith of the Church. Entering into
the life of the Church as fully and as faithfully as is possible for
him—through regular participation in the liturgical and sacramental services of the Church, through continual and fervent
prayer, through diligent study of the various elements of holy

tradition and especially the writings of the great fathers of the Church—the Orthodox Christian must seek an understanding of Holy Scripture which is consistent with and expressive of the spiritual and doctrinal content of the Orthodox faith as a whole. The Orthodox Christian's judgment of scriptural truth must never be a merely private judgment (see 2 Pt 1:20) but must be a judgment in harmony with the mind of the Church as expressed in holy tradition.

CULTURAL COMM. OF ST. MARY'S
UKRAINIAN ORTHODOX CHURCH
54 WINTER ST.
NEW BRITAIN, CT 06051

CHAPTER 2

God's Creation and the Fall of Man: Genesis 1-11

The first eleven chapters of the book of Genesis contain a story of the origins of the world, of mankind and of the people of Israel. During the thirteenth century B.C., as we shall see below, the people of Israel were liberated by God from their slavery in Egypt and were given possession of the promised land of Canaan (or Palestine). The book of Genesis is written from the standpoint of this "Exodus experience," Israel's experience of God's special favor toward his people. Many scholars believe that the present form of Genesis is a compilation and edition of ancient written documents and oral traditions made by Jewish religious authorities in the fifth century B.C. The Orthodox Church does not deny this, but teaches that the entire process by which the book of Genesis (and the other books of Holy Scripture) came into existence—the writing, the editing and the compiling of the documents that make up the biblical text—was guided and inspired by God through the Holy Spirit.

The early chapters of Genesis were not written as a scientific or empirical history, but as a sacred history. Through poetic, symbolic, legendary and even mythological stories, Genesis 1-11 is an attempt to convey certain religious truths concerning the general relationship between God, man and the universe and the special relationship between God and Israel. This section of scripture is not a scientific account of the origins of man and the cosmos, but a *theological interpretation,* within a chronological

27

and genealogical framework, of the human condition and of Israel's role in God's providential plan for the world.

Genesis 1-11 does, of course, contain a number of important factual claims: that God created the universe, that mankind was created in the image of God, that the human race has alienated itself from God as a result of sin, that the sinful world is subject to God's judgment and that God mercifully acts to redeem his creation from the powers of sin and death. It may also be true that Adam, Eve, Cain, Abel, Seth, Noah and other persons named in Genesis 1-11 were indeed historical figures whose names have been preserved in the folklore of ancient Israel; and many scholars believe that the story of the great flood in Genesis 6-8 is based upon the actual occurrence of a major deluge in the ancient Middle East (c. 4000 B.C.). But it is doubtful that God created the world and mankind in the precise manner depicted in Genesis 1-2, that the fall of the human race took place exactly as described in Genesis 3, that the stories of Noah and the flood (Gn 6-9) and of the Tower of Babel (Gn 11) are literally true in all of their details, and so on. Were we to accept every detail of Genesis 1-11 as literally true, we should be committing ourselves to the view that man made his appearance on earth only about 120 hours after the world was created; that daylight existed before the sun came into being (Gn 1:3-5, 14-19); that the universe is surrounded by water (1:6-8); that the universe is no more than six or seven thousand years old (a figure arrived at by tracing the various genealogies found in the Old Testament); and that the various languages of the human race originated at the Tower of Babel, less than four thousand years ago (11:1-9). Such ancient conceptions of the cosmos and of human history have been rendered implausible by modern scientific and historical discoveries. For example, it is practically certain that the universe is millions or even billions of years old and that it is *not* surrounded by water; that mankind appeared on earth approximately two million years ago; and that there was a multiplicity of human cultures and languages long before the time of the Tower of Babel (c. 2000 B.C.).

It may well be that the human writer (or writers) of the book of Genesis believed some or even all of the stories contained in the first eleven chapters of that book to be literally true in every detail. Even so, the primary purpose of Genesis 1-11 is not to insist upon the truth of any particular scientific description of the origins and development of the world, but to proclaim that God is the Creator of the world and of mankind, that the human race has sinfully separated itself from the presence of God and that to be saved from the powers of sin and death man must return to God in a spirit of love and obedience. The cosmological and historical framework of the early chapters of Genesis is merely the vehicle by which the Holy Spirit reveals and communicates certain spiritual truths necessary to the salvation of mankind and the world. Genesis 1-11 is a sacred history that gives "coherent expression to truths and events of a religious nature which cannot possibly be enunciated or described in empirical terms";[1] it is a revelation of God and his nature, a prophetic explanation of the "brokenness" of human existence and a proclamation of God's plan for the redemption of mankind and the world.

The theological content of Genesis 1-11, then, encompasses two major themes: (1) the original relationship between God, man and the universe, prior to the intrusion of sin into the divinely created cosmic order (chapters 1-2); and (2) the disruption of the divine order by sin, God's judgment and condemnation of that sin and his merciful determination to redeem mankind and the world from the bondage of evil (3-11). Genesis 1-2 describes the relationship between God, man and nature *as it was originally intended to be;* while Genesis 3-11 presents that relationship *as it is*—corrupted and subverted by man's sinful rebellion against the love and will of God.

GOD, MAN, AND THE UNIVERSE (GENESIS 1-2)

The central theme of the first two chapters of Genesis is God's creation of the world and of mankind. In Genesis 1, the creative work of God is divided into six "days." After his initial creation of "the heavens and the earth" (1:1), God calls into being the light of day (1:3-5); the earth's atmosphere (1:6-8); the major land masses and vegetation (1:9-13); the sun, moon and stars (1:14-19); the sea creatures and the birds (1:20-23); and, finally, the land animals and mankind (1:24-30). Genesis 2 describes the great Sabbath rest of God following the "six days" of creation (2:1-3), as well as God's preparation of "the garden of Eden" as a dwelling place for mankind (2:4-25).

Most modern biblical scholars believe that Genesis 1-2 contains two different creation stories, derived from two different traditions in ancient Israel. The "six day" creation story of Genesis 1, which concludes with God's "seventh day" rest in Genesis 2:1-3, is followed in Genesis 2:4-25 by what appears to be a second account focusing upon God's creation of the human race and the garden of Eden. What are we to make of this?

According to the widely held "documentary hypothesis," the Pentateuch (that is, the first five books of the Bible) is a compilation of four major "documents" put together in their present form by Jewish priests and scribes during the fifth century B.C. These written documents, which include material composed at various times between the tenth and fifth centuries B.C., represent ancient Israelite oral tradition dating back to the days of Moses (c. 1300 B.C.) and Abraham (c. 2000 B.C.). Thus, the Pentateuch "embraces a great diversity of material which reflects Israel's pilgrimage from the time of Abraham to the [Babylonian] Exile [sixth century B.C.]."[2] The four basic sources interwoven in the Pentateuch are commonly known as J, E, D and P. The J source, so-called because it was composed during the tenth century B.C. in *Judah* (or southern Israel) and because it gives "Jahveh" (or "Yahweh") as the name of God, is the earliest known written form of the religious traditions of ancient Israel. The E source, written in *Ephraim* (or northern Israel) and using "Elohim" for the name of God (and hence "E"), was produced some time between 900 and 750 B.C. The D source constitutes the basis of the book of *Deuteronomy* ("D") and was put into written form in the seventh century B.C. And the P source, which was composed during the sixth and fifth centuries B.C., is a written expression of ancient traditions preserved by the *priesthood* ("P") in Jerusalem. These sources "were woven together in various stages at different times," and the Pentateuch as we know it "represents a composite of these sources, completed about 400 B.C."[3] Since much of the oral tradition represented in these written documents can be traced back to the time of Moses and the Exodus, the ancient Jews and Christians referred to the Pentateuch as "the books of Moses."

The book of Genesis contains materials from J, E and P. Genesis 1:1-2:3 is part of P; and Genesis 2:4-25 is taken from J. And on this basis, it may be said that there are two—different but complementary—accounts of creation in the first two chapters of Genesis. The first account (in Genesis 1) is concerned not only with the place of mankind in God's providential plan, but with the divine creation of the entire cosmos; whereas the second account (in Genesis 2) concentrates exclusively upon God's creation of, and original purpose for, the human race.

God and Creation in Genesis 1-2

As pointed out above, the early chapters of Genesis are not to be read as literal descriptions of historical or scientific fact. What matters most is the *theological meaning* of this portion of Holy Scripture. Genesis 1-2 proclaims that God is a single, transcendent and supremely good being who created the world out of nothing (*creatio ex nihilo*) and who is the universal Lord of all creation. This conception of God is radically different from the pagan theologies of such ancient peoples as the Egyptians, Babylonians, Persians, Indians, Greeks and Romans. In affirming that God is one (monotheism), Genesis 1-2 constitutes a rejection of the pagan belief in the existence of many gods (polytheism). In holding that God is transcendent—that is, above and beyond the world—the theology of Genesis is, in effect, departing from the pagan view that the gods are either part of or identical with the world process (pantheism). And in insisting that God is the Lord not only of Israel but of all the world, Genesis 1-2 stands in opposition to the pagan practice of worshiping one god (the god of the tribe or nation) above others (henotheism). Furthermore, the gods of the ancient pagan religions were frequently conceived of as amoral or even immoral—as very powerful but not necessarily very good—whereas the God of Genesis 1-2 is depicted as absolutely good, righteous and just. From the standpoint of the biblical witness, then, the God of Israel is the *only*

God, and this one God is the transcendent, absolutely good and supreme Lord of the universe.

The biblical claim that God is the Creator of the world in an absolute sense, in the sense that he has created the world "out of nothing," establishes another major difference between the theology of Genesis 1-2 and the ancient pagan theologies. In the pagan religions, the cosmos is depicted either as eternal and therefore as uncreated, or as "created" by divine beings out of some pre-existent "matter." In other words, when the pagan theologies speak of "creation" at all, they present the gods as divine artists, shaping the world out of certain materials (e.g., earth, air, fire, water) which coexist eternally along with the gods themselves. Thus, the gods "create" not out of nothing but out of something, as do human artists. But in the Genesis account of creation, God simply causes the universe to be by an act of his will. "In the beginning God created the heavens and the earth" (Gn 1:1)— not out of eternally preexistent materials, but literally out of nothing. Or perhaps we should say, with Fr. Kallistos Ware, that God created the universe "out of His own self, which is love."[4] In either interpretation, the Genesis account presents God as the absolute source of being, the transcendent and all-powerful originator of all things. Nothing can exist independently or outside of God's being and will. God is not merely a divine artist or craftsman, but the absolute Creator and ground of all being.

The biblical doctrine of creation out of nothing lays special emphasis upon the transcendence of God. The God of Genesis 1-2 exists prior to, above and beyond his creation. He is not a product of, nor is he identical with, the world process. As we have seen, the biblical doctrine of God as transcendent is a direct repudiation of all forms of pantheism. And yet, the early chapters of Genesis also make clear that God is omnipresent, that is, present and active everywhere in his creation. "As creator, . . . God is always at the heart of each thing, maintaining it in being."[5] God is both transcendent and immanent, actively present in all things and yet above and beyond all things.

Another important implication of the biblical doctrine of God as creator is the rejection of all forms of nature worship. In ancient pagan religions, natural objects and forces were commonly worshiped as divine powers. For example, the sun, moon, stars and planets were often regarded as gods and venerated as such by the ancient Egyptians, Greeks and Romans. But in the Genesis account of God's creation, these "celestial lights" are treated simply as natural objects placed in the heavens for the purpose of illuminating the earth (Gn 1:14-19). Also, the various species of animals, which were also sometimes divinized and worshiped in ancient pagan cults, are presented in Genesis 1 as God's creatures—subordinate not only to God but to man as well (1:20-26). Nature, therefore, is not divine but divinely created; not God but the *creature* of God. Thus, the first chapter of Genesis contains an implicit condemnation of nature religion, a condemnation that is made explicit in later portions of Holy Scripture (see, for example, Dt 4:19). To worship nature rather than God—the creation rather than the Creator—is to worship "false gods." Nature religion, from a biblical standpoint, is a form of idolatry. It is on this basis that some of the fathers of the Church (for example, St. Augustine of Hippo) condemned the pseudo-science of astrology: they considered it a kind of nature worship, looking to the forces of nature for "signs" of one's destiny rather than trusting in God for all things.

It is important to recognize, however, that while the world of nature is not God, it would be contrary to Holy Scripture to conclude that nature is not *good*. The six-day creation story in Genesis 1 makes it quite clear that God's creation—the natural order as well as mankind—is fundamentally good. "And God saw everything that he had made, and behold, it was very good" (1:31). From an Orthodox Christian standpoint, therefore, it is a heresy to claim that the material world and human nature are inherently evil, for both man and nature are creatures of God, and God has judged them to be good. As we shall see, the Bible teaches that man and nature now exist in a fallen state, as a result of man's rebellion against God. Yet even when man acts in an evil manner, and when nature fails to display her original and divinely ordained benign order, the basic natures of man and the cosmos, because they are creations of God, remain essentially good.

There is yet another aspect of the theology of creation in Genesis 1-2 that deserves comment. In these initial chapters of the Bible, God is depicted as a *person*. The God of Genesis is not an impersonal cosmic force or world essence. He is a personal being who wills the world and mankind to be, who structures the world according to his own design, who cares for the welfare of man. A person is a self-conscious, intelligent, free and creative being. And the God of Genesis is depicted in these terms. He is intimately and personally related to his creation, he is involved in it, he is concerned about it.

In Orthodox theology, the personhood of God is defined in terms of the doctrine of the Holy Trinity. God is a triune being in whom we must distinguish three persons—God the Father, God the Son and God the Holy Spirit—who are neither three gods (tritheism) nor three parts or modes of God (modalism), but coequally and coeternally God. God is one essence (*ousia*) in three persons (*hypostases*).

Many Orthodox interpreters of the Bible have argued that the first chapter of Genesis contains a revelation of the Holy Trinity in action, of the three divine persons cooperating in the work of creation. "In the beginning God created the heavens and the earth. . . . and *the Spirit of God* was moving [or soaring, or brooding] over the face of the waters. *And God said,* 'Let there be light . . .'" (Gn 1:1-3). The expression "and God said" is repeated nine more times in Genesis 1. God creates the world by his *Word*. "By the word of the Lord the heavens were made, and all their host by the breath of his mouth. For he spoke, and it came to be; he commanded, and it stood forth" (Ps 33:6, 9). In the Gospel according to St. John, the creative Word of God is identified as God the Son, the second person of the Holy Trinity, who "became man" in Jesus Christ:

> In the beginning was the Word, and the Word was with God, and the Word was God. He was in the beginning with God; all things were made through him, and without him was not anything made that was made. In him was life, and the life was the light of men. . . . And the Word became flesh and dwelt among us, full of grace and truth; we have beheld his glory, glory *as of the only Son from the Father.* . . . (Jn 1:1-4, 14)

The Gospel of John is therefore "the indispensable key to the understanding of the first chapter of Genesis."[6] And on this basis,

Orthodox theologians have read Genesis 1 in trinitarian terms: God the Father, brooding or moving in the Holy Spirit, creates the universe through his Son, the divine Word.

God and Man in Genesis 1-2

The relationship between God and mankind is also given special attention in Genesis 1-2. Genesis 1 speaks of this relationship as follows:

> Then God said, "Let us make man in our image, after our likeness; and let them have dominion over the fish of the sea, and over the birds of the air, and over the cattle, and over all the earth, and over every creeping thing that creeps upon the earth." So God created man in his own image, in the image of God he created him; male and female he created them. (1:26-7)

And according to Genesis 2,

> . . . the Lord God formed man of dust from the ground, and breathed into his nostrils the breath of life; and man became a living being [or soul]. And the Lord God planted a garden in Eden, in the east; and there he put the man whom he had formed; and out of the ground the Lord God made to grow every tree that is pleasant to the sight and good for food, the tree of life also in the midst of the garden, and the tree of the knowledge of good and evil. . . . [And the] Lord took the man and put him in the garden of Eden to till it and keep it. And the Lord God commanded the man, saying, "You may freely eat of every tree of the garden; but of the tree of the knowledge of good and evil you shall not eat, for in the day that you eat of it you shall die." (2:7-9, 15-17)

What is the theological meaning of these texts?

The biblical conception of man as the image and likeness of God has played a very significant role in the development of Orthodox theology. As the image and likeness of God (*imago*

Dei), man is a person endowed with a spiritual life, intelligence, moral sensibility, a social nature (as an icon of the trinitarian life of God), freedom and creativity. Each human being is a unique and unrepeatable spiritual subject, who lives in relation to other (divine, angelic and human) persons, and who is capable of conscious, purposive and creative activity. As Fr. Ware puts it, "Man is a finite expression of God's infinite self-expression."[7] God's decree that man is to "have dominion" over all other life forms on earth (Gn 1:26, 28) is the biblical sign of man's "God-like" nature.

Orthodox theology, following the lead of St. Irenaeus of Lyons (c. 130-200 A.D.) and other ancient fathers of the Church, often draws a distinction between the *image* and the *likeness* of God. In Fr. Ware's summary of the patristic preaching, "The image . . . denotes man's *potentiality* for life in God, the likeness his *realization* of that potentiality."[8] Man was not created as a spiritually perfect and immortal being. Originally innocent and good, he was called to become morally and spiritually *perfect,* to become *like* God. The biblical symbol of this moral and spiritual perfection is "the tree of life," that is, the source of immortality. Created as mortal beings like other natural creatures, but, unlike other creatures, endowed with the *image* of God, Adam and Eve were intended to grow into the moral and spiritual *likeness* of God and thus share in the goodness, wisdom and life of God himself. Through freely loving and obeying God, man was to enter into an eternal and ever-deepening communion with the triune God; he was to be united with God by sharing in the eternal life and goodness of the uncreated Trinity. "In other words, man at his first creation was innocent and capable of developing spiritually (the 'image'), but this development was not inevitable or automatic. Man was called to cooperate with God's grace and so, through the correct use of his free will, slowly and by gradual steps he was to become perfect in God (the 'likeness')."[9]

Man's basic need and ultimate purpose, then, is to become *like* God, to become *one* with God. Man was created for communion with God, and thus the final goal of human existence is participation "in the fullness of the divine life."[10] "To believe that man is made in God's image is to believe that man is created for communion and union with God, and that if he rejects this communion he ceases to be properly man."[11] Orthodox theologians employ the term "deification" (*theosis*) when speaking of the process of moral and spiritual growth through which man may achieve union with God. Fr. Thomas Hopko defines deification as "an unending process of growth and development" in which man becomes "through gracious communion with God in freedom all that God is by nature in the superabundant fulness of His inexhaustible and infinite Trinitarian being and life."[12]

The key to man's participation in the divine nature is the incarnation of God the Son in Jesus Christ the man. According to the Orthodox tradition, it was "God's eternal decision to associate man to his own blessedness."[13] But man, as we have seen, although created good, was a finite, incomplete and therefore imperfect being, even in the garden of Eden. And for this reason, many Orthodox thinkers have argued that man's movement toward union with God would have required God's movement toward union with man, even if man had remained faithful to his Creator and therefore free from sin. Only if God condescended to become one with man could man realistically hope to become one with God. Thus, the incarnation of the divine Word—the union of God and man in the person of Jesus Christ—is an essential feature of God's eternal plan for the world. And the incarnation would have taken place even if man had not fallen under the bondage of sin and death (as described symbolically in Genesis 3). What man's rebellion against God's divine order did was to separate man from "the tree of life," thereby making the *death* of Christ necessary. In the incarnation, God identifies himself with the human race. And to identify himself fully with a fallen and sinful humanity, God had to identify himself with human mortality; he had to enter into our death in order to raise us to eternal life. Had he not sinned against God, man would have remained free to partake of "the tree of life," and God's union with man in the incarnation would not have required the death of Christ. But the incarnation would have taken place nonetheless.

In Christ, then, God and man become one. Insofar as a human being is "in Christ"—through faith and through full participation in the life of the Church—he is one with God, because Christ's humanity is one with God. And it is through the gracious work of the Holy Spirit that the Christian believer is brought into an ever-developing and ever-deepening communion with God. The deification of man, therefore, is a process of moral and spiritual growth toward God the Father, through God the Son and in God the Holy Spirit. In this way, man may become a "partaker of the divine nature" (2 Pt 1:4), a participant in the energies and eternal life of the triune God.

It is implicit in the preceding analysis that, while the Bible holds quite an exalted view of human nature, man is, after all, a creature who exists and thrives only by the mercy and grace of God. Human "creatureliness" is expressed in several ways in Genesis 1-3. In the first place, man is dependent for his very existence upon the creative will and activity of God (1:26-27 and 2:7). In the second place, man's harmony with God and the world requires his recognition of his subordination to and dependence upon God. While man is to "have dominion" over the earth, he is to exercise this dominion in the name of God. In Genesis 2:15, God places man in the garden of Eden and commands him "to till it and keep it." Man's dominion, in other words, is the dominion of stewardship—a dominion exercised by a steward under the authority of his Lord. And the garden of Eden is symbolic of man's original harmonious relationship with God and nature, prior to the disruption of the cosmic order wrought by human sin. In the third place, man's creatureliness is revealed in the fact that, in God's original dispensation, both men and animals are prohibited from killing one another. Both were to be vegetarians (see 1:29-30), living together under the divine rule of their Creator. Once again, man's earthly dominion is shown to be limited, rather than absolute. And in the fourth place, man's physical and spiritual well-being is contingent upon his faithful and loving obedience of God. This aspect of man's creatureliness is given its most striking expression in the story of the two trees in Genesis 2. To disobey God in pursuit of the worldly wisdom derived from "the tree of the knowledge of good and evil" is to depart from "the tree of life," to lose the source of eternal life.

The divine prohibition against man's eating the forbidden fruit (see Gn 2:17), which emphasizes the lordship of God and man's need to obey his Creator, requires some explanation. Why should the acquisition of the knowledge of good and evil separate man from the life of God? In biblical thought, to know is to experience, to be involved or immersed in, to partake of the object of one's knowledge. Knowledge, for the human authors of the Bible, is not the abstract comprehension of concepts and theories, but the active and "existential" interpenetration of the knower and the known. Thus, when the Bible speaks of a man "knowing" a woman (for example, in Gn 4:1), it is referring to the act of sexual intercourse. To "know" good and evil, then, is to be personally engaged in the performance of both good *and* evil acts. This immersion of oneself in the ways of the world—where good and evil are mixed together—is symbolized in the Bible by "the tree of the knowledge of good and evil" and is, even now, forbidden by God.[14]

Thus, the Bible presents man both as the image and likeness of God *and* as one of God's creatures. The task of human life is to grow toward communion with God on the basis of faith, love and obedience—always keeping in mind the fundamental creatureliness of human nature.

An implicit sub-theme in Genesis 1-2 is a depiction of the original (prelapsarian) relationship between man and woman. Genesis 1:27-28 makes it clear that both men and women are created in the image of God, and that both are to exercise dominion over the earth. This text also stresses God's commandment that the human race is to "be fruitful" in multiplying itself —that is, in the procreation of children. Bearing children is a great blessing from the biblical point of view.

In Genesis 2:18-25, the relationship between man and woman is described in some detail. This text stresses the social nature of man: "It is not good that the man should be alone" (2:18). It also emphasizes that man's social nature—his need for companionship—cannot be fulfilled in his relationships with the animal world (2:19-20). While man is less than God, he is more than an animal. Man needs the presence of members of his own species—"bone of my bones and flesh of my flesh"—to satisfy his longing for fellowship. More particularly, man needs woman (and vice-versa) in order to be a complete human being: in the institution of marriage, man and woman "become one flesh"— one person, a completed image of God. In referring to the un-

ashamed nakedness of the first man and woman (2:25), the
Bible speaks symbolically "of their guiltless relation to God and
to one another."[15]

Before the fall, then, the relationship between man and
woman was one of equality, mutuality and harmony under the
divine order of God. One of the original tasks of man and
woman was to preserve, strengthen and deepen this divinely ordained relationship. But because of sin, as we shall see, the
primal communion between man and woman—and between the
human race and God—was subverted and destroyed.

THE FALL, THE SPREAD OF EVIL, AND A NEW BEGINNING (GENESIS 3-11)

The early chapters of Genesis contain several images of God's
righteous condemnation of sin and his redemptive purpose for
man and nature. In Genesis 3 there is the account of man's
"original sin" and his consequent separation from the eternal
life of God. After the expulsion of Adam from paradise, Genesis
traces the spread of evil throughout virtually the entire world,
leading up to the story of Noah and the great flood. Even the
flood, however, does not halt the continuing activity of evil in
the world; yet God in his mercy decides to work out the redemption of the world through a "chosen people," the nation of Israel.
All these biblical images of divine judgment and redemption
in response to human sin are, in effect, depictions of the human
condition and of the human need for salvation from evil and
reconciliation with God.

Genesis 3: The Fall of Man

Genesis 3 does not mention the devil or the name of Satan.
But the Christian tradition has always considered the serpent of
this chapter to be a symbolic reference to the devil. And, indeed,
other passages of the Bible, when speaking of the devil, identify
him with the serpent in the garden of Eden (see Ws 2:24, Jn
8:44, and Rv 12:9 and 20:2). Before the creation of the human

race, one of God's angels (sometimes referred to as Lucifer), seeking to take God's place, led an angelic rebellion against God. But the rebellion was put down by St. Michael the archangel and his legions, and the rebellious angels were cast out of heaven. Thenceforth, the leader of the fallen angels was known as Satan (which means adversary, accuser, or enemy) and as the devil (Greek, *diabolos,* "he who takes a bite," the biter).[16] Ancient Jewish and Christian traditions also hold that Satan was originally the angel appointed by God to guard the earth, and especially the garden of Eden (see Ezk 28:11-19). And God, for reasons of his own, has continued to allow Satan and his angelic underlings (now known as demons) to intervene in and influence earthly affairs.

According to such fathers of the Church as St. Irenaeus of Lyons and St. Gregory of Nyssa, the satanic rebellion was a response to God's revelation of his intention to identify himself with mankind and to exalt human nature above the angels in the incarnation and ascension of Christ. The mystery of the incarnation is "the self-abandonment of the divine Person of the Word, a 'little lower than the angels' (Hebrews 2:7)." And the mystery of the ascension is "the exaltation of human nature above all the worlds of the angels." This "double mystery" overthrows "the natural order of things" and "throws the angels into a state of astonishment."[17] The sin of the fallen angels was that they refused "to recognize the dignity of Adam created in the image of God" and to "accept the future prospect of an Incarnation of the Word."[18] If this is true, then the satanic promise that by partaking of the forbidden fruit of "the tree of the knowledge of good and evil" Adam and Eve would become "like gods" (Gn 3:5, Septuagint rendering) is quite fitting. The term "gods" in this context refers to members of God's heavenly court—that is, angels. By enticing Adam and Eve to membership in the angelic choirs rather than to union with God himself, the devil, having failed in his attempt to replace God in heaven, seeks to console himself by causing the intended beneficiaries of God's glorious plan for the deification of man to rebel against that plan, to desire what they cannot have and what is contrary to the divine will. Thus, "there has been a double fall: first of the angels, and then of man."[19]

The satanic temptation of man takes the form of a distortion of divine truth. In enticing Eve to partake of the forbidden fruit, the serpent, who was "more subtle than any other wild creature that the Lord God had made," assured her by saying: "You will not die. For God knows that when you eat of it your eyes will be opened, and you will be *like gods,* knowing good and evil" (Gn 3:1, 4-5). Thus, the devil seeks to arouse doubt, suspicion and pride in the minds of men. He questions the truth of God's warning that to partake of the forbidden fruit is to die; he implies that God's prohibition against eating the forbidden fruit is based upon an unjust desire to exclude mankind from the angelic choirs in heaven; and he promises that the forbidden fruit—which is "good for food, a delight to the eyes, and able to make one wise"—will exalt Adam and Even into the ranks of the angels. Man is thereby led to doubt God's truth, to suspect God's motives and to pridefully seek his own self-aggrandizement rather than the purposes of God.

The same pattern of deception is present in the satanic temptation of Christ (see Mt 4:1-11 and Lk 4:1-13). But Christ, unlike Adam and Eve, successfully resists the enticements of the devil. Indeed, from an Orthodox perspective, man does in Christ what he failed to do in Adam. But let us postpone this part of our discussion until a later chapter.

The Nature of Sin and Evil. Genesis 3 also teaches us a good deal concerning the nature of sin and evil. Sin is presented not as a natural weakness but as a moral failure. The biblical conception of sin presupposes the reality of human and angelic freedom. Sin is thus an act of the will leading to a revolt against God, "a *conscious* act of disobedience, a *deliberate* rejection of God's love, a *freely-chosen* turning from God to self."[20] Before the satanic rebellion and the fall of man, evil was present in God's creation only as a "subsistent potentiality," in order to make the moral and spiritual freedom of angels and men real—for where there is no possibility of making a wrong choice, there can be no moral or spiritual freedom. In God's original dispensation, evil was merely possible, "contingent upon a morally [and spiritually] wrong choice."[21] Evil became an "existent actuality" not through the direct activity of God but through the abuse of freedom by angels and men. God permits evil in the form of morally and spritually wrong choices and actions because he respects our freedom; but it would be misleading (or even contradictory) to say that God, who is supremely good, is the direct cause of evil.

The Consequences of Sin. Man's disobedience of God leads to a world in which the forces of disorder, incoherence, contradiction, hostility, fragmentation, suffering, death and anxiety reign. According to the biblical text, the first consequence of human sin is a sense of exposure and shame: Adam and Eve experience their nakedness, which previously connoted their openness to one another and to God, as a kind of vulnerability deriving from their guilty transgression of God's will (Gn 3:7). After allowing themselves to be "clothed" with the false promises of the devil, they can now "see through" their own pretensions and are vividly aware that God will be able to discern their complete moral and spiritual impoverishment. Their nakedness is no longer a symbol of their innocence and their intimate relationship with God but rather a sign of their guilt and their consequent alienation from their divine Father. Their moral and spiritual nakedness leads Adam and Eve to cover themselves up with garments made of fig leaves, to hide from God and to evade their own responsibility for having sinned against their Creator (Gn 3:7-13).

Also in the biblical account, Adam blames Eve for his sin, and Eve seeks to shift the burden of her own guilt to the serpent. Adam actually suggests that the responsibility for his transgressions belongs not primarily with his wife, but with God: "The woman whom *thou* gavest to be with me, she gave me fruit of the tree, and I ate" (3:12). Instead of emphasizing his own deliberate activity, Adam chooses to concentrate upon what Eve has done and even upon what God has done. Thus, sin leads to guilt, and guilt is evaded through the concoction of excuses, which constitute a refusal to accept responsibility for one's own actions. "Men have always tried to shuffle out of responsibility for their failures. We blame our instincts, our environment, our parents, our wives or our neighbors, and if all else fails we can always blame God."[22]

But the human "cover-up" does not work. Needless to say,

God is not fooled by the fig leaves and the excuses; man's transgression is judged and condemned. The harmonious relationship between the sexes is disrupted, and the husband becomes the "ruler" of his wife (Gn 3:16). As a result of sin, the original union of man and woman is broken, and the "war between the sexes" begins. On a deeper level, this "division" of man and woman may be viewed as a division of human nature itself. As pointed out earlier, the divine image in man is expressed in the union of "male and female" (1:27) and of husband and wife (2:24-25). The disjunction of man and woman as a consequence of sin is therefore a sundering of the integrity of human nature itself. Furthermore, the smooth interaction between man and nature which prevailed before the advent of sin is undermined. Woman's pain in childbearing (3:16) and the fact that man must toil and struggle in order to eke out a living from the soil (3:17-19) are images used to illustrate the postlapsarian conflict between man and the natural order.

But the most grievous result of man's sin is his alienation from God and his consequent loss of access to eternal life. Man's original mortality, which he was to overcome by growing toward the *likeness* of God, is now made permanent (Gn 3:19), "an inevitable fate that haunts man throughout life."[23] The story of man's expulsion from the garden of Eden (3:22-24), his loss of immediate contact with God and thus with "the tree of life," is crucial to an understanding of the Orthodox perspective on the human condition. Adam and Eve, as God's creatures, owed their love and obedience to God alone. But they submitted their wills to the temptations of the devil and devoted themselves to self-love rather than to the love of God. As a result of this rebellion against and rejection of God (symbolized by man's partaking of the forbidden fruit), the human race has been separated from the presence and life of God. And since the postlapsarian world is a broken world, a world conditioned by sin and death, "a world in which it is easy to do evil and hard to do good,"[24] it is impossible for man to work himself back into paradise through his own moral and spiritual efforts. And because the human race was created in the image of the tripersonal God—and is therefore an "interdependent and coinherent" society of persons—the "original sin" of Adam and Eve "affects the human race in its entirety."[25]

The solidarity of the human race, the corporate nature of man, is therefore the ontological basis of our "Adamic inheritance." This does not mean that we are *guilty* of the sins of others or of Adam's "original sin." We are born into a world conditioned by Adam's sin and by the accumulated sins of others; we are *involved in* and *influenced by* that world; and our lives are often shaped by the ongoing consequences of human sinfulness. But we are *guilty of*—and therefore morally and spiritually *responsible for*— our own actual sins, and not the sins of others. The human tendency to sin is "original" (or "congenital") in that it is a natural consequence of being born into a fallen world. In this restricted sense, we may be "born sinful," but we are not "born guilty." The Orthodox Church has always repudiated the doctrine of "original guilt"—that is, the view that all men share not only the *consequences of* but also the *guilt for* the sin of Adam and Eve.

The Protoevangel—God's Promise of Redemption. Although Genesis 3 is primarily concerned with the theological interpretation of man's expulsion from paradise, the text also contains a suggestion of God's continuing concern for the welfare of the human race. In Genesis 3:15, God says to the serpent, "I will put enmity between you and the woman, and between your seed and her seed; he shall bruise your head, and you shall bruise his heel." This verse has been understood by Orthodox theologians and other Christian scholars as a "shadow" of the gospel of Christ, as a "protoevangel." "This is the first promise of a Redeemer. The conflict of the ages is predicted—a conflict between the seed of the woman and the seed of the serpent. The Redeemer will finally bring ruin to Satan and his seed although in the process Satan will bruise the Redeemer, . . . as took place at Calvary."[26] It is also interesting that the mention of the woman's seed in this verse is the only example of such an expression in all of scripture. Many commentators have interpreted this unique passage as a reference to the virgin birth of Christ.

The protoevangel is also present in Genesis 3:21, where God, in recognition of man's lost innocence and consequent moral and spiritual exposure, clothes Adam and Eve in animal skins prior to driving them out of Eden. This may be viewed as still another sign of the lapsed harmony between God, man and nature in that

animals have to die in order that man might live. But the text
has also been interpreted as a symbol of God's continuing providential care for mankind even in a time of judgment. And the
"garments of skins" (God-given and not man-made like the ineffective aprons of fig leaves) have been regarded as a typological
image of Christ. If man is ever to return to the presence of God,
he will have to put off his old nature (Eph 4:22) and "put on
the Lord Jesus Christ" (Rm 13:14). Sinful man must be clothed
with the righteousness of Christ if he is to regain his place in the
divine order. And the "shadow-gospel" of Genesis 3:15 and 21
appears to be the first scriptural promise of God's redemption of
man and the world from satanic bondage.

Genesis 4-8: The Proliferation of Evil and the Great Flood

Another depiction of divine judgment and redemption is
contained in Genesis 4-8. The biblical account of man's expulsion
from God's paradise is followed immediately by the story of the
first murder (4:1-16). Cain, the first son of Adam and Eve, slays
his younger brother Abel. Without going into the details of this
section of Genesis, we may say that "man's revolt against God
leads to his revolt against his fellow man; the crime of murder
confirms the fallen state of man."[27]

After murdering his brother, Cain is removed still further
from the presence of God. He is sent off, away from his parents,
to "the land of Nod, east of Eden" (Gn 4:16). The human race
is, at this point, divided into two parts, as is indicated in the two
genealogies in Genesis 4-5. A distinction is made here between
the "Cain line" (4:17-24) and the "Seth line" (4:25-5:32). The
Cain line is characterized by the cries of vengeance and the murder-
ous acts of Cain himself and of his great-great-great-grandson,
Lamech (see 4:23-24). The Seth line—Seth was the third son of
Adam and Eve (4:25)—is presented as the true line of descent
from Adam (5:3) and is characterized by its initial holiness
(5:18-24) and devotion to God (4:26). With the advent of Seth
and his offspring, the sons of Adam "began to call upon the name
of the Lord" (4:26). In other words, while the Cain line is cut
off from "the generations of Adam" and steeped in evil, the

Seth line is the legitimate continuation of Adam's seed and is oriented toward the worship of God.

Genesis 6 tells of the growing wickedness of the world in those days and of God's decision to destroy human civilization by sending a great deluge upon the earth. The chapter begins, in verses 1-4, with a strange and difficult passage:

> When man began to multiply on the face of the ground, and daughters were born to them, the sons of God saw that the daughters of men were fair; and they took to wife such of them as they chose. Then the Lord said, "My spirit shall not abide in man for ever, for he is flesh, but his days shall be a hundred and twenty years." The Nephilim were on the earth in those days, and also afterward, when the sons of God came in to the daughters of men, and they bore children to them. These were the mighty men that were of old, the men of renown.

Some interpreters have held that the "sons of God" referred to in this text were fallen angels (or demons) who married human women and "spawned a mixed race" of giants or monsters. But since angels and demons are pure spirits—who may *appear* in human form (see Gn 18-19) but who cannot be actually "incarnate" in a material body[28]—it is difficult to see how they could impregnate "the daughters of men." A more natural reading of the text would indicate that "the sons of God" were descendants of Seth who were guilty of intermarriage with women descended from Cain. From this point of view, the progeny of these unholy marriages are not giants or monsters, but "strong, violent, tyrannous men of great wickedness."[29] Given the emphasis upon the divinely ordained separation of the Cain and Seth lines in Genesis 4:17-5:32, the mixing of the two stocks would certainly be an abomination in the sight of God and a fitting introduction to the tale of corruption, judgment and catastrophe contained in Genesis 6:5-7:24.

In resolving to destroy the disordered and wicked world brought into existence by human sin, God chooses to save a remnant of men and animals as the basis for a "new world" (Gn 6:5-22). Noah, a righteous descendant of Seth (5:28-32), "finds

favor in the eyes of the Lord" (6:8) and is instructed to build a
great ark in order to save himself, his family and a large number
of birds and beasts from the coming destruction (6:9-22). The
biblical description of the great flood appears in Genesis 7-8.
The flood raged for 150 days, covering the entire planet to a
depth of five miles and leaving only Noah and those with him in
the ark alive.

Again, we must remind ourselves that the first eleven chapters
of Genesis are made up of legendary stories and parables aimed
at the revelation of religious truths concerning God, man and
nature, not scientific accounts of the history of mankind and the
world. What appears in this section of the Bible is the folklore
of ancient Israel, organized in such a manner as to serve theological purposes. Many contemporary biblical scholars regard the
story of the great flood in Genesis 6-8 as "the Hebrew version of
a much older Babylonian myth, which related the adventures . . .
of one Utnapishtim, a Babylonian worthy who is warned by the
God Ea of an impending deluge, builds an ark and is saved in
the same manner as Noah."[30] Archeological studies have indicated that this ancient Near Eastern legend is based upon the
actual occurrence of a major flood in Mesopotamia about 4000
B.C.; but the evidence also makes it clear that this inundation was
a local one and that it did not cover the entire earth.

It must be emphasized, however, that there are important
differences between the biblical and the Babylonian flood stories.
The Babylonian version reflects a pagan religious and mythological perspective: "There are many gods who decree the flood for
no apparent reason. The hero is warned by one of them, again
for no apparent moral reason." But in the biblical account, "the
one God, supreme lord of the situation, decrees the flood because
of man's sin. Noah is saved because of his justice."[31] The aim of
the biblical account is to emphasize God's judgment and condemnation of sin and his steadfast love for the righteous—his refusal
to tolerate the unrequited practice of evil and his merciful redemption of that remnant of the human race which strives to
conform to the divine will. Thus, in religious and moral content
the biblical story of the great flood is entirely different from, and
infinitely superior to, the Babylonian version.

There is a relationship—in the Bible and in Orthodox theology

—between the story of the great flood and the sacrament of baptism. Indeed, the great flood might also be called "the great baptism." In the Bible, water is often employed as a symbol of the world, especially the fallen world, which has been infected by chaos, evil and death. St. Matthew's account of Jesus walking on the sea is an illustration of this point. Jesus invites Peter to join him on the surface of the water. And at first Peter also walks on the water, "but when he saw the wind, he was afraid, and beginning to sink he cried out, 'Lord, save me.' Jesus immediately reached out his hand and caught him, saying to him, 'O man of little faith, why did you doubt?'" (Mt 14:28-31). Here, Peter's sinking into the sea, and his need to be saved from drowning, is symbolic of man's loss of life as a result of losing faith in God. When Peter takes his eyes off Jesus, the Son of God incarnate, he begins to slip into the chaos and death of the waters, he faces being swallowed up by a fallen world and he needs to be lifted up again by the Lord himself.

In the sacrament of baptism, a person is immersed in water. This immersion is an entering into the death of Christ. And emergence from the waters of baptism is a participation in the resurrection of Christ from the dead. As we have seen, sinful man has been alienated from the life of God. But through the incarnation of God in Christ, man is given a second chance to unite himself to God in faith, love and obedience. In dying for us upon the cross, Christ enters into our death and transforms it into a path to new life. Christ's death destroys death itself, because Christ is *Life*. Through Christ's immersion in "the waters of chaos, evil, and death," those waters—which may also be taken as a symbol of the entire fallen world—are "filled with the presence of God."[32] The waters of baptism, therefore, represent not only death, but a world which has been transfigured by the incarnate life of God. Through the baptismal rite, we die to sin and rise to eternal life in Christ.

St. Peter makes the relationship between the great flood and the sacrament of baptism explicit. He says that Christ's saving work was foreshadowed "in the days of Noah, during the building of the ark, in which a few, that is, eight persons, were saved through water. Baptism, which corresponds to this, now saves you, not as a removal of dirt from the body but as an appeal to

God for a clear conscience, through the resurrection of Jesus
Christ" (1 Pt 3:18, 20-22). The great flood is a symbol of God's
eternal judgment of sin. St. Peter depicts Noah as a type of those
who look to God in faith and are thus mercifully redeemed from
the destruction which sin brings. And the ark of Noah is a type
of Christ, in whom the faithful remnant is "saved through water."

Genesis 9-11: A New Beginning

The parable of the great flood is followed by the story of
God's covenant with Noah (Gn 9:1-17). According to the Bible,
God has entered into a number of "covenants" (or agreements)
with human individuals, nations and the human race in general.
These covenants are "sovereign pronouncements" which establish
"relationships of responsibility" between God and men. In his
covenants, God sets down the conditions of human existence and
makes promises concerning the future. Some of these promises
will be fulfilled unconditionally, while the fulfilment of others
depends upon man's faithful response to the commandments of
God. Each covenant, moreover, is accompanied by a sign or seal
given by God as evidence that an agreement has been made. Three
such covenants are given explicit consideration in the Pentateuch.
The covenant with Noah (Gn 9:1-17) is unilateral in that it is
not conditioned upon man's faithful response to God, it is extended to all creation, "and its sign is a natural phenomenon"—
the rainbow. *The covenant with Abraham* (Gn 12:1-3; 13:14-17;
15:1-7, 18-21; and 17:18) "presupposes his personal commitment to God, is extended only to his descendants, and its sign
is circumcision." *The covenant with Israel* (Ex 19-24) "requires
continuing loyalty . . . is extended to the nation, and its sign is
the Sabbath observance" (see Ex 31:16-17).[33]

The Noahic covenant is based upon God's presupposition of
the moral and spiritual disorder caused by sin, for "the imagination of man's heart is evil from his youth" (Gn 8:21). The
Lord's decree is that man's dominion over nature will be "exercised, not in peace, but through fear."[34]

The fear of you and the dread of you shall be upon every

beast of the earth, and upon every bird of the air, upon everything that creeps on the ground and all the fish of the sea; into your hand they are delivered. Every moving thing that lives shall be food for you; and as I gave you the green plants, I give you everything. Only you shall not eat flesh with its life, that is, its blood. (Gn 9:2-4)

The killing and eating of animals—which had been forbidden in God's original dispensation—is now acknowledged as a central feature of human culture. Man is, however, prohibited from devouring the blood of animals; for, in biblical thought, blood is considered the essence of life, and life ultimately belongs not to man but to God.

The covenant also prohibits the murder of human beings and establishes capital punishment as a divinely ordained institution. "Whoever sheds the blood of man, by man shall his blood be shed; for God made man in his own image" (Gn 9:6). The hostile relationships between man and animals and between man and man, which are alluded to in these texts, are symbolic of the corruption of the world wrought by human sinfulness.

The scope of God's covenant with Noah is universal—that is, it extends beyond Noah to his descendants and indeed to all animal life (Gn 9:8-10). And the promise of this covenant is "that never again shall all flesh be cut off by the waters of a flood, and never again shall there be a flood to destroy the earth" (9:11). This promise does not mean that God will not continue to judge, condemn and punish sin. But it does mean that God's creation will not be finally destroyed by the powers of evil. God's redemptive purpose will prevail. And as has already been noted, the sign of the Noahic covenant is the rainbow (9:11-17), a sign of God's promise of redemption to Noah and to all the world.

The Continuing Challenge of Evil. We have seen that the Noahic covenant presupposes the continuing presence and operation of sin in the world, even after the great flood. Genesis 9:18-11:9 amply illustrates the ongoing sinfulness of the human race.

First, there is the strange tale of the sin of Ham, one of Noah's three sons, in Genesis 9:20-27:

Noah was the first tiller of the soil. He planted a vineyard; and he drank of the wine, and became drunk, and lay uncovered in his tent. And Ham, the father of Canaan, saw the nakedness of his father, and told his two brothers outside. Then Shem and Japheth took a garment, laid it upon both their shoulders, and walked backward and covered the nakedness of their father; their faces were turned away, and they did not see their father's nakedness. When Noah awoke from his wine and knew what his youngest son had done to him, he said, "Cursed be Cannan; a slave of slaves shall he be to his brothers." He also said, "Blessed by the Lord my God be Shem; and let Canaan be his slave. God enlarge Japheth, and let him dwell in the tents of Shem; and let Canaan be his slave."

There are two major puzzles contained in this text: What, exactly, was the nature of Ham's offense? And why does Noah pronounce his curse on Canaan, Ham's son (10:6), rather than upon Ham himself?

The essence of Ham's sin is expressed in the phrase, "saw the nakedness of his father," a phrase which must be understood in the light of chapter 18 of the book of Leviticus. In that text, God proclaims that it is an abomination for a man to "uncover the nakedness" of his father, his mother, his sister, his children, his grandchildren, his aunts and uncles, his sisters-in-law and his daughters-in-law (Lv 18:6-16). What is condemned here is any act of incest. And it is quite clear that the expression "uncover the nakedness" refers to various forms of sexual intercourse. It should also be noted that homosexuality is condemned in Leviticus 18:22 and 20:13, and in Romans 1:26-27. What Ham did, then, was to engage in some form of incestuous and homosexual intercourse with his father. (It is, by the way, interesting that the Bible contains no suggestion that Noah's drunkenness was in any way reprehensible.)

Noah's curse upon Canaan is quite consistent with the ancient Near Eastern view that a man's proudest hope lies in the future prosperity of his descendants (his "seed"). Thus, the curse upon Canaan *is* a curse upon Ham. And the Bible tells us that the sexual atrocities that later became common among the Canaanite tribes of ancient Palestine resulted from the sin of Ham and led to the eventual conquest of the Canaanites by the people of Israel. The Israelites were, as we shall see, descendants of Shem, who is blessed and named by Noah as the conqueror by whom Canaan will be enslaved.[35] This scandalous profile of sin and congenital sexual disease is an extraordinarily dramatic and apt example of the depth of human sinfulness.

The continuing challenge of evil in the postdiluvian age is also portrayed in Genesis 10. The descendants of Noah are divided into three major groups: the sons of Japheth (10:1-5), the sons of Ham (10:6-20) and the sons of Shem (10:21-32). And these three groups are further subdivided into a multitude of peoples, cultures and nations. These genealogies may, of course, constitute a primitive attempt to account for the geographical and ethnological distribution of the world's human population. But the theological significance of this rather undramatic section of Genesis is its emphasis upon the division, separation and fragmentation of the human race, which is one of the fundamental conditions of "man's inhumanity to man." The forces of cultural chauvinism, ethnocentrism and nationalism are, indeed, among the most obvious signs of humanity's loss of its unity under God. And this loss of original unity is surely one of the major symptoms of human sinfulness.

The story of the Tower of Babel in Genesis 11:1-9 is a final illustration of the human corruption that prevails in the world after the flood. This legendary tale is based upon a well-known fact: human beings speak various languages, and, even among those who share the same tongue, effective and meaningful communication is always difficult and sometimes impossible. Human beings, therefore, suffer from a "confusion of tongues" and often cannot understand one another. This "crisis of communication," the Bible tells us, is a sign of man's fallenness, a "symbol of mankind's effort to proclaim their independence from God."[36] It is a further expression of man's sinful rebelliousness against God and of God's consequent judgment of man and his world.

In this chapter, we have surveyed the great themes of Genesis 1-11: God's creation of man and the cosmos; the sinfulness of man and his consequent alienation from God; God's eternal

judgment, condemnation and punishment of sin; and God's redemptive purpose for man and the world. The overall message
of Genesis 1-11 is that man's failure to love and obey God, his
desire to live "on his own" without the presence of God, is the
source of all the anxiety, meaninglessness, and horror of human
existence. The centrality of God in biblical thought reminds us
that God is the foundation and the fountain of life, and that the
love of God is the fulfilment of man, for only in God can we
find our true selves and our salvation.

The genealogy which traces the descent of the Semites from
Shem to Abraham (Gn 11:10-32) is the final sign of God's
redemptive work presented in Genesis 1-11. In Abraham, God
chooses a new remnant. The descendants of Abraham will be
the people of Israel, the chosen people. And it is from the chosen
people that the Redeemer promised in Genesis 3:15 will come.
The "seed of the woman" derives from the long line of Adam,
Seth, Noah, Shem, Abraham, Isaac, Jacob, Judah and David.
Jesus Christ, the "son of David," born of a virgin, will be the
greatest in the line of "the sons of God" (see Mt 1:1-18 and Lk
3:23-38). And this genealogical progression is carried forward
significantly in the eleventh chapter of Genesis. In the coming
of Abraham there is new hope, for the movement of God's
redemptive will is accelerated in the direction of the "new and
everlasting covenant" of Jesus Christ.

CHAPTER 3

The Old Testament History of Ancient Israel

Of the forty-nine books that make up the Old Testament, twenty-three are devoted to the history of ancient Israel. The period from Abraham to Moses is described in the Pentateuch, beginning with the twelfth chapter of Genesis and running through the books of Exodus, Leviticus, Numbers and Deuteronomy. The books of Joshua, Judges and Ruth tell the story of Israel's conquest and settlement of the land of Canaan (or Palestine). The rise of the Hebrew empire under Saul, David and Solomon and the collapse of that empire under Solomon's descendants is discussed in great detail in 1 and 2 Samuel, 1 and 2 Kings, 1 and 2 Chronicles, Tobit and Judith. The history of the Jews from the sixth century B.C. to the time of Christ—during which time Palestine was dominated successively by the Babylonians, Persians, Greeks and Romans—is told in the books of Ezra, Nehemiah, Esther, 1 Esdras and 1, 2 and 3 Maccabees. The noncanonical books of 2 Esdras and 4 Maccabees also contain information pertaining to this late phase of Old Testament history.

From the standpoint of Orthodox Christianity, the historical writings of the Old Testament point toward the incarnation of God the Son in Jesus Christ. The Old Testament as a whole is a foreshadowing of the New Testament revelation, a preparation for the advent of Christ. St. Paul stresses the Christocentric nature of the Old Testament revelation in 2 Timothy: "From childhood," he writes, "you have known the Holy Scriptures, which are able to make you wise for salvation through faith in Christ Jesus" (2 Tm 3:15). These words were written in 67 or 68 A.D., when the New Testament had not yet been completed. Thus, the "Holy Scriptures" mentioned here by St. Paul are the writings of the Old Testament, writings which, he says, lead us to salvation in Christ. Following St. Paul and other New Testament writers, the Orthodox Church regards the Old Testament as a preliminary revelation of God's providential plan for the salvation of the world. The Bible, both Old Testament and New Testament, is the book of salvation; and salvation comes through Jesus Christ. Thus, the Bible as a whole is about Christ. The Old Testament tells of God's promise to save through Christ; and the New Testament tells of the fulfilment of that promise. God has acted to save mankind and the world through Israel, his chosen people, and through the Messiah of Israel, Jesus of Nazareth.

God's intention to identify himself with the human race in the incarnation required his identification with one of the many nations of the world. If God the Son was to be "made man" in a fallen and fragmented world of many cultures and nations, he would have to be born into one of those cultures or nations. In choosing Israel as his people, and in promising to send a Messiah who would save Israel and all the world from the forces of evil, God began the process that would culminate in the birth and redemptive work of Jesus Christ. The Bible does not tell us why God chose Israel as his people rather than some other nation; it is simply revealed that this is what he has done. And the Old Testament history of ancient Israel, in describing and interpreting God's dealings with his people from the days of Abraham to the Roman conquest of Palestine, is a revelation of the manner in which both Israel and the world were made ready for the coming of Christ, the Son of God incarnate.

In the following pages of this chapter, we shall, first, survey the history of ancient Israel as presented in the Old Testament, and, second, we shall attempt to decipher the theological significance of that history from an Orthodox Christian point of view.

THE HISTORY OF ISRAEL FROM THE PATRIARCHS
TO THE POSTEXILIC ERA

For the purposes of analysis and interpretation, it is convenient to distinguish between six major periods or stages in the history of ancient Israel: (1) the age of the patriarchs (c. 2000-1700 B.C.); (2) the era of Moses and the exodus of Israel from Egypt (c. 1290-1250 B.C.); (3) the conquest of Canaan by Israel (c. 1250-1200 B.C.); (4) the period of the twelve-tribe confederacy (c. 1200-1025 B.C.); (5) the rise and fall of the Hebrew empire (1025-538 B.C.); and (6) the period from the Babylonian exile of the Jews to the Roman conquest of Palestine (538-37 B.C.), often referred to as the "restoration period."

The Age of the Patriarchs (c. 2000-1700 B.C.)

The story of the patriarchs (or fathers) of Israel is told in the book of Genesis, chapters 12 through 50. The central theme of these chapters is God's covenant with Abraham and the renewal of that covenant with Abraham's descendants, the people of Israel. (The Latin term *testamentum,* from which the Old and New Testaments are named, means "covenant.") In Abraham, the nation of Israel was elected as the people of God and was promised "everlasting possession" of the land of Canaan (or Palestine). Through faith in and obedience to God, Israel was to enjoy liberty, peace and happiness in the "promised land."

The development of the covenant relationship between God and Abraham is recorded in Genesis 11:10-25:18. God called Abraham to be the father of the chosen people, promising him that ". . . I will make of you a great nation, and I will bless you, and make your name great, so that you will be a blessing. I will bless those who bless you, and him who curses you I will curse; and by you all the families of the earth shall bless themselves" (Gn 12:2-3). The Bible also tells us that Abraham was chosen by God to be the patriarch, not only of the nation of ancient Israel, but of "a multitude of nations" (17:4-6). In Genesis 17:7-8, God tells Abraham that ". . . I will establish my covenant between me and you and your descendants after you throughout their generations for an everlasting covenant, to be God to you and to your descendants after you. And I will give to you, and to your descendants after you, the land of your sojournings, all the land of Canaan, for an everlasting possession; and I will be their God." According to Genesis 17:9-14, the fulfilment of God's covenant promises is contingent upon the faith of Abraham and his descendants, and the rite of circumcision was instituted as a sign of the covenant between God and his people. From the standpoint of Orthodox Christianity, it was through Christ and his Church that Abraham became the father of many nations, and it is those who live in faithful union with Christ who are the descendants of Abraham. In Christ, the rite of circumcision has been transcended by the sacrament of baptism; and those who are baptized into Christ will inherit the true promised land, the kingdom of heaven, of which the biblical land of Canaan (or Palestine) was a physical symbol.

Genesis 25:19-36:43 describes God's renewal and continuation of the Abrahamic covenant with Abraham's son Isaac and with Isaac's son Jacob. The Bible testifies to the strength of Abraham's faith in God and to Isaac's spiritual steadfastness and innocence. But Jacob was a sinful man whose faith in God was weak and impure. The Bible depicts his early life as a long and roundabout journey toward righteousness and fellowship with God. Jacob is pictured as one who has "striven with God and with men"; and God renames him "Israel," which means "he who strives with God" (Gn 32:28). This change of name is made in recognition of Jacob's victorious spiritual struggle to conquer his own sinful nature and to achieve reconciliation with God and his fellow man.

Jacob, or "Israel," fathered twelve sons: Reuben, Simeon, Levi, Judah, Dan, Naphtali, Gad, Asher, Issachar, Zebulun, Joseph and Benjamin. The "sons of Israel" are also the fathers of the twelve tribes of Hebrews which constituted the ancient nation of Israel. Thus, "Israel" is a name for the descendants of Abraham as well as the name of an individual (Jacob).

The history of the sons of Israel is recounted in Genesis 37-50. Joseph, the second youngest son of Jacob, is the major figure in this history. His elder brothers, resentful because Jacob "loved Joseph more than any other of his children," cast him into a pit.

Joseph was rescued by traveling merchants, who took him to Egypt and sold him as a slave. There he found favor with his master, Potiphar, until he was falsely accused by Potiphar's wife of trying to seduce her, and as a result of this charge, Joseph was thrown into prison. Then Pharoah (the king of Egypt) had a troubling dream which no one could explain to him. Hearing that Joseph possessed a special gift of interpretation, Pharoah sent for the young prisoner. Joseph interpreted Pharoah's dream, predicting that seven years of plenty would be followed by seven years of famine, and he advised that large amounts of food be carefully stored away as a reserve. Pharoah then put Joseph in charge of the storage project, which was successfully carried out. And as a result of his success, Joseph became a prominent and powerful man in the land of Egypt.

When the predicted famine arrived, Joseph's brothers were among those foreigners who came to Egypt to purchase food. Joseph forgave them for their sin against him and sent for his father, Jacob (Israel). Thus, Israel and his people went to dwell in the land of Egypt. And the nation of Israel continued its sojourn in Egypt from the time of Jacob and Joseph until the time of Moses.

Moses and the Exodus from Egypt (1290-1250 B.C.)

The biblical account of Israel's exodus from Egypt and return to the land of Canaan is contained in the books of Exodus, Leviticus, Numbers and Deuteronomy, which were written, edited and compiled by Jewish priests and scribes between the tenth and fifth centuries B.C.

The book of Exodus is divided into two main parts: chapters 1-18 describe the oppression of the Israelites in Egypt and their deliverance from their Egyptian yoke under the leadership of the prophet, Moses; and chapters 19-40 describe God's renewal of his covenant with Moses and the people of Israel.

The oppression of Israel by Egypt is described in Exodus 1. After the death of Joseph and his brothers, the people of Israel prospered in Egypt—"they multiplied and grew exceedingly strong, so that the land was filled with them" (1:7). Then "there arose a new king over Egypt, who did not know Joseph" (1:8). This king, probably Seti I (1309-1290 B.C.), feared the strength and numbers of the tribes of Israel. He therefore enslaved them and ordered that their male infants be drowned.

It was into this situation that Moses was born. His parents were Israelites, members of the tribe of Levi. His mother sought to save his life by hiding him among the reeds at the brink of the Nile River. The child was found by Pharoah's daughter, who adopted him and gave him the name of Moses, which means "to draw out." He who was "drawn out" of the river would live to draw his people out of Egypt (see Ex 2:1-10). Although he was brought up in the Egyptian court, Moses somehow discovered his Hebrew roots and developed a strong sense of loyalty to his own people. As a young man, he killed an Egyptian whom he saw beating an Israelite; and, when his act was made known to Pharoah, Moses was forced to flee to the land of Midian (that is, present-day Saudi Arabia). In Midian, he married the daughter of a Midianite priest and became a shepherd (2:11-22). Moses' family life and settled pastoral existence were, however, soon disrupted. For God appeared to him in a burning bush, and commanded him to return to Egypt, where he would be the Lord's instrument in delivering the people of Israel from their bondage (2:23-4:31).

The deliverance of Israel from Egypt is recounted in Exodus 5-15. Returning from Midian to Egypt, probably during the reign of Ramses II (1290-1224 B.C.), Moses called upon Pharoah to let the people of Israel go. But Pharoah refused to release the Israelites from their bondage. Thus, God sent a series of ten plagues upon Egypt in order to change Pharoah's mind. The people of Israel were unaffected by these calamities, and, after the tenth plague—the death of all the first-born of Egypt, both man and beast—Pharoah agreed to Moses' demand that the Israelites be set free.

Thus, the people of Israel, led by Moses, began their exodus from the land of Egypt. As Israel moved eastward from Egypt toward the Sinai peninsula, Pharoah regretted that he had granted his Hebrew slaves their liberty. Mobilizing his military forces, Pharoah pursued the Israelites as they made their way toward "the Red Sea." (The Hebrew phrase which is commonly translated as "Red Sea" might be more accurately rendered as "sea of reeds," which was not the Red Sea itself, but a shallower body of water farther north.) When Moses and the people of God, followed by the Egyptian host, reached the sea, Moses, upon the command of the Lord, "stretched out his hand over the sea; and the Lord drove the sea back by a strong east wind all night, and made the sea dry land, and the waters were divided" (Ex 14:21). The terrified Israelites were therefore able to cross the sea. But when Pharoah's forces tried to pursue the fugitive Hebrews, the Lord caused the waters of the sea to return to their "wonted flow," and the Egyptians were utterly destroyed (see 14:22-31). And the people of Israel, finally and decisively delivered from bondage in Egypt, "feared the Lord; and they believed in the Lord and in his servant Moses" (14:31).

The story of the exodus contains two images that have played important roles in the development of traditional Christian sacramental theology. First, there is the feast of Passover, instituted by God during the tenth plague inflicted upon Egypt. The details of the feast are contained in Exodus 12, where the Lord instructs the Israelites on how to prepare the Passover lamb:

> Your lamb shall be without blemish, a male a year old. . . .
> The whole assembly of the congregation of Israel shall kill
> their lambs in the evening. Then they shall take some of
> the blood, and put it on the two doorposts and the lintel
> of the houses in which they eat them. . . . And you shall
> eat it in haste. It is the Lord's passover. For I will pass
> through the land of Egypt that night, and I will smite all
> the first-born in the land of Egypt, both man and beast. . . .
> The blood shall be a sign for you, upon the houses where
> you are; and when I see the blood, I will pass over you,
> and no plague shall fall upon you to destroy you, when I
> smite the land of Egypt. (12:1-13)

Orthodox sacramental theology interprets the Passover events as symbolic foreshadowings of the holy eucharist. The Passover lamb is sacrificed and eaten, and the people of Israel are saved from God's wrath by the blood of the lamb. In the New Testament, Christ is the Passover lamb, whose death on the cross saves mankind from sin and death. And in the Christian sacrament of holy communion, the people of God, in eating and drinking the consecrated bread and wine, partake of the very body and blood of the Lord Jesus Christ—"the Lamb of God, who takes away the sin of the world" (Jn 1:29).

The story of Israel's miraculous crossing of the sea has also been interpreted in sacramental terms. The story is, in effect, an icon of the sacrament of baptism. The people of God enter the sea, which ordinarily would mean certain death; but they are delivered from the Egyptians through the intervention of God. As indicated in chapter 2, the sacrament of baptism, which requires immersion in and emergence from water, is a participation in the death and resurrection of Christ. And the Exodus account of the crossing of the sea is one of several important Old Testament images that prepare the way for the full New Testament development of the baptismal theme.

Following their liberation from the land of Egypt, the people of Israel were led by Moses across the Sinai desert toward Mount Sinai (Ex 15-18). The journey was a difficult one, and the people complained frequently against Moses. But time and again, when it seemed that they would be overcome by their hunger and thirst, the Israelites were sustained by miraculous interventions by God. The Lord provided them with fresh water (see 15:22-27, 17:1-7), and with meat and bread (see chapter 16). He also gave the people of Israel victory in their battle against the Amalekites, a fierce desert tribe that sought to destroy and plunder the wandering Hebrews (17:8-16). And thus, with God's help, Moses and Israel reached Mount Sinai, a site, as we shall see, of great spiritual significance. Again, these stories of God's sustenance of his people in the desert are commonly interpreted by Orthodox commentators as images and foreshadowings of the definitive work of salvation which was effected by Jesus Christ centuries after the time of Moses.

Exodus 1-18, which tells of the deliverance of Israel from Egypt, is followed by an account of God's renewal of his covenant with Moses and the people of Israel (Ex 19-40). As we have seen, the covenant relationship between God and Israel began with Abraham. In Exodus, that relationship is renewed and significantly extended. At Mount Sinai, God spoke to Moses, saying,

"Thus you shall say to the . . . people of Israel: '. . . If you will obey my voice and keep my covenant, you shall be my own possession among all peoples; for all the earth is mine, and you shall be to me a kingdom of priests and a holy nation'" (19: 3-6). Here, God's covenant with Abraham is extended to the entire nation of Israel (Abraham's descendants) and is conditioned upon the nation's faithful and obedient response to the Word of the Lord.

Following Israel's acceptance of the covenant, God called Moses to the top of Mount Sinai and revealed to him the divine law, which is recorded in Exodus 20-23. The law, as expressed in the book of Exodus, is divided into two parts: the Ten Commandments (20:1-17) and the Covenant Code (20:21-23:33). The Ten Commandments, which are stated in Exodus 20 and also in Moses' reflections upon the law in Deuteronomy 5:6-21, constitute a revelation of the moral nature of God, of his holiness and righteousness and of the standards he expects his people to live up to. They also serve as a preface and introduction to the Covenant Code. This code, sometimes called the "Book of the Covenant," contains a collection of detailed and specific commandments concerning religious worship and ritual, the treatment of slaves and servants, murder, criminal assault, theft, property rights, usury, slander, witchcraft, sexual conduct, idolatry, the observance of the Sabbath, and so on.

All in all, the divine law, as set down in Exodus 20-23, is a revelation of God's will for his people—that by obeying the Word of the Lord they might become "a kingdom of priests and a holy nation" (19:6), worthy of possessing the land promised them in Abraham. And upon hearing the laws of God spoken by Moses, the people of Israel proclaimed, "All that the Lord has spoken we will do, and we will be obedient" (Ex 24:3-8).

In response to Israel's apparent commitment to the covenant and the law, and in fulfilment of his promise that the descendants of Abraham were to be his chosen people, God commanded Moses to have a tabernacle (a portable, tent-enclosed sanctuary) constructed. The biblical account of the building of the tabernacle of the Lord is contained in Exodus 25-40. The tabernacle was to house the Ark of the Covenant, a wooden chest containing stone tablets upon which the Ten Commandments were engraved.

The religious services of Israel were conducted in the tabernacle by priests selected from the tribe of Levi. The first members of the Israelite priesthood were Aaron, the brother of Moses, and Aaron's sons (see 28:1-4). Most importantly, God himself was present in the tabernacle in a "cloud of glory," which filled the holy place and remained over the Ark of the Covenant (see 40:34-38). During the wilderness wanderings of Israel, the forty-year preparation period prior to their occupation of the land of Canaan, the Lord dwelt with his people and guided them in their quest for a homeland. "For throughout all their journeys the cloud of the Lord was upon the tabernacle by day, and fire was in it by night, in the sight of all the house of Israel" (40:38).

It was pointed out already that the Lord's covenants with men are always accompanied by a sign or seal confirming that a covenant relationship has been established. This is also true of God's covenant with Israel during the days of Moses. Indeed, this covenant seems to be sealed by three signs. First, the Lord commands Israel to observe the Sabbath day as "a sign between me and you throughout your generations, that you may know that I, the Lord, sanctify you" (see Ex 31:12-18). Second, there is the law of God, given to Moses and Israel both as a sign and as an extension of the covenant. And third, the covenant is completed with the building of the tabernacle, a sign in the most literal sense of God's presence with his people.

Leviticus, the book of the Levites or the Hebrew priesthood, describes the religious organization of Israel under the leadership of Moses and his brother, the high priest Aaron. The central theme of this book is God's absolute holiness, the sinfulness of man and the way of atonement. The first sixteen chapters of Leviticus contain the ritual law of ancient Israel, which is presented as "the way of approach to God," a means by which sinful man can be reconciled with his Lord. Through rituals of purification, worship, sacrifice and service—conducted under the guidance of the Levitical priesthood—the spiritual and moral failures of Israel were repented of by the people and forgiven by God. In Leviticus 16, the institution of the "Day of Atonement" (or Yom Kippur), a major observance of historic Judaism, is described: "And it shall be a statute for you for ever that in the seventh month, on the tenth day of the month, you shall afflict yourselves, and shall do no work, either the native or the stranger who sojourns among you; for on this day shall atonement be made for you [by the priest], to cleanse you; from all your sins you shall be clean before the Lord" (16:29-30). And, indeed, atonement, or *at-one-ment*, between a holy God and sinful man is the whole purpose of the ritual law of Leviticus 1-16.

Leviticus 17-27 contains an extended analysis of the relationship between the ritual law of the tabernacle and general moral conduct. Such matters as marriage, chastity, respect for parents, the treatment of the poor, relationships between neighbors, the proper performance of national religious observances such as the Sabbath and Passover and tithing are discussed in detail. This section of Leviticus is sometimes called the "Holiness Code" because of its stress upon the need for personal piety and moral purity.

The book of Numbers (so called because of the numberings of the Israelites in chapters 1 and 26) is concerned with the social and political organization of Israel under Moses; and it also describes the preparations that were made for the occupation of the land of Canaan. "Most of the events in Numbers occur in the second and fortieth years of the forty-year period between the exodus and the entering of Canaan. Aside from two events, the thirty-eight weary years in the wilderness are passed over in silence."[1] Because of their sins against God, their lack of faith and failure to obey God's law, the people of Israel were not permitted to enter the Holy Land immediately after the renewal of the covenant at Mount Sinai. Instead, they had to go through a forty-year period of testing, a period of wandering in the wilderness to the south of Canaan. Numbers emphasizes the importance of religious devotion, of personal holiness and of a well-ordered community in its account of God's preparation of Israel for the entry into the promised land.

From a Christian point of view, Israel's forty-year sojourn in the desert and eventual conquest of the Holy Land constitute a typological image of the satanic temptation of Christ, which took place during a forty-day period (see Mt 4:1-11 and Lk 4:1-13). Like ancient Israel, "Jesus was led up by the Spirit into the wilderness to be tempted by the devil" (Mt 4:1). Unlike Israel, however, Jesus was guilty of no sin. But as the incarnation of

God the Son—that is, in identifying himself with the human condition—Christ had to enter into the desert created by man's sin. And upon his victory over Satan in the wilderness, Christ returns to the world to found the Church, the new Israel, and to lead her into the kingdom of God, the true Holy Land of which biblical Canaan is a physical symbol.

Deuteronomy (that is, the "Second Law"), the fifth and final book of the Pentateuch, is devoted mainly to the final teachings of Moses on the content and meaning of the covenant and the law. The book contains three Mosaic addresses to the tribes of Israel: first, an interpretation of the wilderness wanderings of God's people, which emphasizes their faithless failure to love and obey God (Dt 1:1-4:43); second, an exposition of the law (4:44-26:19); and third, a discourse on the meaning of the covenant (chapters 27-30). The last days of Moses' life and his death are recounted in Deuteronomy 31-34. The fundamental message of Deuteronomy, and indeed of the entire Pentateuch, is epitomized in the following question asked by Moses: "And now, Israel, what does the Lord your God require of you, but to fear the Lord your God, to walk in all his ways, to love him, to serve the Lord your God with all your heart and with all your soul, and to keep the commandments and statutes of the Lord...?" (10:12)

The Conquest of Canaan (c. 1250-1200 B.C.)

The Israelite conquest of the land of Canaan in the thirteenth century B.C. is described rather systematically in the book of Joshua, which was put into its present written form during the fifth century B.C. The book is named for its central character, Joshua, a member of the tribe of Ephraim, who succeeded Moses as the spiritual and military leader of Israel. In describing Israel's success in the occupation of the promised land, the book of Joshua portrays that success as a fulfilment of God's covenant commitment to his people.

Many readers of the Old Testament are dismayed at God's favor toward Israel and his wrathful condemnation and abandonment of the Canaanites. The Bible tells us, however, that the peoples of Canaan had become utterly corrupt and degenerate, and that their religions were concerned entirely with idolatry and demon worship (including the practice of human sacrifice). They appear as far more ungodly and depraved than the other peoples of the ancient Middle East. It was not impossible for the Canaanites to repent of their evil ways and to turn toward God for salvation (see Jos 2 and Rt 1-4). But, according to the Bible, very few Canaanites were interested in repentance and holiness. And it was for this reason that the Lord delivered them into the hands of the tribes of Israel.

The book of Joshua is composed of three major sections: first, an account of the invasion and conquest of Canaan by Israel (chapters 1-12); second, a description of the manner in which the promised land was partitioned among the tribes of Israel (13-21); and third, a rendition of Joshua's farewell address to the people of God prior to his death (22-24). The farewell address contains a renewal of the covenant between God and Israel, and it insists upon the necessity of steadfast faith in and obedience to God. The perils of faithlessness and disobedience are given an especially heavy emphasis. And indeed, the Bible testifies repeatedly that the people of the old covenant did not maintain their faith in God, nor were they consistently obedient to God. "The melancholy history of Israel is a clear example of failure to believe God and to obey Him. Judgment, dispersion among the nations, and the withdrawal of the blessing of God inevitably followed."[2] This faithlessness and disobedience constitute the basis upon which the old covenant with ancient Israel was ultimately superseded by "the new and everlasting covenant of our Lord and Savior Jesus Christ."

The story of Joshua leading the old Israel into the promised land is yet another Old Testament icon of the person and work of Jesus Christ. The name "Joshua" (or *Yehoshua*) is a Hebrew word meaning "Yahweh is salvation." And the Greek rendering of "Joshua" is "Jesus." Just as Joshua led God's people to victory in the land of Canaan, so Jesus has brought victory to his Church —the new Israel—and is, even now, leading her into the true promised land, the kingdom of heaven.

*The Period of the Twelve-Tribe Confederacy
(c. 1200-1025 B.C.)*

The books of Judges and Ruth recount the history of Israel from the death of Joshua to the time just prior to the establishment of the Hebrew monarchy under Saul, David and Solomon. During this period, those parts of Canaan that had been occupied by Israel were partitioned among the twelve tribes, and the land was loosely organized and ruled by a tribal confederacy.

The book of Judges was put into final written form during the seventh and sixth centuries B.C. The first part of the book (1:1-2:5) emphasizes Israel's limited hegemony in Canaan, the failure to complete the process of occupation begun during the days of Joshua. This failure is explained as a result of Israel's sinful blending of the worship of God with the pagan religious practices of the non-Hebrew tribes dwelling in Canaan. The people of Israel began to venerate Baal, the chief god of the Canaanites, and Astarte, the Canaanite goddess of fertility and war (see 2:11-15). Thus, the Lord God did not allow them to complete their conquest of the land. Because the Israelites did not obey the Lord's command to "make no covenant with the inhabitants of this land" and to "break down their altars," God proclaimed that he would "not drive . . . [the Canaanites] out before you; but they shall become adversaries to you, and their gods shall be a snare to you" (2:1-5).

Thus, disobedience and faithlessness bring judgment and condemnation. But God, while he judges and condemns the sins of Israel, is also merciful. He sends spiritual and political assistance to his people in the persons of the judges—those charismatic spiritual, military and political leaders who emerged during the period of the twelve-tribe confederacy to deliver Israel from her Canaanite enemies and from her own sinful apostasy. The second part of the book of Judges (2:6-16:31) tells of the emergence of the judges and of the dialectic of apostasy and deliverance—the seemingly endless cycle of sin, judgment, repentance and forgiveness—which characterized the life of Israel during the twelfth and eleventh centuries B.C. The judges who are mentioned are Othniel of Judah, Ehud, Shamgar, Deborah, Barak, Gideon of

Manasseh, Tola of Issachar, Jair of Gilead, Jephthah, Ibzan, Elon, Abdon and Samson. The book of Judges does not explain whether some of these leaders ruled consecutively or contemporaneously. The last of the judges was Samuel, as the book of Samuel indicates.

Even under the guidance of the judges, however, something was amiss in the nation of Israel. The third part of Judges (chapters 17-21) describes the anarchic social and religious conditions that prevailed throughout the era of the twelve-tribe confederacy. Many Israelites rejected God's law and the leadership of the judges. They were faithless and disobedient, adopting the culture, values and religious practices of the Canaanites. The consequences of this apostasy and paganization were social and political disorder, corruption and instability among the tribes of Israel. In rejecting the terms of God's covenant, Israel was judged by God and accordingly condemned to a life of almost utter insecurity. The concluding sentence of Judges states both the basis for the anarchic conditions of the time and the direction in which God was leading his people during that age of crisis: "In those days there was no king in Israel; every man did what was right in his own eyes" (21:25). The era of anarchy was bringing Israel ever closer to the time when the nation would be united under and ruled by a king.

The coming of the Hebrew monarchy is given further emphasis in the book of Ruth, which was probably composed during the sixth century B.C. but which contains a story set in the days of the judges. The story of Ruth testifies to the presence of God in the lives of his faithful children, even during a period generally characterized by unbelief, apostasy, lawlessness and disorder. And the relationship between the Israelites and the Canaanites is presented from a point of view that is rather different from that of the book of Judges.

The events described in the book of Ruth took place during the late twelfth or early eleventh century B.C. Seeking to escape a famine in the region of their native Bethlehem, a family of Israelites from the tribe of Judah—Elimelech, his wife Naomi and their two sons, Mahlon and Chilion—moved into Moab, which lay in the southeastern portion of the land of Canaan. The Moabites were descended from Moab, the son of Lot (Abraham's nephew) and his daughter (see Gn 19:30-38). Their incestuous origins marked the Moabites as alien to the ways of God. In Moab, Elimelech died, and his sons married Moabite women, Orpah and Ruth. "They lived there about ten years; and both Mahlon and Chilion died, so that the woman [Naomi] was bereft of her two sons and her husband" (Rt 1:4-5). Hearing that the famine in Bethlehem had ended, Naomi decided to return to her native country. And although her daughters-in-law wished to accompany her, Naomi urged them to return to their own people. Orpah agreed to remain in Moab, but Ruth clung to Naomi, saying, "Entreat me not to leave you or to return from following you; for where you go I will go, and where you lodge I will lodge; your people shall be my people, and your God my God" (1:16). Having thus become an Israelite through love and faith, Ruth traveled to Bethlehem with Naomi. In Bethlehem, the young Moabitess found favor in the eyes of Boaz, a "man of wealth" and kinsman of Elimelech. Thus, Boaz and Ruth were married—and their son Obed was the father of Jesse, who became the father of David, the greatest of all the kings of ancient Israel (see Rt 2-4). And through David, Ruth became an ancestress of Jesus Christ himself. Her name is mentioned explicitly in the genealogy of Christ presented in Matthew 1:1-17.

The book of Ruth has two major purposes: first, to trace the ancestry of King David (keeping in mind that the book was written long after the events it describes); and second, to proclaim that the love and mercy of God extend to all, Israelite and non-Israelite, who turn to him in faith and who seek his protection. The death of Elimelech and his sons in Moab is a sign of God's condemnation of Israel's move toward paganism, whereas Naomi's return to Bethlehem and the consequent conversion of Ruth is a sign of the only acceptable form of integration between Israel and the Canaanites. This second aim of the book of Ruth is in no way inconsistent with the perspective of the book of Judges. The latter book condemns the paganization of the Israelites, their turning from the true God to the idols of the Canaanites; but Judges never suggests that the conversion of Canaanites to the religion of Israel is either impossible or contrary to the will of God.

The Rise and Fall of the Hebrew Empire (1025-538 B.C.)

The fifth stage in the Old Testament history of ancient Israel —the emergence and eventual collapse of the Hebrew monarchy —is described in great detail in 1 and 2 Samuel, 1 and 2 Kings, Tobit and Judith. The books of Samuel and Kings were compiled in written form between the tenth and fifth centuries B.C., and the books of Tobit and Judith were composed during the second century B.C. Since the material contained in these texts is both very detailed and very complex, we shall have to rest content here with a sketch of the broad outlines of this important era in the history of God's people. The history of the Hebrew empire can be divided into three parts: first, the emergence and establish-ment of the Hebrew monarchy, often called the "united mon-archy" (1025-931 B.C.); second, the division of the empire into two kingdoms (930-586 B.C.); and third, the final destruction of the Hebrew empire by the Babylonians (586-538 B.C.).

The Establishment of the Hebrew Monarchy (1025-931 B.C.). During the eleventh century B.C., the anarchic conditions that characterized the twelve-tribe confederacy became ever more severe and difficult to live with. The people of Israel became in-creasingly discontented with the leadership of the judges, and they began to cry out for "a king to govern us . . . that we may also be like all the nations" (1 Sm 8:5, 20). This demand for a king, however, was in effect a rejection of God's theocratic rule through his judges (see 1 Sm 8:7-9). It was not the rule of the judges that made the era of the confederacy unstable, but rather the faithlessness and disobedience of the people of Israel them-selves. Yet God allowed the Israelites to have their king; and he directed the last great judge, Samuel (see 1 Sm 1-7), to name Saul, a member of the tribe of Benjamin, as the first king of Israel (1 Sm 8-10).[3] The reign of Saul (1025-1000 B.C.), which is described in 1 Samuel 8-31, was a mixed blessing for Israel. King Saul consolidated the Hebrew monarchy and waged war with the Philistines and other Canaanite peoples. But he failed to eliminate intertribal strife among the Israelites; and he was ultimately de-feated by the Philistines, leaving his nation thoroughly exposed to foreign domination. When Saul committed suicide after losing the Philistine war, the kingdom of Israel was on the verge of collapse. Thus, as a result of their desire for a king (that they might be "like all the other nations"), the people of Israel were left even worse off than they had been under the leadership of the judges.

But, once again, God intervened to save his people from disaster. David, the great-grandson of Boaz and Ruth, was raised up to rule Israel as God's anointed king. The reign of David (1000-965 B.C.) is chronicled in 2 Samuel and in the first two chapters of 1 Kings. David was far from perfect, either morally or spiritually (see 2 Sm 11-12); but he was "deeply aware that God alone . . . [was] Israel's true king and that he himself, like every other citizen of Israel, . . . [was] subject to God's cove- nant."[4] And under his highly effective military and political leadership, the Philistines and other enemies of Israel were defeat- ed and driven back, and the tribes of Israel were welded into a unified, prosperous and powerful nation.

When David died, he was succeeded by his son, Solomon (965-931 B.C.). The biblical account of Solomon's kingship is contained in 1 Kings 3-11. Under Solomon, the territory con- trolled by Israel was greatly extended, and many alliances and trade agreements with foreign powers (such as Egypt) were made. Thus, the kingdom became an empire. Solomon also or- dered the construction of the great Temple in Jerusalem, which replaced the tabernacle as the location of the Ark of the Covenant and as Israel's center of religious worship. But, in spite of his many years of glory and faithfulness to God, Solomon turned away from the Lord in his old age. He brought "many foreign women" into his harem and allowed himself to be enticed into idolatry by some of his pagan wives (see 1 Kg 11). Because of Solomon's sin, God raised up adversaries against the king; and when Solomon died, the civil strife he had brought upon his kingdom was inherited by his son and heir, Rehoboam.

The Division of the Empire (930-586 B.C.). Rehoboam (931- 913 B.C.) did not rule wisely, and the Hebrew empire was soon torn apart by civil war. The empire was divided into two king- doms: a northern kingdom, called Israel, and a southern kingdom, called Judah. The northern kingdom was made up of the ten tribes of Reuben, Simeon, Dan, Naphtali, Gad, Asher, Issachar, Zebulun, Ephraim and Manasseh (the latter two were half-tribes resulting from an earlier division of the tribe of Joseph—see Gn 48). The two southern tribes, Judah and Benjamin, maintained their loyalty to the house of David and constituted the kingdom of Judah. The tribe of Levi, from which the priesthood of the Israelites was drawn—and because of its religious role in the life of God's people—had been dispersed among the other tribes during the days of Joshua (see Jos 21). Thus, there were Levites living in both the northern and southern kingdoms following the civil wars of the late tenth century B.C.

The kingdoms of Israel and Judah coexisted from 930 to 722 B.C. (see 1 Kg 12-2 Kg 16). In 723 B.C., the kingdom of Israel was attacked by the Assyrians, and within a year, the northern kingdom had been utterly defeated (see 2 Kg 17 and Tb 1-14). The ten northern tribes were enslaved and transported eastward to the outer reaches of the Assyrian empire, which stretched as far as present-day Iran. The lands of the vanquished Israelites were subsequently settled by Assyrian colonists, and the area was thenceforward known as Samaria. These Assyrian settlers adopted the God of Israel as their God, but accepted only the first five books of the Old Testament (the Pentateuch) as their scriptures and considered Mount Gerizim in Samaria their holy place rather than Jerusalem. The descendants of these colonists were the Samaritans of later times, who were regarded as Gentiles by the people of Judah. In effect, the Assyrian conquest of the northern kingdom meant the disappearance from history of the ten tribes of Israel that had been located in that kingdom. After the Assyrian destruction of the kingdom of Israel, only the tribes of Judah and Benjamin and those members of the tribe of Levi dwelling in the southern kingdom remained in existence. This historical fact is the foundation of all later legends concerning the lost tribes of Israel. And because the surviving kingdom was named Judah, her people came to be called "Jews" throughout the Middle East, and her culture and religion came to be known as "Judaism."

The Babylonian Exile (or Captivity) of the Jews (586-538

B.C.). After the Assyrian conquest of the northern kingdom, the kingdom of Judah continued as an autonomous state from 722 to 586 B.C. (see 2 Kg 18-24). The Assyrian empire, which had tried unsuccessfully to destroy Judah, was overthrown by the Babylonians (or "Chaldeans") in 612 B.C. And the Babylonians, under the leadership of Nebuchadnezzar (605-562 B.C.), succeeded where the Assyrians had failed: they overwhelmed the kingdom of Judah in the summer of 586 B.C., destroyed the great Temple which had been built during the reign of King Solomon and the Ark of the Covenant which was housed in the Temple and deported many Jews as slaves to the eastern regions of Babylonia (see 2 Kg 23:36-24:30 and Jdt 1-16). With the Babylonian exile, which lasted nearly fifty years, the Hebrew empire was finally and decisively annihilated, and the empire became a thing of the past, to haunt the imaginations of Jews for centuries thereafter.

The Restoration Period (c. 538-37 B.C.)

The Babylonian domination of the Holy Land came to an end in 539 B.C., when the Babylonian empire was conquered by the Persians. The period of Persian hegemony over Palestine is presented in biblical perspective in the books of 1 and 2 Chronicles, Ezra, Nehemiah, Esther and 1 Esdras, which were written between the fifth and second centuries B.C. The Persian empire, under Cyrus the Great (555-530 B.C.), was the largest empire the world had yet seen. "The new empire was conceived as a commonwealth of provinces enjoying a large degree of autonomy under the control of their viceroys or satraps."[5] In the year 538 B.C., Cyrus issued an edict allowing the Jews who were enslaved in Babylon to return to their homeland: "Thus says Cyrus king of Persia: The Lord, the God of heaven, has given me all the kingdoms of the earth, and he has charged me to build him a house at Jerusalem, which is in Judah. Whoever is among you of all his people, may his God be with him, and let him go up to Jerusalem, which is in Judah, and rebuild the house of the Lord [the Temple]. . . ." (Ezra 1:2-3). The rebuilding of the Temple was accomplished by 515 B.C. (see Ezra 1-6). Jerusalem itself was then largely reconstructed, the work on the city being completed in 443 B.C. (see Ne 1-7). Judah was ruled by the Persians from 539 to 330 B.C., but the Jews were, within limits, virtually self-governing.

The Persian empire was destroyed by the armies of Alexander the Great in 330 B.C. And thus, Egypt and the entire Middle East, including Judah, passed into the hands of the Greeks. Alexander died in 323 B.C., and "in the ensuing struggle for Alexander's succession, Judea [and all of present-day Palestine] was claimed by the Ptolemies of Egypt [who were of Greek extraction], until it passed under the allegiance of the Seleucids of Antioch [also ethnically Greek] in 198 B.C., when Antiochus the Great defeated the Egyptian forces at Panias."[6] The Seleucids attempted to impose Hellenistic culture and values upon the Jews, and sought to destroy the Jewish religion. This policy led to the Maccabean revolt of 165-153 B.C. The revolt was begun by Mattathias the Levite and his five sons, John, Simon, Judas, Eleazar and Jonathan. The sons of Mattathias have come to be known as "the Maccabees," because *Makkabaios* is the Greek form of Mattathias. The revolt was largely successful, and it ended with the establishment of an independent Jewish state in Palestine ruled by the family of the Maccabees (known as "the Hasmonean dynasty," since the family name of the brothers Maccabee was "Hasmon") until 37 B.C. The Greek and Maccabean phases of the restoration period are reflected in the books of 1, 2 and 3 Maccabees, which were composed during the second and first centuries B.C.

The period of Jewish independence under the Hasmoneans was short-lived. After 63 B.C., the Roman empire began to expand into the Middle East. And with the coming of the Romans to the Holy Land after 40 B.C., the Old Testament history of ancient Israel draws to a close. For it was during the Roman era that the "old covenant" was to be transcended by the "new covenant" of Jesus Christ.

THE THEOLOGICAL SIGNIFICANCE OF THE HISTORY OF ANCIENT ISRAEL

As we have seen, the first eleven chapters of the book of

Genesis constitute a theological reflection upon the original harmonious relationship between God, man and nature and the disruption of that relationship by the sinful rebellion of men and fallen angels against the love and will of God. Genesis 1-11 depicts man's loss of eternal life in God and his bondage to the devil. Man is alienated from God and subject to the tyranny of sin and death; and he is powerless to extricate himself from this fallen state of existence. Thus, Genesis 1-11 (and, indeed, the entire Bible) is a revelation of the human condition and of the human need for salvation. Those earliest chapters of Holy Scripture also reveal God's intention to redeem mankind and the world through his chosen people—the people of Israel—and through the Messiah of Israel, who would lead the entire human race back into fellowship with God. The Old Testament history of ancient Israel, which we have surveyed, traces the process by which God prepared the world for the coming of the Messiah, our Lord and Savior Jesus Christ. For this reason, the history of Israel from Abraham to the Roman conquest of Palestine (from Gn 12 through 3 Mc) is frequently and quite properly called a "salvation history," a history with a theological purpose containing a promise of salvation from the world, the flesh and the devil.

The message of salvation contained in the Old Testament history of ancient Israel may be broken down into a number of major themes. We shall now turn to a discussion of several specific theological ideas as they relate to that history.

The Nature of God

Holy Scripture presupposes the existence of God. For the "scriptural mind," the reality of God and of the supernatural is obvious, a fact of religious experience. Thus, the Bible contains no arguments for the existence of God. The existence of spiritual beings was not problematic for the writers of scripture and other citizens of the ancient world. Their question was not, "Does God exist?" but rather, "Where can I find the true God, and what is the nature of that true God?" We have already presented the perspective of Genesis 1-2 on the nature of the true God.[7] The historical texts of the Old Testament express a view of God's nature that is essentially identical with the theological perspective of Genesis 1-2 and which is, in fact, common to the entire biblical corpus.

Building upon holy tradition and upon the biblical revelation of the Lord and his mighty works, Orthodox theologians have developed a detailed description of the activity and fundamental attributes of God. The central declaration and constant affirmation of the Orthodox Church is that God *is,* that God *lives* and that God *acts.* And the being, life and activity of God are directed both toward himself and toward his creation. That is, God is, lives and acts in and of himself (within his own essence); and God also is, lives and acts toward and in his created order ("the heavens and the earth . . . all things visible and invisible"[8]). Thus, God's being, life and activity are both *transcendent* and *immanent.* And because they are immanently present in the created order, it may be said that God—who is, in and of himself, "ineffable, inconceivable, invisible, [and] incomprehensible"[9]— "shows" or "reveals" himself in and to his creation. God reveals himself *in* the creation at large and *to* those of his creatures who are endowed with intelligence (that is, humans and angels). From the standpoint of Orthodox Christianity, then, it is not enough to say that God is an eternally real, living and active being; we must also affirm that *God has revealed himself to us,* in holy tradition and in Holy Scripture.

For the Orthodox Christian, then, the God of the Bible is a single, supremely perfect, spiritual (that is, immaterial), and personal being possessing all holiness, truth, goodness, joy and power. Thus, God is one, personal and spiritual; his being is infinite, eternal and immutable; he is all-powerful (omnipotent) and all-knowing (omniscient); he is all-present (omnipresent), and yet he is above and beyond the world (transcendent); and he is the absolutely good (omnibenevolent) and perfectly free Creator of the universe. In addition to these fundamental attributes of the divine nature, Orthodox biblical theology also holds that Holy Scripture reveals the trinitarian being of God. This is certainly true of the New Testament, where there are many references to the three persons of the Holy Trinity. There are also several places in the Old Testament where the triunity of God seems to manifest itself—for example, in the work of creation as depicted in Genesis 1, where God creates the universe in the Spirit and through his Word;[10] and in Genesis 18, where the Lord appears to Abraham in the tripersonal form of "three men."

The Old Testament historical writings contain four distinctive emphases with regard to the nature and activity of God. In the first place, God is presented again and again as the one, personal and universal Lord of all creation. This emphasis upon a strict personal monotheism is especially clear in the "revelation" of the burning bush (Ex 2:23-3:22), in which the absolute and universal sovereignty of God was made known to Moses. In that revelation, which transformed Moses from fugitive to prophet, the God of Israel—the God of Abraham, Isaac and Jacob—encountered Moses as the great "I AM." Moses asked God his name, and the Lord replied, "I AM WHO I AM" (Ex 3:13-15). That is to say, the God of Israel is the ground of all being, the source of all things—the one, universal and absolute Creator of the world. The God of Israel is not merely a local or tribal deity, one god among a multitude of other divine beings, but the absolute and universal Lord of all creation. And this supreme Lord has made his covenant with Israel and called Moses to be his agent in liberating the people of God from the oppression of Egypt. Such is the central content of the revelation at the burning bush, a central theme throughout the entire Old Testament history of Israel.

In the second place, the absolute holiness and righteousness of God are made manifest in the revelation of the law as recorded in the books of Exodus, Leviticus, Numbers and Deuteronomy. The Lord's repeated judgment and condemnation of the sinfulness of Israel during the long period following the death of Moses and prior to the advent of Christ is a further expression of his moral perfection and supremacy. In the third place, however, the mercy and compassion of God, which are also aspects of his absolute goodness, are revealed in his abiding love for his people. While God judges and condemns sin, he also, time and again, forgives and redeems the children of Israel. And in the fourth place, the love of God for Israel is actually an expression of his love for the entire human race. For in Israel, the Lord was preparing the world for salvation from sin and death. In Israel, the existence, nature and saving activity of God were to be proclaimed to the world; and through Israel, the final redemption of man and nature was to be effected in the person and work of the Messiah, of Christ. Thus, God's special relationship with Israel, as described in the historical literature of the Old Testament, was preparatory to the reconciliation of "all things" to God in and through Christ.

God's Covenant with Israel

God's special relationship with ancient Israel is grounded upon his covenant with Abraham and the renewal and extension of that covenant at Mount Sinai during the time of Moses. The renewed and extended relationship between God and his people is sometimes called "the covenant with Israel." In the covenant, God promised his people deliverance from their enemies and a free, peaceful and happy life in Canaan, the land of fulfilment; and the fulfilment of God's promise was contingent upon Israel's faithful and obedient response to the Lord's love and will. Thus, because of the repeated disobedience and apostasy of ancient Israel, the covenant promises were never perfectly fulfilled during Old Testament times.

The failure of the Israelites to live up to the terms of their covenant relationship with God was, from a Christian point of view, a part of the divine plan for the salvation of the world. The all-knowing Lord of creation foresaw the faithlessness and disobedience that would make Israel's everlasting possession of the promised land impossible; and through the historical pilgrimage of Israel from the time of Abraham to the coming of Christ, God sought to make it clear to the human race that salvation could never be won by human effort alone. Only in the perfect faith and obedience of the Messiah, Jesus Christ, would an Israelite measure up to the standards of the divine law. Only through the perfect and personal union of God and man in Jesus could the requirements of God's covenant with his people be met. The incarnation was necessary to the fulfilment of the covenant with Israel, because no man could perfectly obey the divine law unless God became man. And that, according to the Christian faith, is exactly what happened in Jesus Christ.

In Christ, then, the covenant with Israel was fulfilled, transformed and transcended. After the coming of the Messiah—the incarnation of God the Son—only those who are "built into Christ" are counted among the people of God. In Christ, the old Israel is superseded by the Christian Church, the new Israel, the body of Christ; the old covenant is completed in the new covenant in and through Jesus Christ. And Jesus—"the second Adam," the new Joshua, "the son of David," "the son of Abraham"— fulfils the old covenant and leads his people, the Church, into the true promised land, the kingdom of heaven. Through the Messiah of Israel, and through his fulfilment of the old covenant, a new covenant is established between God and the human race. In Christ, God's covenant with Abraham is extended, not only to the old Israel, but to the entire human race. But like the covenant with Israel, the new covenant requires steadfast faith and an obedient spirit in those who would be reconciled to the Lord of all creation. And like all covenants between God and man, the new covenant in Christ is sealed with a sign: the sign of the cross.

The Revelation of the Divine Law

The giving of the law—as recorded in Exodus, Leviticus, Numbers and Deuteronomy—is a revelation of the holiness of God, of the desperate sinfulness of man and of the human need for salvation. The standards of the Old Testament law are extremely high; they are reflective of the moral and spiritual perfection of the Lord himself. The Old Testament history of ancient Israel makes it quite clear that mankind is incapable of living up to the standards of God's law. As the ancient Israelites sinned repeatedly against the divine law, so do we all fall short of the perfect righteousness of God. As we have seen, the Old Testament law contains a ritual code (Lv 1-16) which establishes a way of atonement for the sins of Israel, a means by which violations of God's will might be forgiven. Thus, man's inability to measure up to the holiness of the Lord is both implicitly and explicitly recognized in the law itself.

Jesus, quoting Deuteronomy 6:5 and Leviticus 19:8, summarized the divine law as follows: "You shall love the Lord your God with all your heart, and with all your soul, and with all your mind. This is the great and first commandment. And a second is like it, You shall love your neighbor as yourself. On these two commandments hang all the law and the prophets" (Mt 22:37-40; see also Mk 12:29-31). We are to love God with all the passion of our hearts, with all the life of our souls and with all the power of our minds. And, on that basis, we are to love our neighbors as ourselves—that is, we are to place the desires, interests and needs of others on at least an equal footing with our own. To believe that we are able to save ourselves through our own works of righteousness is to be subject to the most extreme moral and spiritual delusion; it is to ignore the entire content of Holy Scripture. For, in the words of the prophet Isaiah, "We have all become like one who is unclean, and all our righteous deeds are like a polluted garment. We all fade like a leaf, and our iniquities, like the wind, take us away" (Is 64:6). God's law shows us that, as St. Paul puts it, "None is righteous, no, not one; no one understands, no one seeks God. All have turned aside, together they have gone wrong; no one does good, not even one" (Rm 3:10-12). Thus, "no human being will be justified in . . . [God's] sight by works of the law [that is, through self-produced righteousness], since through the law comes knowledge of sin" (Rm 3:20).

To meditate upon the law of God, and upon the repeated failure of Israel to obey that law, is to see the difference between things as they ought to be and things as they are. Most of us, most of the time, are fixated upon the contrast between things as we think they are and things as we would like them to be. The Old Testament history of ancient Israel is therefore a spiritual and moral challenge to us: it challenges us to look at the world, ourselves and God with a "scriptural mind." The revelation of God's law in the Old Testament is, in an important sense, a disturbing revelation. Many of us would like to believe that the Lord demands nothing of us except that we be "nice people," living according to the commonly accepted moral, legal and religious standards of our society. But our society and its standards, from a biblical point of view, are aspects of a fallen world that has departed from the path of God's righteousness. To conform oneself to the ways of the world is to set oneself in opposition to God and his law. The law of God, as expressed in the Old Testament historical literature, challenges us to face up to our desperate situation, to discern the vast differences between the way we are and the way God wants us to be, the way we ought to be. If we will acknowledge our lack of righteousness in the eyes of God, our utter failure to conform to the standards of God's absolute holiness, we will at least realize that we are far from the kingdom of heaven and that we will never enter that kingdom except through the mercy and grace of the Lord.

The law was given that Israel and all mankind might realize their need for salvation. For the law, when seen for what it is, shows us that "all have sinned and fall short of the glory of God" (Rm 3:23). And thus, the Old Testament revelation of the divine law is intended to direct our spirits toward the redemption God has made possible in Jesus Christ. Only through faith in Christ, our Savior and Lord, can man even begin to make progress in his quest for the moral and spiritual perfection that will transform him into the "likeness of God" (see Ga 3-4).

The Tabernacle and the Temple: God's Presence with His People

God's presence in the lives of his people is a constant theme of the Old Testament history of ancient Israel. He is present in the world, which is his creation; he is present in the covenant with Israel and in the divine law which was given during the days of Moses; he is present in his prophets, priests, judges and kings. But most of all the Lord is present, first, in the tabernacle, which was the center of Israel's existence from the time of Moses to that of Solomon; and, later, in the Temple, which was constructed during the reign of Solomon (965-931 B.C.). The Temple of Solomon was destroyed by the Babylonians in 586 B.C.; but with the support of the Persians, who liberated the Jews from their Babylonian captivity, it was rebuilt during the late sixth century B.C.

The biblical material on the tabernacle, the Temple of Solomon and the rebuilt Temple of the postexilic era describes a change in the relationship between God and his people—a change based upon the failure of Israel to live up to the terms of her covenant with the Lord. In the tabernacle, God was literally present with his people in the cloud of glory which hovered over the sanctuary and the Ark of the Covenant. In Solomon's Temple, the Ark of the Covenant and the tables of the law remained as symbols of God's presence with and concern for Israel, but there is no cloud of glory, no literal presence of the Lord (see 1 Kg 8). In the reconstructed Temple of the late sixth century B.C., even the Ark of the Covenant and the tables of the law were missing, having been destroyed during the Babylonian conquest of 586 B.C. And during the sixth century B.C., the prophet Ezekiel began to dream of the building of a new and heavenly temple in which "the glory of the Lord" would once again be literally present with his people (see Ezk 40-48).

The tabernacle-temple theme in the historical texts of the Old Testament points to the human need for the literal, and even physical, presence of God. Ezekiel's prophetic dream of the heavenly temple filled with "the glory of the Lord" was fulfilled in the coming of Jesus Christ. The gradual distancing of God from Israel during the Old Testament era was a preparation for the advent of Christ, in whom "the glory of the Lord" was made literally, physically and personally present in the world. In Christ, God became man; and this man is the true temple of the Lord (see Jn 2:13-22). In the incarnation, God united himself with the human race; the divine nature and human nature were made one in the person of Christ. Christ's body is therefore the temple of God (see Jn 2:19-21). And insofar as a man joins himself to Christ in faith and obedience, he becomes a member of the new Israel, the Church. St. Paul refers to the Church as "the body of Christ" (1 Co 12:27; Eph 1:22-23 and 5:30). As "the glory of the Lord" was literally and physically present in the person of Christ, so is that glory literally and physically present in the community of those who have "put on Christ." Through union with Christ, the Church has become "the mystical body of Christ," "the fulness of him who fills all in all" (Eph 1:23). In Christ and his Church, the full significance of the Old Testament tabernacle-temple imagery is made manifest, and the human need for the presence of God is satisfied.

The Human Need for Atonement

Sinful man needs reconciliation with God. The Old Testament history of ancient Israel insists upon the absolute holiness of God, the sinfulness of man and the human need for atonement. In failing to obey the law of God, man's life is forfeit. But the Lord, in his mercy, provides a way of atonement that permits the sinner to save his life. Instead of shedding his own blood, the reprobate may make atonement for his sins through animal sacrifice. For blood, in the Old Testament, is the symbol of life, and life is the property of God. The blood sacrifices commanded by the law (see Lv 1-16) involved the ritual killing of unblemished and healthy male animals (lambs, rams, bulls, goats). The blood of these animals was accepted by God in place of the blood of men. And the blood, as the essence of life, symbolized the rededication of the sinner's life to the service of God and his covenant. This form of atonement is often called "substitutionary" or "vicarious" atonement. In the sacrificial rituals of the old covenant, the blood of innocent animals was substituted for the blood of sinful men. And through this vicarious sacrifice, if offered in a repentant spirit, the sinner was able to achieve reconciliation, or "at-one-ment," with God.

The New Testament presents the crucifixion of Christ in terms reminiscent of the Old Testament code of ritual atonement. Christ is our passover lamb, our "sin-offering" to God. Christ died for our sins that we might live to be reconciled with God. "All this is from God, who through Christ reconciled us to himself and gave us the ministry of reconciliation; that is, in Christ God was reconciling the world to himself, not counting their trespasses against them [because those sins had been atoned for by the blood of Christ], and entrusting to us the message of reconciliation. . . . For our sake he made him to be sin who knew no sin, so that in him we might become the righteousness of God" (2 Co 5:18-21). Should a sinner acknowledge Christ as his Savior and offer the blood of Christ to God as atonement for his sins, his transgressions against the Lord will be forgiven and he will enter into the reconciliation between man and God wrought by the work of Christ. "Therefore, if any one is in Christ, he is a new creation; the old has passed away, [and] behold, the new has come" (2 Co 5:17).

According to the Bible, a sinner "lies under the wrath of God and is therefore lost and undone." The ritual code of blood sacrifice in the Old Testament is a response to the human need for atonement. But, from a Christian point of view, the animal sacrifices of the old covenant were not fully effective in bringing about an "at-one-ment" between man and God. Those ritual sacrifices point toward the death of Christ as the ultimate and final sacrifice of atonement. For "by the grace of God, provision was made for Christ to offer Himself as a sin-bearer . . . and God [the Father] was willing to accept the atonement of Christ so that the sinner himself secures the benefits of forgiveness, peace, and fellowship with God."[11] Christ "bore our sins in his body on the tree [or cross], that we might die to sin and live to righteousness. By his wounds you have been healed. For you were straying like sheep, but have now returned to the Shepherd and Guardian of your souls" (1 Pt 2:24-25). In this sense Christ's death counts as a "vicarious atonement" for our sins.

The Emergence of the Messianic Ideal

The Old Testament history of ancient Israel presents us with five archetypical human figures, representing several aspects of the ideal of a Messiah who would emerge from Israel to lead the world back to God. These figures are Moses the prophet, Aaron the priest, Joshua the conqueror, Samuel the judge and David the king. During the centuries after the reign of David, the people of Israel, led by the prophets, began to long for and to expect the coming of a Savior called the Messiah (or "anointed one"). And the Messiah was to be all that Moses, Aaron, Joshua, Samuel and David were—and more. As Moses was perhaps the greatest of the prophets, the Messiah would be the perfect prophet (referred to by Moses himself in Dt 18:15-19) and would proclaim "the Word of the Lord" to all the universe. As Aaron, the first of the Levitical priests, made atonement for his people through animal sacrifices, the Messiah would, as perfect priest, make universal atonement for the sins of the whole world.[12] As

Joshua the conqueror had led Israel into the land of Canaan, the Messiah would be a perfect conqueror, defeating the powers of sin and death and leading all faithful people into the kingdom of God. As Samuel had judged the tribes of Israel, the Messiah would be the perfect judge of the entire human race. And as David had been a great (and almost messianic) king, the Messiah would be the perfect king, governing his people with an abiding love and an everlasting justice.

The relationship between the idea of kingship and the messianic ideal in the historical writings of the Old Testament requires special emphasis. In the period between the Exodus from Egypt and the rise of the Hebrew monarchy, Israel was ruled theocratically—that is, by God and his appointed agents such as Moses, Joshua and the judges. But as their faithlessness and disobedience led them further and further into anarchy, the people of Israel began to demand a king who might put things in order. For "in those days there was no king in Israel; [and] every man did what was right in his own eyes" (Jg 21:25). Although this demand was itself a failure to grasp the real causes of Israel's troubles, and at the same time a sinful rejection of God's theocratic rule, the Lord condescended to give his people what they wanted. Thus, the Hebrew empire came into existence; and the divine King was replaced by a dynasty of human kings.

The ideal of a divinely anointed king, who would rule over Israel and save the nation from destruction, was very nearly fulfilled in the reign of David. The books of Samuel and Kings were written in the light of Israel's memory of David, and this section of scripture depicts the great king as a messianic figure. This tendency, in the books of Samuel and Kings, to present David as an anointed savior-king is often referred to by biblical scholars as "royal messianism."[13] As later Hebrew monarchs failed to live up to the standards set by David, a series of failures documented in 1 and 2 Kings, the people of Israel began to long for the coming of a "new David." The great prophets of the eighth, seventh and sixth centuries B.C. predicted the eventual emergence of a king like David, a *Messiah* (the "anointed one"), who would save his people from evil and destruction. This prophecy, as we shall see, was fulfilled in the person and work of Jesus Christ.

Although the Hebrew monarchy had its good moments—for example, in the reigns of David (1000-965 B.C.) and Solomon (965-931 B.C.)—the empire constructed during the tenth century B.C. was utterly destroyed within a period of 350 years following Solomon's death. Thus, human kingship, like the theocracy it had succeeded, did not bring the peace and happiness sought by the people of Israel.

The movement from theocracy through human kingship in the Old Testament historical writings seems to be a revelation of the human need for a king who is both divine *and* human. Apparently, an exclusively divine kingship is too demanding for the human race, which has been morally and spiritually weakened by sin; and a merely human kingship—that is, rule by men who are themselves sinful and thus morally and spiritually weak—cannot establish the conditions of life that would make peace and happiness possible. Again, therefore, an Old Testament theme directs our attention to the person of Christ, in whom the divine nature and human nature are united. Only he, the Bible seems to tell us, can serve as a king who can bring us perfect deliverance from evil and lead us into the land of fulfilment, the kingdom of God. In Christ, theocracy and human kingship are made one.

Throughout this chapter, we have emphasized the future-oriented (or "eschatological") and Christocentric orientation of the Old Testament history of ancient Israel. The fulfilment of the Old Testament longing for deliverance and happiness is to be found in Jesus Christ. Addressing the Pharisees, who were careful students of the Old Testament, Jesus said: "You search the Scriptures [that is, the Old Testament], because you think that in them you have eternal life; and it is they that bear witness to me; yet you refuse to come to me that you may have life" (Jn 5:39-40). Thus, Christ himself tells us that the Old Testament is a preparation for and a foreshadowing of the proclamation of the New Testament.

Man longs for peace and happiness, for perfect fulfilment, for infinite completeness. This longing is expressed, but not fully articulated, in the Old Testament historical literature. It is clear that this human quest for redemption and salvation points toward union with God. For only in God, who is infinitely complete, can man discover his "promised land." God, and not Canaan, is the true promised land. And the message of the New Testament is that the incarnation of God in Christ makes possible the union of man and God. Through Christ, who is both true God and true man, we can be adopted as "sons of God" (or children of God) and attain the infinite completeness which, in our heart of hearts, we so deeply yearn for.

"Whenever we read the Bible, we must look for Christ. And we must go on looking until we see and so believe."[14] This is true of the Old Testament as well as of the New Testament. For the Old Testament was a preparation for the advent of the Lord Jesus Christ.

CHAPTER 4

Wisdom and Prophecy in the Old Testament

The theme of salvation, which was rather thoroughly developed in the Old Testament historical writings, underwent a significant transformation in the wisdom literature and the prophetic writings, which together make up the final phase of the Old Testament revelation. By the eighth, seventh and sixth centuries B.C., it was beginning to dawn upon many devout followers of God that God's covenant promises were not going to be fulfilled as expected by the majority of their fellow Israelites. It was not an Israel of the flesh but rather an Israel of the spirit which was called to be God's chosen people. And the promised land into which the chosen people were to be led was not the land of Canaan but the kingdom of God, a spiritual kingdom which stood beyond the world as then constituted and whose realization would require the radical transcendence and reconstruction of the fallen world order. The wisdom literature and the prophetic writings of the Old Testament look beyond the old Israel toward a new Israel and toward the coming of the universal kingdom of God. Thus, biblical scholars, especially Christian biblical scholars, speak of an "eschatological" transformation of the biblical message of redemption in the Old Testament wisdom books and prophetic writings. *Eschaton* is a Greek word meaning "end," "goal" or "last thing." And "eschatology," therefore, is the theory or doctrine of the last things, a conception of the final destination of the world process. This future orientation

89

is the most striking characteristic of the wisdom literature and the writings of the prophets in the Old Testament.

THE WISDOM LITERATURE OF THE OLD TESTAMENT

The Old Testament presents two perspectives on the nature of "wisdom." In the first place, wisdom is viewed as the ability to establish a practical and meaningful relationship between oneself and God, other human beings, and the world in general. Old Testament wisdom, in this context, is not philosophical or intellectual wisdom, but rather "the practical wisdom which enables a man to live a good life both in the eyes of men and the sight of God."[1] The Old Testament wise men sought "to interpret for the people [of Israel] the meaning of life and human existence in the light of what the Law and Prophets had taught."[2]

In the second place, the Old Testament conceives of wisdom as a divine and metaphysical (or mystical) power, an "emanation of the glory of the Almighty," the "divine purpose by which the universe is directed." In much of the Old Testament, the principle of wisdom is given a personal character and is closely associated with the being of God himself. In Proverbs 8:22-36, wisdom is personified and depicted as having been with God before the creation of the world and as being the key to eternal life. The book of the Wisdom of Solomon also speaks of wisdom in personal terms as an intelligent, holy, subtle lover of the good who is an expression of the purity, power, glory, light and goodness of God himself (see Ws 7:22-8:1). Wisdom is also referred to as "the fashioner of all things," the "word" by whom "all things" were made (Ws 7:22, 9:1). On the basis of such Old Testament passages, New Testament writers such as St. Paul, along with many fathers of the Church, regarded the Old Testament principle of wisdom as the living Word of God, the second person of the Holy Trinity, who became incarnate in the person of Jesus Christ. Thus, in 1 Corinthians 1:24-30, St. Paul speaks of Christ as the power and wisdom of God, who has made possible "our righteousness and sanctification and redemption." And in the Divine Liturgy of the Orthodox Church, Christ is addressed as the "Wisdom, Word, and Power of God."[3] The principle of wisdom is, then, of both practical and mystical significance from a biblical point of view.

The Wisdom Books of the Old Testament

The Old Testament contains seven books which are collectively known as the wisdom literature.[4] The book of Job, which dates from the tenth or ninth century B.C., is a philosophical and theological reflection upon "the problem of the righteous sufferer." Why do the righteous suffer and the unrighteous prosper in a world created by God? The argument of the book of Job in response to this problem is, roughly, that there is a divinely created cosmic order and pattern within which the injustices of the world will be, in the long run, turned to good. God will ultimately bring the righteous to victory and the unrighteous down to defeat. Exactly how this recompense will be wrought is not specified in the text as we have it.

The book of Psalms (or "Songs") has played a very great part in the liturgical life of the Orthodox Church. It is often called "the hymnbook of the second temple" because it was compiled in its present form during the days of Ezra (fifth century B.C.) for use in the services of the rebuilt Temple in Jerusalem. The book contains hymns of praise, prayers for times of crisis and songs of faith; and it has as its central theme the relationship between God and the meaning of human existence. To discover the meaning of one's own existence, one must be related intimately and harmoniously to the Lord, the ground of all being and the source of all meaning.

The book of Proverbs is a collection of aphorisms and poems dealing with the relationship between wisdom, righteousness and religious devotion. Proverbs was put into its final written form during the third century B.C., but earlier versions of the book were in use throughout the entire postexilic era. During that period, this compendium of maxims and wise sayings was employed by rabbis in the moral and religious training of Jewish youth.

The book of Ecclesiastes, written in the fifth century B.C., is the most pessimistic book in the Bible. But in spite of its author's deep reservations concerning the prospects and meaning of this life, Ecclesiastes leads the mind toward God as the only real source of hope and meaning. Only God can reveal to us the significance of our lives; and only in God can we realistically hope to gain deliverance from the vanities of this life and from the bondage of sin and death (see Ec 12). Ecclesiastes contains a hint of the hope for immortality (see 12:7), but this theme is not highly developed.

The Song of Solomon was written some time between the time of Solomon (tenth century B.C.) and the third century B.C. It is a long psalm dealing with the relationship between human and divine love. This poetic tale of the true love of a man and a woman was interpreted by the fathers of the Church as an iconic depiction of the Old Testament relationship between God and Israel, and of the New Testament relationship between Christ and his Church.

The book of the Wisdom of Solomon is an extended discussion of the principle of wisdom and of the meaning of human existence. Its composition has been dated as late as the first century B.C. The book prophesies victory and immortality for the righteous and judgment and condemnation for the wicked (chapters 1-5); depicts and praises wisdom as a divine-mystical principle, a manifestation of God himself (6-9); traces wisdom's guidance of God's people from the days of Adam to the Mosaic era (10-12); and emphasizes God's love for his people (16-19).

The final component of the Old Testament wisdom literature is the book of the Wisdom of Jesus ben Sirach, also called Ecclesiasticus. This is a late expression (second century B.C.) of the wisdom tradition enshrined in the book of Proverbs. Wisdom is interpreted as a practical understanding of God's law, which makes possible a good life under the authority of God.

The Overall Message of the Wisdom Literature

The Old Testament wisdom literature assumes without argument the existence of God, which is considered as self-evident and thus indubitable. God is depicted as all-powerful, all-knowing, omnipresent, eternal, infinite, perfectly good, perfectly just and perfectly merciful. God is the almighty Creator of the world, the Father of mankind, who reveals himself to man in both nature and history, especially in the history of Israel, the people of God.

The wisdom literature argues that the meaningfulness and fulfilment of human existence depends upon man's relationship with God. Sin alienates man from the presence of God, whereas repentance and obedience lead to reconciliation with God. Man's sinfulness is the major obstacle to the fulfilment of human hopes and needs.

The wisdom literature also ties the theme of man's salvation to the theme of life after death (see, for example, Ws 3:1-9 and Ps 16, 17, 49 and 73). This linkage marks a new stage in the Old Testament understanding of God's redemptive plan. The theme of personal immortality, of hope beyond death, of the future life, is not highly developed in most of the writings of the Old Testament. Having lost access to the eternal life of God, the ancient Israelites apparently interpreted the covenant promises of God entirely in this-worldly terms. The "promised land" was nothing more than the land of Canaan; and the happiness promised by God was nothing more than peace and contentment in this world. But in the wisdom literature (and in some of the writings of the prophets), there is a realization that the happiness of this life, which is ended so soon by death, is an insufficient fulfilment of the promises of God. Only if death can be defeated will true happiness be possible. This insight was made fully explicit in the New Testament and in the teachings of the Christian Church.

The central concern of the Old Testament wisdom literature, however, is with the problems of evil, suffering and meaninglessness. Human finitude and dependence are set off against God's transcendence and power; and the severe limitations of human understanding are strongly emphasized. Man's radical need for God is continually underlined. The proper responses to the difficulties and pains of life are *faith, hope* and *obedience: faith* in God's ultimate justice and mercy (see the book of Job); *hope* for redemption from evil, suffering, meaninglessness and death (see Ecclesiastes, Psalms and Wisdom); and *obedience* to the law of God (Torah) as a way of avoiding evil, suffering and meaninglessness (see Proverbs and Ecclesiasticus).

The wisdom books offer us an existential choice between meaning and meaninglessness, between hope and despair. Life may be ultimately meaningful, or it may be ultimately meaningless. Neither possibility can be objectively or scientifically verified. According to the wisdom books, we must *choose* between meaning and meaninglessness—we must decide to live either in hope or in despair. And for the Old Testament wise men, the way of faith, hope and obedience is the proper choice because it is a response to a historically and existentially experienced invitation from God.

THE WRITINGS OF THE OLD
TESTAMENT PROPHETS

The Greek word *prophetes* means "one who speaks for another," and especially for God. And the Hebrew word for "prophet" is *nabi,* "a person who communicates, or pours forth, the Divine will."[5] Thus, a prophet is one who speaks for God and communicates the divine will. The task of the Old Testament prophet was "to declare the will of God to his fellow men, to reveal God's secrets, and to announce what shall come to pass."[6] The prophets were those who were *called* by God to proclaim the divine word and will to ancient Israel. And the necessity of this "prophetic call" is insisted upon in the Old Testament (see, for example, 1 Sm 3; Am 7:14-15; Ho 1-3; Is 6; Jr 1:4-10; and Ezk 1:1-3:21).

The Old Testament prophets sought to pour forth the word of the Lord, to declare the will of God, to apply God's word to the situations in which they and their contemporaries lived. Futuristic (or predictive) prophecy, the announcement of "what shall come to pass," was only one phase of the overall mission and ministry of the prophets. They were primarily concerned with illuminating and evaluating the conditions of their time on the basis of the word of God, and with calling their fellow man out of apostasy and back to faith in and obedience to the Lord.

The Greek version of the Old Testament (the Septuagint)

contains nineteen books of prophecy in the following order: Isaiah, Jeremiah, Lamentations (attributed to Jeremiah), the Letter of Jeremiah (also attributed to Jeremiah), Baruch, Ezekiel, Daniel, Hosea, Joel, Amos, Obadiah, Jonah, Micah, Nahum, Habakkuk, Zephaniah, Haggai, Zechariah and Malachi. Isaiah, Jeremiah, Ezekiel and Daniel are sometimes referred to as the "major" prophets, because their books are greater in length than those of the "minor" prophets. It should also be noted that the Hebrew version of the Old Testament does not classify Daniel as one of the prophets—the book of Daniel is placed among a collection known as "The Writings" at the end of the Jewish canon. And the Hebrew Bible does not include the Letter of Jeremiah or the book of Baruch at all, since these texts are regarded as uncanonical by the Jews.[7]

The nineteen books listed above represent the era of "classical prophecy"—the prophetic activity of the eighth through the second centuries B.C., during which Old Testament prophetic thought reached its highest point of development. There was also an era of "early prophecy," running from the thirteenth through the ninth centuries B.C. The major "early prophets" were Moses, the prophetic bands and lone seers of the period of the judges and the nonwriting prophets of the early monarchical period, such as Samuel, Elijah and Elisha (see 1 and 2 Samuel and 1 and 2 Kings).

The "classical prophets" emerged during and after the period of the decline and fall of the Hebrew empire. With the late tenth century B.C. division of the empire into a northern kingdom (Israel) and a southern kingdom (Judah), the people of the old covenant entered into a long era of corruption, decadence, and social, political and religious disorder. The nation faced a mounting cultural and spiritual crisis, as the people introduced pagan and idolatrous elements into their religious practice and as immorality increased in both the northern and southern kingdoms. It was into this age of crisis that the prophets were sent. Their mission was to apply the word of God to the situation into which Israel had fallen, to elucidate the theological and human meaning of the grave troubles that had been visited upon the descendants of Abraham. Their general message in this context was a reiteration of the argument of the Old Testament historical books:

Israel was in danger of forfeiting her covenant relationship with the Lord, of losing the kingdom of God, because of her unrepentant faithlessness and lawlessness.

The historical development of classical prophecy may be analyzed into three major periods as follows: the preexilic era; the exilic era; and the postexilic era.

Classical Prophecy during the Preexilic Era. During the eighth and seventh centuries B.C., the kingdoms of Israel and Judah were menaced, first by the Assyrians and later by the Babylonians. The Assyrians destroyed the northern kingdom in 722 B.C. and were themselves destroyed by the Babylonians in 612 B.C. And then, the Babylonian empire conquered the kingdom of Judah in 586 B.C. and held the Jews in captivity (the "Babylonian exile") for nearly fifty years thereafter. The major prophets of the preexilic era—Amos, Hosea, Isaiah, Micah, Zephaniah, Nahum and Habakkuk—were sent by God to warn the kingdoms of Israel and Judah of the calamities that were to overwhelm them if they did not return from apostasy to an obedient faith in the Lord. From a biblical standpoint, the Assyrian and Babylonian empires were instruments by which a just and angry God punished his people for their gross sinfulness.

Amos (fl. c. 750 B.C.) was a herdsman and cultivator of sycamore trees from the kingdom of Judah who was, however, called to prophesy in the northern kingdom. He denounced the oppression of the poor by the rich and other social injustices, as well as the pagan and idolatrous religious practices that prevailed in the kingdom of Israel, and he warned of the divine judgment and punishment that would fall upon the people of God (in both the northern and southern kingdoms) as a result of their sin. The book of Amos contains an indictment of the sins of God's people and of other nations (chapters 1-2); an extended denunciation of the immorality and ungodliness of the kingdom of Israel in particular (chapters 3-6); and five visions of the impending judgment of the northern kingdom (chapters 7-9).

Another prophet who was active in the north during the time of Amos was Hosea (fl. c. 740 B.C.). In an age marked by gross immorality and religious apostasy, Hosea compared the relationship between God and his people to a marriage in which a faithful husband has been severely wronged by his adulterous wife (chapters 1-3 and 4-13). But should the woman (Israel) repent of her infidelity, then, the prophet predicts, her husband (God) will most surely forgive her and bless her. The woman's repentance, however, will have to be both real and constant (chapter 14).

Isaiah was active in Judah for more than fifty years (c. 740-687 B.C.). The book of Isaiah is divided into two main parts (chapters 1-39 and chapters 40-66), and many contemporary scholars believe that the second part was not written by Isaiah but by a later disciple of his during the sixth century B.C. The first part of Isaiah contains prophecies concerning the destiny of Judah (chapters 1-12) and other nations of the ancient Middle East (chapters 13-23); a vision of the last judgment and of the kingdom of God (chapters 24-27); and a prediction of the eventual downfall of the Assyrian empire (chapters 28-39). The second part of the book looks forward to God's deliverance of his people from their Babylonian exile (chapters 40-48); and to the emergence of a new Israel (chapters 49-55) which will be led by the Messiah into the promised kingdom (chapters 56-66).

Micah's prophetic ministry was contemporaneous with that of Isaiah (c. 740-687 B.C.). He spoke "the word of the Lord" both to Judah and to Israel. His book contains prophecies of doom against the two kingdoms (chapters 1-2); a promise of ultimate salvation for mankind through the advent of the Messiah and the eventual establishment of the kingdom of God (chapters 3-5); and a poetic discourse on the relationship between divine punishment and divine mercy (chapters 6-7).

Zephaniah (fl. 625 B.C.) wrote his book in Judah approximately one century after the Assyrian conquest of the northern kingdom. He prophesies the Babylonian exile of the Jews and their eventual deliverance from that exile (chapters 1-2); and he looks toward the final salvation of the faithful by the Lord (chapter 3).

Nahum, like Zephaniah, lived in Judah during the late seventh century B.C. His prophecy, written c. 620 B.C., predicts with amazing accuracy the Babylonian destruction of the Assyrian empire in 612 B.C. His prophetic denunciation of Nineveh (the capital city of the Assyrian empire) is symbolic of God's wrath against all nations that depart from the divine law.

The last prophet of the preexilic era was Habakkuk (fl. 600 B.C.), who explained the impending conquest of Judah by the Babylonians as an act of God against his apostate people (chapter 1). Habakkuk also prophesies the eventual destruction of Babylon herself (chapter 2), and he looks, in faith, for the final deliverance of all repentant sinners who turn to God for redemption (chapter 3).

Classical Prophecy during the Era of the Babylonian Exile. The period of the Babylonian captivity (586-538 B.C.) saw the emergence of three important prophets: Jeremiah, Ezekiel and Obadiah.

Jeremiah prophesied both before and during the exile. His book (which he dictated at various times to his amanuensis, Baruch) predicts the fall of Judah and the Babylonian captivity (chapters 1-25); and it contains biographical material on the prophet's long and difficult ministry (chapters 26-36), a narrative account of his experiences at the time of the Babylonian destruction of Jerusalem (chapters 37-45), a series of prophecies against foreign nations (chapters 46-51) and an appendix reviewing the early exilic period (chapter 52). The book of Lamentations and the deuterocanonical Letter of Jeremiah have also been attributed to Jeremiah. Both books reflect the thought of Jeremiah, but neither was actually written by him. Lamentations is an elegy expressing great grief over the fall of Judah and was composed c. 540 B.C. The so-called Letter of Jeremiah, a diatribe against the sin of idolatry, was written in the late fourth century B.C.

The book of Ezekiel was written between 593 and 573 B.C. Ezekiel describes in detail the divine call that transformed him into a prophet of God (chapters 1-3); he explains the Babylonian exile as a divine judgment against the apostasy of Judah (chapters 4-24); he prophesies against the foreign nations surrounding the Holy Land (chapters 25-32); and he predicts the future restoration, not only of the Jews to Canaan, but of all the people of God (Jew *and* Gentile) in the kingdom of heaven (chapters 33-48). Ezekiel 40-48 describes a mystical vision of the heavenly temple of God which awaits the faithful at the end of time.

Scholars are divided concerning the date of the book of Obadiah. It was written either during the Babylonian exile or shortly thereafter. It is a short book, only twenty-one verses long. Obadiah prophesies destruction for the Edomites, a tribe located in the southeastern part of the land of Canaan, and indeed for all the nations of the world that set themselves apart from the law of God. The prophecy seems to point toward the end of days, the last judgment, when all the ungodly will be cast into the outer darkness. At that time, Obadiah tells us, only the Israel of God (that is, those who have been faithful and obedient to the Lord) will enter into the kingdom of heaven (see verses 15-21).

Classical Prophecy during the Postexilic Era. The later, postexilic prophets were Haggai, Zechariah, Malachi, Jonah, Joel, Daniel and Baruch.

Haggai and Zechariah were prophets of the late sixth century B.C. who urged the Jews of the early postexilic period to work diligently and enthusiastically in their rebuilding of the Temple in Jerusalem. Haggai's prophecy is a collection of four highly passionate messages on the importance of the Temple in the life of God's people. His insistence upon the rebuilding of the Temple is a testimony to the human need for the presence of God, for a house of worship in which the divine might be encountered (see Haggai 1-2). The book of Zechariah contains two main divisions. In chapters 1-8, the prophet encourages the Jews to continue the work of rebuilding God's Temple in Jerusalem and warns them of the Lord's wrath toward all sinners, whether Gentile or Jew. And in chapters 9-14, Zechariah prophesies the coming of the Messiah and the establishment of the kingdom of God at the end of the ages.

Malachi lived and wrote during the mid-fifth century B.C., a time of drought and famine in the land of Palestine. In response to the difficult social and economic conditions of the time, the Jews, once again, began to grumble that God's goodness and justice were not apparent, and they became spiritually lax and apathetic. Malachi warned the remnant of Israel that their spiritual and moral indifference was verging upon outright apostasy from the Lord, and that such sacrilege would not be tolerated by the Almighty (chapters 1-2). He sought to encourage his people to return to the worship of God with a resolute and enthusiastic heart; and he prophesied the advent of the Messiah and of "the great and terrible day of the Lord" when all evildoers will be destroyed and all the righteous redeemed (chapters 3-4).

The book of Jonah was written in the late fifth century B.C., although the events it depicts are set in the eighth century B.C. The prophet Jonah, the book tells us, was called by God to warn Nineveh (the Assyrian capital) of the destruction that was to come upon her if she did not repent of her sins and turn to God for forgiveness. Jonah, a pious Israelite, did not wish the Assyrians to repent and thus be saved; so he resisted God's call and sought to escape his prophetic responsibility. But, in the end, urged on by the Lord, Jonah confronted the people of Nineveh and delivered God's message to them. And as a result of his prophecy, the Assyrians renounced their evil ways and promised to follow the law of God. Thus, the destruction of Nineveh was, for the time being, averted. (Assyria evidently returned to her spiritual and moral outlawry later on, for she was conquered by the Babylonians in 612 B.C.). The purpose of the book of Jonah is to show that God's righteous condemnation of sin and his gracious forgiveness of repentant sinners is applicable not only to Israel but to all nations. Through repentance and an obedient faith, all mankind can become a part of the people of God (see Jonah 1-4).

The book of Joel was written during the late fifth or early fourth century B.C. Joel emphasizes the divinely ordained punishments visited upon sinners (chapter 1), and he interprets these punishments as foreshadowings of the Lord's final judgment and condemnation of all unrepentant sinners (chapter 2). But with the coming of "the day of the Lord," the Spirit of God will be poured out on all faithful people, and they will dwell in "the house of the Lord" forever (chapters 2-3). Like most of the classical prophets, Joel offers us both dark warnings of judgment and happy promises of redemption; and whether the warnings or the promises shall be fulfilled depends upon our response to "the word of the Lord." Faith and obedience will bring salvation; and ungodliness will bring destruction.

Most contemporary biblical scholars believe that the book of

Daniel was written during the second century B.C., although it may well contain material written by Daniel himself, who lived during the time of the Babylonian exile. The book is a highly symbolic and visionary work, emphasizing the supreme power of God and his steadfast intention to redeem mankind and the world from the bondage of evil. The central focus of the entire prophecy is the advent of the "everlasting kingdom" in which all faithful people will be ruled by God himself. The book is divided into two sections: chapters 1-6 describe "the experiences of Daniel and his friends while in exile in Babylon"; and chapters 7-12 contain four spectacular visions of the future course of human history leading up to the establishment of the universal kingdom of God.

The book of Baruch, named after the secretary of the prophet Jeremiah, was written during the latter half of the second century B.C. The book interprets the sufferings of Israel as the result of the nation's apostasy from God (1:15-3:8); praises wisdom as a divine principle which, if followed, will lead God's people to salvation (3:9-4:4); and prophesies the ultimate redemption of all faithful people (4:5-5:9). Like the Letter of Jeremiah, the book of Baruch is a deuterocanonical text which is counted among the works of the prophets in the Greek version of the Old Testament (the Septuagint). The ancient Hebrew version of the Old Testament, as pointed out earlier, did not include the deuterocanonical books in its canon of sacred scripture.

THE MESSAGE OF THE PROPHETS

It is possible to discern a number of major themes in the prophetic literature of the Old Testament, and to six of these we shall now turn in the following pages.

The Insistence upon an Absolute and Uncompromising Monotheism

The classical prophets emerged in Israel during an age of apostasy and idolatry. The Israelites had compromised their religious principles and had blended the worship of the true God—the God of Abraham, Isaac, Jacob, and Moses—with the cultic beliefs and practices of the pagan peoples around them. Ancient Middle Eastern religion was polytheistic—that is, based upon the worship and veneration of many gods. The gods of the Canaanite pantheon were nature deities, personifications of natural objects such as heavenly bodies and animals and natural processes such as fire, thunder, rainfall and fertility. By contrast, the God of the Bible is one and transcendent, the Creator and Lord of nature. In adopting elements from the religions of surrounding pagan cultures, the Israelites were confusing God and nature; they were worshiping the creation rather than the Creator. And in following this path, they were separating themselves from their one true hope for salvation and happiness and bringing themselves under the wrathful judgment and condemnation of God.

Thus, the prophets, reacting against the polytheistic nature worship that had infected the tribes of Israel, proclaimed the unity and absolute supremacy of the Lord. The God of Israel is described by Isaiah as the incomparable, unique and absolute Lord of all being. The Lord is everlasting, without beginning or end, and "all the ends of the earth" are his creation. It is only God who can save. Mankind is not to look to the forces of nature—"all the ends of the earth"—for salvation, since nature is a creature of God, subordinate to his authority (see Is 40:25, 28; 41:14; 43:10-11; 44:6; 45:21-22).

The lordship of God over the natural order is also given expression by the prophet Amos: "He who made the Pleiades and Orion, and turns deep darkness into the morning, and darkens the day into night, who calls for the waters of the sea, and pours them out upon the surface of the earth, the Lord [Yahweh] is his name" (Am 5:8). And this Lord of the universe, "the Holy One of Israel," is, Isaiah tells us, our only Redeemer, the only true God—"there is no other." The classical prophets, therefore, sought to revive the teaching of Moses: "Hear O Israel: The Lord our God is one Lord; and you shall love the Lord your God with all your heart, and with all your soul, and with all your might" (Dt 6:4-5). The gods of paganism, then, are false deities. From a Christian point of view, they are either deluding figments of the fallen human imagination or demons in the service of

Satan. In either case, polytheism is a radical and dangerous departure from the theology of the prophets and of Holy Scripture in its entirety.

The Righteousness of God and the Meaning of Human History

The Lord of the universe is also the Lord of history, "a God of justice who stands within history, and who will vindicate his truth and punish the cruel and rebellious nations of the world."[8] The prophets consistently explained the woes of Israel and of the world in general as evils following from the freely willed sins of men and permitted by God as retribution for those sins (see, for example, Am 1-2). The sufferings of ancient Israel, in particular, were interpreted as divinely ordained punishments for the transgressions of the chosen people against their God (see Am 2:4-16 and Is 1-6).

The sin of idolatry—the worship of false gods—was, according to the prophets, the most grievous of Israel's many violations of the divine law. In his prophecy to the kingdom of Israel in the eighth century B.C., Hosea compared the idolatry of the nation to the adultery of a faithless wife. He urged Israel to turn away from her harlotry "lest . . . [the Lord] strip her naked . . . and make her like a wilderness, and set her like a parched land, and slay her with thirst" (Ho 2:3). Should Israel continue her adultery with her false lovers (the gods of paganism), the prophet argued, the Lord "will hedge her way with thorns; and . . . build a wall against her, so that she cannot find her paths. She shall pursue her lovers [the false gods], but not overtake them; and she shall seek them, but shall not find them" (2:6-7). God's affliction of his people was intended to return them to their senses—to bring a fallen Israel to the point where she would say, "I will go and return to my first husband [God], for it was better with me then than now' " (2:7).

Hosea's message concerning the unsteady course of Israel's history is supported by Amos, who also prophesied in the northern kingdom during the eighth century B.C. According to Amos, the sufferings of Israel were divine punishments aimed at motivating

a sinful nation to return to her Lord. Through Amos, God proclaimed to his people:

> Seek me and live. . . . Seek God, and not evil, that you may
> live; and so the Lord, the God of hosts, will be with you.
> . . . Hate evil, and love good, and establish justice in the
> gate; it may be that the Lord, the God of hosts, will be
> gracious to the remnant of [Israel]. (5:4, 14-15)

Both Hosea and Amos, then, warned the kingdom of Israel
that if the nation remained apostate and unrepentant, she would
be swept away into oblivion. The northern kingdom, however,
did not heed the warnings of the prophets and was utterly
destroyed by the Assyrians in the late eighth century B.C. Thus,
the history of the northern kingdom is an icon of the dangers of
idolatry and of the final destiny of those who fail to love the
Lord above all things, to "have no other gods" before him.

The kingdom of Judah was also guilty of the sin of idolatry.
The book of Jeremiah contains a harsh indictment of the southern
kingdom:

> There is revolt among the men of Judah and the inhabi-
> tants of Jerusalem. They have turned back to the iniquities
> of their forefathers, who refused to hear my words; they
> have gone after other gods to serve them; the house of
> Israel and the house of Judah have broken my covenant
> which I made with their fathers. . . . For your gods have
> become as many as your cities, O Judah; and as many as
> the streets of Jerusalem are the altars you have set up to
> shame, altars to burn incense to Baal. Therefore . . . The
> Lord of hosts, who planted you, has pronounced evil
> against you, because of the evil which the house of Israel
> and the house of Judah have done, provoking me to anger
> by burning incense to Baal. (11:9-14, 17)

The evil pronounced by God against the southern kingdom was,
of course, the Babylonian captivity of the sixth century B.C. But
the nation of Judah was not totally annihilated by the Babylo-

nians. The nation survived and lived on to continue its mission in bringing God's message of salvation to the world.

The history of ancient Israel, then, from the standpoint of the classical prophets, is a revelation of the righteousness of God, of humanity's need for communion with God through faith and obedience and of the ultimate meaning of human history. The God of Israel is present in history, and it is through the historical process that he unfolds his plan for the redemption of mankind and the world. The history of Israel is an object lesson for the whole human community. Unbelief in God, the practice of idolatry and immorality are the primary causes of the sufferings of Israel and of the human race. Only through repentance and a renewed and obedient faith in God's redemptive purpose will mankind arrive at the intended goal of history: a kingdom of peace and harmony under the lordship of God.

The prophets explained the upheavals and sufferings of human history as the judgment of a righteous God upon a sinful world. But what of the sufferings of those who struggled against their own sinful selves, who avoided idolatry and who continued to trust in the promises of the Lord? Why do the righteous lovers of God, such as Job, come under the oppression of evil?

The prophets of the Old Testament struggled with this problem and sought to account for the plight of "the righteous sufferer." The book of Habakkuk contains one of the most direct prophetic analyses of the problem of undeserved suffering, and Habakkuk's perspective on this problem stands in the tradition of the book of Job. The suffering of the innocent and the righteous, he argues, is a testimony to "the cost of discipleship"[9] in a fallen world, and that suffering will be rewarded in the kingdom of God which is to come at the end of days. God's punishment of Israel and the other nations of the world for their sins takes the form of historical crises and political calamities that inevitably affect the righteous as well as the unrighteous (see Hab 1-2). But the Lord will make good the suffering of the innocent in the long run. This mysterious recompense, however, is hidden beyond the prophet's comprehension in the future:

For still the vision awaits its time; it hastens to the end—
it will not lie. If it seems slow, wait for it; it will surely

come, it will not delay. Behold, he whose soul is not upright in him shall fail [on the day of judgment], but the
righteous shall live by his faith. (Hab 2:3-4)

This analysis of the problem of the righteous sufferer clearly
implies the reality of life after death. For how will the righteous
who have died throughout the ages of history gain their reward
in God if there be no resurrection of the dead? Habakkuk does
not make this point explicitly, but simply places his trust in the
ultimate and redemptive righteousness of God. The theme of
hope beyond death was not fully expressed in the writings of the
prophets,[10] but only on the basis of a fully developed doctrine of
personal resurrection and immortality for all mankind could it
be said, with St. Paul, "that the sufferings of this present time
are not worth comparing with the glory that is to be revealed to
us" (Rm 8:18).

Still another dimension of the problem of the righteous sufferer was addressed by the prophet Isaiah. The suffering of the
righteous, he seems to say, is a living historical symbol of the
sufferings of the Messiah who was to redeem mankind and the
world from sin and death. The Messiah is depicted by Isaiah as
the "Suffering Servant" of God who was to save "all things"
from the tyranny of evil (see Is 49-57). "Christians of all ages
have interpreted this as a prediction of the sufferings of Christ,"[11]
through which atonement was made once and for all for the
sins of the whole world. In Christ, the righteousness of God and
the sufferings of the innocent are made one, and the full meaning and goal of human history are made decisively and finally
explicit. In the kingdom of God, the righteous will be vindicated
and will enter into the everlasting glory of heaven.

The Prophetic Conception of True Religion

True religion, according to the prophets, is not legalistic
moralism; it is not merely a love of beautiful rituals and im-
pressive ceremonies; it is not primarily a passion for elegant
liturgical form. True religion must be based upon a real and
personal encounter with God, which issues in an obedient faith.

And an obedient faith in God must manifest itself in good moral works as well as in liturgical worship. A lover of God must strive to live a righteous and holy life, devoting himself to prayerful worship of the Lord and to the service of his fellow man. His love for God must show itself in "works of love"[12]—that is, in efforts to share the love of God with others, to assist those who are in spiritual or material need, to institute the conditions of justice wherever possible.

Thus, good works are the expression of an authentic and living faith, and the Old Testament prophets were scathingly critical of the empty, formalistic, and merely ceremonial religion of their time. The prophet Amos, for example, denounced the social injustices that prevailed in the eighth century B.C. in both Judah and Israel. And he made it clear that the Lord would not accept the liturgical worship of his people in the absence of a real passion for moral righteousness. The moral wantonness of Judah and Israel, moreover, made their elaborate religious services into a mockery with no spiritual significance. Through Amos, God proclaimed:

> I hate, I despise your feasts, and I take no delight in your solemn assemblies. Even though you offer me your burnt offerings and cereal offerings, I will not accept them, and the peace offerings of your fatted beasts I will not look upon. Take away from me the noise of your songs; to the melody of your harps I will not listen. But let justice roll down like waters, and righteousness like an everflowing stream. (5:21-24)

God expects us to express our faith both in liturgical worship and in works of righteousness. A merely ceremonial religion, expressing itself in the grandest liturgical forms, is spiritually insufficient. A faith that does not result in moral works as well as in devotional form is not, in biblical terms, a real or authentic faith. The Bible commands the believer "to do justice, and to love kindness, and to walk humbly with your God" (Mi 6:6-8). To engage in moral effort without worshiping God is, of course, a spiritually dangerous indifference to the supreme glory of the Lord. But to engage in a ceremonial religious worship of no prac-

tical and moral consequence in our daily lives is to treat God as
a mere ornament of no real significance to human conduct in
the world.

The New Covenant and the Kingdom of God

God's covenant with Israel was discussed in detail in chapter
3. In Abraham, Israel was elected as the people of God (Gn
12), and through faithful obedience to God's law she was to
become "a kingdom of priests and a holy nation," calling all
mankind to the Lord (Ex 19-24). By accomplishing her priestly
mission to the nations, Israel was to be vindicated in the sight of
all the world, and was to enter into possession of the "promised
land" forever (Gn 17).

In the writings of the Old Testament prophets, the theme of
Israel's election and covenant relationship with God, her mission
to the world and her ultimate vindication, are reinterpreted in
eschatological terms. That is, the salvation of Israel is understood
as a future event that will include all the nations of the world.
Human history is viewed as moving toward a final day of judgment—"the day of the Lord"—when the unfaithful will be separated from the faithful. And the "promised land" is conceived
in spiritual terms as the kingdom of God, in which "all things"
will be made new and will be in harmony with the Lord.

The classical prophets lamented Israel's failure to accomplish
her mission to the world, and they sought to reawaken the nation
to her priestly call. Isaiah emphasized that Israel was given by
God "as a light to the nations, that . . . [the salvation of the
Lord] may reach to the end of the earth" (49:6). God's covenant
with Israel was to be a covenant with all mankind: "I have given
you as a covenant to the people, a light to the nations, to open
the eyes that are blind, to bring out the prisoners from the dun-
geon, from the prison those who sit in darkness" (42:6-7). And,
according to the prophet Micah, God's covenant with Israel was
a promise of the ultimate salvation of all faithful people—both
Jew and Gentile—in the coming kingdom of God (see Mi 4:1-3).

But ancient Israel, as the Old Testament reveals, did not
keep the terms of her covenant with God. Instead of acting as

"a light to the nations" and witnessing to the universal lordship of God, the people of the old covenant abandoned their priestly mission to the world and went chasing after the false satisfactions of pagan culture and religion. As we have seen, this apostasy led to the overthrow and destruction of the ancient Hebrew kingdoms of Israel and Judah. And on the basis of this historical failure by Israel to fulfil her divinely ordained mission, the classical prophets began to look toward the advent of a "new covenant" between God and the "remnant" of Israel—that is, between the Lord and those few descendants of Abraham who, after the Babylonian exile, continued to witness to God's truth and to hope for his coming kingdom.

In the eighth century B.C., Isaiah prophesied both the destruction of the Hebrew kingdoms and the salvation of a holy remnant with whom God would renew his covenant (see Is 10:20-23). And, according to the prophet Micah, this "remnant of Jacob"—the righteous remnant of the postexilic era—will carry on the covenanted mission of God's people and will be counted as the living representative of the fallen kingdoms of Israel and Judah (see Mi 5:7-8).

The covenant with the righteous remnant will be, according to Jeremiah, a "new covenant."

> Behold, the days are coming, says the Lord, when I will make a new covenant with the [remnant of] the house of Israel and the house of Judah, not like the covenant which I made with their fathers when I took them by the hand to bring them out of the land of Egypt, my covenant which they broke, though I was their husband, says the Lord. But this is the covenant which I will make with the house of Israel after those days, says the Lord: I will put my law within them, and I will write it upon their hearts; and I will be their God, and they shall be my people. And no longer shall each man teach his neighbor and teach his brother, saying, "Know the Lord," for they shall all know me, from the least of them to the greatest, says the Lord; for I will forgive their iniquity, and I will remember their sin no more. (Jr 31:31-34)

In the new covenant, which God will make with his people, the law of God will not be written on tables of stone, but rather in the hearts of men (see Rm 11:26-36 and Heb 8:8-12).

Through the remnant of Israel and the new covenant, "all nations and tongues" will be gathered and will see the glory of the Lord (Is 66:18). The righteous remnant will be a sign to the nations of the world, and they will bring converts from all lands "as an offering to the Lord . . . just as the Israelites bring their cereal offering in a clean vessel to the house of the Lord" (Is 66:19-20). It would appear, then, that the bringing of an unbeliever to belief in God is as significant an offering to the Lord as the offerings made in religious services. And through the new covenant, which will be an everlasting covenant, people from all nations will come to know that the God of Israel is the Lord of all creation: his "dwelling place shall be with them," and he "will be their God," and they shall be his people (see Ezk 37:26-28).

From an Orthodox Christian point of view, of course, these prophecies concerning the remnant of Israel and a "new covenant" between God and mankind are premonitions of the advent of Christ and of the foundation of his Church. The first followers of Christ, almost all of whom were Jews, were expecting the coming of the Messiah and recognized Jesus as the fulfilment of their expectations. And after his death, resurrection and ascension, this "righteous remnant," the early Church, proclaimed God's message of salvation through Christ to all the world and brought people of all nations to trust in the divine promises of the new covenant. The Church, then, is the new Israel, made up of descendants of Abraham and of many other peoples. And membership in the Church is based upon faith, not upon genealogical lineage; the Church is an Israel of the spirit, and not an Israel of the flesh. "For he is not a real Jew who is one outwardly, nor is true circumcision something external and physical. He is a Jew who is one inwardly, and real circumcision is a matter of the heart, spiritual and not literal" (Rm 2:28-29; see also 9:6-8).

In looking toward the establishment of a new covenant, the Old Testament prophets also spoke repeatedly of the coming kingdom of God and of "the day of the Lord," which would precede the advent of the kingdom. The "day of the Lord" is the day of the last judgment, a day which is announced again and again in the writings of the prophets. The words of Zephaniah are representative of the prophetic proclamation of the last judgment:

> The great day of the Lord is near, near and hastening fast; the sound of the day of the Lord is bitter, the mighty man cries aloud there. A day of wrath is that day, a day of distress and anguish, a day of ruin and devastation, a day of darkness and gloom, a day of clouds and thick darkness, a day of trumpet blast and battle cry against the fortified cities [of our lives] and against the lofty battlements [of our selves]. I will bring distress on men, so that they shall walk like the blind, because they have sinned against the Lord; their blood shall be poured out like dust, and their flesh like dung. Neither their silver nor their gold shall be able to deliver them on the day of the wrath of the Lord. In the fire of his jealous wrath, all the earth shall be consumed; for a full, yea, sudden end he will make of all the inhabitants of the earth. (1:14-18; see also Jl 2:1-2, 3:2, 2:12-13, 2:32; and Am 5:18-20)

The words of the prophets concerning "the day of the Lord" are vivid and powerful. To escape the wrathful judgment of God at the end of days, they seem to tell us, we must recognize our sinfulness, repent and "call upon the name of the Lord" with faith (Jl 2:32) and "in fear and trembling" (Ph 2:12). Only then will we stand a chance of being saved from final condemnation and eternal separation from our heavenly Father on the great and dreadful day of judgment.

Following the day of judgment, the prophets proclaim, the kingdom of God will be established. The coming of the kingdom is depicted in the book of Isaiah. In that great kingdom of peace, "the wolf shall dwell with the lamb, and the leopard shall lie down with the kid . . . They shall not hurt or destroy in all my holy mountain; for the earth shall be full of the knowledge of the Lord as the waters cover the sea" (Is 11:6-9). The nations of the world "shall beat their swords into plowshares, and their spears into pruning hooks; nation shall not lift up sword against

nation, neither shall they learn war any more" (2:4). And therefore:

> You will say in that day: "I will give thanks to thee, O
> Lord, for though thou wast angry with me, thy anger
> turned away, and thou didst comfort me. Behold, God is
> my salvation; I will trust, and not be afraid; for the Lord
> is my strength and my song, and he has become my salva-
> tion." With joy you will draw water from the wells of
> salvation. And you will say in that day: "Give thanks to
> the Lord, call upon his name; make known his deeds
> among the nations, proclaim that his name is exalted . . .
> for great in your midst is the Holy One of Israel." (12:1-
> 6)

There are many such glimpses of the kingdom of God in the
prophetic literature of the Old Testament. And what is most interesting about these prophecies is the way in which the old
Israel's quest for the "promised land" is transfigured into the
new Israel's entry into the heavenly kingdom. This theme of
God's coming kingdom, in which there will be "new heavens and
a new earth" (Is 65:17), is the ultimate object of the eschatological vision of the Old Testament prophets.

The Coming of the Messiah

Yet another—and supremely important—element in the prophets' eschatological reinterpretation of the covenant relationship
between God and his people is the theme of the advent of the
Messiah. The prophets look to the Messiah, God's anointed one,
for the salvation of Israel and of all the world. And the messianic
proclamations of the Old Testament prophets are, from the
standpoint of historic Christianity, announcements of the coming
of Jesus, who was the expected Christ (see Lk 4:16-30).

There are three major images of the Messiah in the writings
of the prophets: first, he is spoken of as a great king like David,
who will bring about the deliverance and vindication of Israel;
second, he is depicted as one who will suffer (and even die) in

order to atone for the sins of the human race; and third, the Messiah is described as the very presence of God himself in the midst of his people.

The image of the Messiah as Davidic king is present in many of the prophetic texts. Isaiah speaks of the Messiah as "a shoot from the stump of Jesse [that is, David's father]," a king of David's line (11:1). The image of the messianic king is also developed in the books of Jeremiah and Ezekiel.

> Behold, the days are coming, says the Lord, when I will fulfil the promise I made to . . . [my people]. In those days and at that time I will cause a righteous branch to spring forth for David; and he shall execute justice and righteousness in the land. In those days . . . [the people of God] will be saved and . . . will dwell securely. . . . (Jr 33:14-16)

> And I will set up over them one shepherd, my servant David, and he shall feed them: he shall feed them and be their shepherd. And I, the Lord, will be their God, and my servant David shall be prince among them; I, the Lord, have spoken. . . . My servant David shall be king over them; and they shall all have one shepherd. They shall follow my ordinances and be careful to observe my statutes. (Ezk 34:23-24; 37:24)

The prophets also tell us that the kingly Messiah will be born in the town of Bethlehem—David's birthplace (Mi 5:2), and that he will one day ride humbly into Jerusalem on the back of a donkey (Zc 9:9). Jesus, proclaimed by the New Testament as the Christ, was descended from the house of David (Mt 1:1-17), was born in Bethlehem (Lk 2:1-7) and made his triumphal entry into Jerusalem riding on a donkey (Mt 21:1-11).

The image of the Messiah as he who will suffer for the sins of his people is most clearly and profoundly presented in those chapters of the book of Isaiah that speak of the "Suffering Servant" of God (chapters 42, 49-50, 52-53).

> Behold my servant, whom I uphold, my chosen, in whom

my soul delights; I have put my Spirit upon him, he will
bring forth justice to the nations. He will not cry or lift up
his voice, or make it heard in the street; a bruised reed
he will not break, and a dimly burning wick he will not
quench; he will faithfully bring forth justice. He will not
fail or be discouraged till he has established justice in the
earth; and the coastlands wait for his law. (Is 42:1-4)

And the Servant of God, the Messiah, will make God's salvation
available, not only to the descendants of Abraham and Jacob, but
also to all peoples of the world (see, for example, Is 49:6).

The sacrificial suffering of the Servant of God, through which
the salvation of the whole world is to be effected, is predicted in
Isaiah 52:13-53:12 (see also 50:4-11). And Christians have always understood this passage to be a prophecy of the passion
and death of Christ (see, for example, Ac 8:26-40).

Behold, my servant shall prosper, he shall be exalted and
lifted up, and shall be very high [as a result of his suffer-
ing]. . . . He was despised and rejected by men; a man of
sorrows, and acquainted with grief; and as one from whom
men hide their faces he was despised, and we esteemed
him not. Surely he has borne our griefs and carried our
sorrows; yet we esteemed him stricken, smitten by God,
and afflicted. But he was wounded for our transgressions,
he was bruised for our iniquities; upon him was the chas-
tisement that made us whole, and with his stripes we are
healed. All we like sheep have gone astray; we have turned
every one to his own way; and the Lord has laid on him
the iniquity of us all. He was . . . like a lamb that is led
to the slaughter. . . . He poured out his soul to death, and
was numbered with the transgressors; yet he bore the sin
of many, and made intercession for the transgressors.

Adding to Isaiah's description of the sufferings of Christ, Zechariah speaks of the piercing of his body (12:10), and the book of
Psalms refers to the piercing of his hands and feet (22:16). The
writers of the New Testament saw these texts from Isaiah,

Zechariah and Psalm 22 completed in the death of Christ (see Mt 8:17; Rm 4:25; Heb 9:28; 1 Pt 2:24).

A close reading of Isaiah's prophecies concerning the Servant of God will reveal a certain ambiguity of reference in the prophet's vision. Sometimes the Servant is depicted as the entire nation of Israel, sometimes as the righteous remnant of the postexilic era, and sometimes as the Messiah who will bring God's plan of salvation to its climax. According to Adam W. Miller, Isaiah's "Servant Songs" present the Servant as "the chosen instrument of God through which his will and purpose are revealed. . . . Israel as a nation is looked upon as the servant. Her sufferings were to benefit the world. Also, the faithful remnant of Israel is thought of as a servant. This faithful remnant constituted the servant through which true religion would be kept alive and desseminated throughout the world. But Israel as the servant, and the faithful remnant as the servant, are steps leading to the climax of introducing the suffering Servant of Yahweh as an individual. The Servant is first the nation, then the true Israel or faithful remnant, and finally the One who suffers for the world's sin and misery."[13]

The image of the Messiah as the presence of God in the world—as a divine being—appears in several of the Old Testament prophetic books. The prophet Micah says of the messianic king who would be born in Bethlehem that his "origin [or going forth] is from old, from ancient days" (Mi 5:2). The fathers of the Church interpreted this prophetic text as a confirmation of the New Testament claim that Jesus Christ was the incarnation of God the Son, who was begotten of God the Father from all eternity (see Jn 1:1-18). And in a passage from the book of Daniel which has been read as a messianic prophecy by both Jews[14] and Christians, the following vision is recorded:

> . . . and behold, with the clouds of heaven there came one like a son of man, and he came to the Ancient of Days and was presented before him. And to him was given dominion and glory and kingdom, that all peoples, nations, and languages should serve him; his dominion is an everlasting dominion, which shall not pass away, and his kingdom one that shall not be destroyed. (7:13-14)

Here, he who should come into the world as the Messiah is a divine being in human form, closely associated with "the Ancient of Days" (God the Father); and to this divine "son of man," eternal dominion over all things is given. The many New Testament references to Jesus as "the Son of Man" (see, for example, Mt 12:8; Lk 26:64; and Jn 3:13-14) are intended to show that Daniel's vision of a divine Messiah has been fulfilled in Christ.

The divinity of the Messiah is also strongly suggested in the book of Malachi, where God's messianic "messenger" is presented as intimately involved in the divine judgment of the world. "Behold, I send my messenger to prepare the way before me, and the Lord whom you seek will suddenly come to his temple; the messenger of the covenant in whom you delight, behold, he is coming, says the Lord of hosts" (3:1).

But perhaps the most striking Old Testament references to the Messiah as a divine king are to be found in the book of Isaiah. Isaiah tells us (according to the Greek text) that "a virgin shall conceive and bear a son, and shall call his name Emmanuel [or Immanuel]" (7:14). St. Matthew applies this verse to the miraculous birth of Jesus, and points out that the name "Emmanuel" means "God with us" (Mt 1:23). Jesus, whose name means "Yahweh is salvation," is also "Emmanuel"—God with us!

> For to us a child is born, to us a son is given; and the government will be upon his shoulder, and his name will be called "Wonderful Counselor, Mighty God, Everlasting Father, Prince of Peace." Of the increase of his government and of peace there will be no end, upon the throne of David, and over his kingdom, to establish it, and to uphold it with justice and with righteousness from this time forth and for evermore. The zeal of the Lord of hosts will do this. (Is 9:6-7)

Thus, the prophets of the Old Testament looked forward to the coming of a Messiah who would reign as a king in the tradition of David; who would, through his own suffering, make atonement for the sins of Israel and all mankind; and who would, in his own person, make the power and presence of God manifest in the world. And it is the faith of the historic Christian Church that, in Christ, these prophetic expectations have been more than fulfilled.

The Resurrection of the Dead

A final element in the theology of the prophets is the theme of life after death—of resurrection and immortality. We have touched upon this theme earlier in this chapter, but we must return to it now, for it is a significant aspect of the prophetic conception of the new covenant and the coming kingdom of God.

The prophets' belief in the condemnation of the unrighteous on "the day of the Lord" and in the salvation of the righteous in the kingdom of God presupposes the resurrection of the dead and personal immortality. This presupposition—this article of faith and object of hope—receives explicit formulation in the books of Isaiah, Daniel and Ezekiel. Describing the salvation of the faithful, Isaiah prophesies that the Lord will ultimately destroy the curse of death which covers all peoples: "He will swallow up death for ever. . . . Thy dead shall live, their bodies shall rise. Oh dwellers in the dust, awake and sing for joy!" (Is 25:6-9, 26:19). And Daniel, referring to both the saved and the damned, proclaims: ". . . those who sleep in the dust of the earth shall awake, some to everlasting life, and some to shame and everlasting contempt" (Dn 12:2).

But by far the most dramatic and glorious Old Testament vision of the resurrection of the dead is recorded in Ezekiel 37:1-14. Ezekiel was taken, by "the Spirit of the Lord," to a great valley full of dry bones. And God said to the bones: "Behold, I will cause breath to enter you, and you shall live. And I will lay sinews upon you, and will cause flesh to come upon you, and cover you with skin, and put breath [or spirit] in you, and you shall live; and you shall know that I am the Lord" (37:1-6). And then the Lord lifted the veil of the future and revealed to Ezekiel the final resurrection of the dead (37:7-10). Ezekiel presents God's promise of resurrection in the following terms:

> Behold, I will open your graves, and raise you from your
> graves, O my people; and I will bring you home into the

land of Israel. And you shall know that I am the Lord, when I open your graves, and raise you from your graves, O my people. And I will put my Spirit within you, and you shall live, and I will place you in your own land [the coming kingdom]; then you shall know that I, the Lord, have spoken, and I have done it, says the Lord. (37:11-14)

With this remarkable verbal icon of the final entry of God's people into the eternal life of the kingdom of God, the covenant-kingdom theology of the Old Testament prophets is completed. The next stage in the biblical record of the mighty acts of God will proclaim the fulfilment and transcendence of the Old Testament revelation of the Lord's redemptive purpose in the "new covenant" established by "the revelation of Jesus Christ" (Rv 1:1).

In this chapter, we have surveyed (briefly) the wisdom literature of the Old Testament and (at length) the writings of the Old Testament prophets. In these inspired texts, the biblical theme of salvation was reinterpreted in "eschatological" terms. The promises of God in the old covenant are given a radically futuristic and mystical significance in the writings of the Old Testament wise men and prophets. The old covenant is to be transfigured into a new covenant; and the Messiah—in whom the wisdom, word, and power of God are to be made present to the world—will come to lead his people into the eternal life of the kingdom of God. Such is the overall theological message of the books of wisdom and prophecy.

The Old Testament as a whole presents God as the absolute Lord of the universe, the Creator of all things, and man's ultimate good. Man has alienated himself from the Lord through sin and is thus in desperate need of salvation. And God has acted to save man from evil, suffering and death by revealing himself to the world and by preparing the way, through Israel, for the advent of the Messiah, who will reconcile "all things" to the Lord. Thus, God's disclosure of himself to the human race—in nature, in history and in Holy Scripture—points toward the person and work of Jesus Christ, the incarnation of God the Son. The long period between Adam and the postexilic era was, then, from a Christian point of view, one long wait for the coming of Christ. But in waiting, we have been blessed, for "they who wait for the Lord shall renew their strength, they shall mount up with wings like eagles, they shall run and not be weary, they shall walk and not faint" (Is 40:31).

CHAPTER 5

The Message of the Synoptic Gospels: St. Matthew, St. Mark and St. Luke

The New Testament, like the Septuagint version of the Old Testament, was composed in Greek. And the word "testament" (Latin, *testamentum*) is a translation of a Greek term, *diatheke,* which means "covenant." The Old Testament tells of the "old covenant" between God and ancient Israel, and the New Testament is a proclamation of a "new covenant" between God and the "new Israel," which is the Christian Church. The prophets of ancient Israel, as we have seen, looked forward to the coming of the Messiah and the establishment of a new covenant between God and his faithful people. And, according to the New Testament, Jesus of Nazareth was the Messiah (or Christ)—the divine-human king in whom the promises and prophecies of the Old Testament have been "summed up, confirmed, and transcended."[1]

The new covenant makes salvation available to all who acknowledge Jesus as Christ and Savior and who submit to him as Lord of their lives. In Christ, who "reflects the glory of God and bears the very stamp of his nature" (Heb 1:3), the divine promise of salvation, first revealed in the Old Testament, is fulfilled. Christ is the incarnate Son of God, "the mediator of . . . [the] new covenant" (Heb 9:15), who brings salvation to the world. And by the grace of God, the human race is called to respond to Christ in faith and obedience. Those who so respond are "the heirs of salvation, the covenant people . . . the Israel of God, the Church."[2] Such is the central message of the New Testament.

THE MAKING OF THE NEW TESTAMENT

The New Testament contains twenty-seven books: the four gospels of SS. Matthew, Mark, Luke and John; the book of Acts, a history of the early Church written by St. Luke; twenty-one letters or "epistles" by St. Paul and other writers; and the Apocalypse or book of Revelation, a vision of the final fulfilment of God's cosmic purpose, attributed to St. John. All of these documents were written in Greek—not classical Greek, but the common Greek (*koine*) of the Hellenistic age. The gospels were composed later than many of the epistles. Most of St. Paul's letters—and perhaps the letters of St. James, St. Peter and St. Jude[3]—were written prior to 65 A.D.; whereas the four gospels were composed between 65 and 90 A.D. The book of Acts was detached and treated as a separate book during the second century, when the gospels were "brought together and began to circulate as a fourfold record [of Christ's ministry]."[4] The letters of St. John and Revelation were written c. 90-95 A.D.

While the apostles and other immediate disciples of Christ still lived, the Bible of the Church was the Greek Old Testament. And the Old Testament revelation was interpreted by the Church in the light of the apostolic message concerning the person and work of Christ. The major events of Christ's life, as well as his teachings, were remembered by the apostles and were incorporated into their preaching during the mid-first century A.D. This oral tradition was "received by the apostles from their Lord and delivered by them in turn to their converts."[5] In time, the "apostolic tradition" began to be set down in writing—in early collections of the sayings of Jesus, in catechisms used for doctrinal instruction, in liturgical texts employed in the conduct of Christian worship and in letters written by major figures in the apostolic Church. As the apostles began to grow old and die, the Church's need for a written expression of the apostolic witness became more and more apparent. This perceived need gave impetus to the writing of the four gospels and other documents during the latter first century, and led to the collection of the corpus of St. Paul's letters (excluding Hebrews) between 80 and 85 A.D.

In seeking to preserve the apostolic tradition in written form, the Church did not, at first, intend to establish a definitive canon of scripture. But with the late first and early second-century proliferation of Christian and quasi-Christian literature, and with the rise of heretical movements claiming apostolic authority,[6] many early fathers of the Church began to call for the formation of a canonical collection of "New Testament" scriptures. To be considered as canonical, a document had to pass three tests: (1) it had to have been written by an apostle or by an immediate disciple of an apostle; (2) it had to be recognized as authentic by at least one leading ecclesiastical community in the ancient Church; and (3) it had to be consistent with apostolic doctrine—that is, with the rule of faith preserved in the living tradition of the Church.

During the second and third centuries—largely through the efforts of St. Irenaeus of Lyons, Hippolytus of Rome, Tertullian, Clement of Alexandria and Origen—the idea of a New Testament canon was established, but the constitution of that canon was widely disputed. It was agreed that the four gospels, the book of Acts, the letters of St. Paul, 1 Peter and 1 John were canonical; but some leading authorities of the day doubted the canonicity of Hebrews, James, 2 and 3 John, Jude and Revelation. Furthermore, some documents that were ultimately excluded from the New Testament—for example, the *Shepherd of Hermas,* the *Epistle of Barnabas,* and the *Apocalypse of Peter*—were accepted as canonical by a few ecclesiastical writers.[7]

By the fourth century, however, the Church had resolved the disputes concerning the constitution of the New Testament, and the process of canonization was brought to completion. In his Paschal Letter of 367, St. Athanasius of Alexandria declared the twenty-seven books of the New Testament as we know it to be "exclusively canonical."[8] And a synodal decree in conformity with the declaration of St. Athanasius, prompted by the arguments of St. Augustine of Hippo, was issued at Carthage in 397. Thenceforth, the New Testament—as the divinely inspired, written expression of the apostolic witness—was accepted by all Orthodox Christians as a central and normative feature of the holy tradition of the Church.

The Four Gospels

The first division of the New Testament, as we have seen, contains the four gospels. The English word "gospel" is a modernization of an Old English term meaning "good story" or "good news," which was itself a translation of *euaggelion,* the Greek word for "glad tidings." The latter term is used throughout the New Testament to designate the "glad tidings" of salvation through Jesus Christ, the "joyful news" proclaimed in the preaching of the apostles and other early disciples of Christ.

The New Testament never uses the term *euaggelia,* the plural of *euaggelion;* for there is only one message of salvation. But with the expression of the apostolic message of salvation in written form, those writings which described the major teachings and acts of Christ came to becalled *euaggelia,* or "gospels." Thus, in the New Testament, we find the Gospel *according* to St. Matthew, *according* to St. Mark, *according* to St. Luke and *according to* St. John—one gospel proclaimed in four distinct books, rooted in one common, apostolic faith. The authors of the gospels "differ from one another in their approaches and expressions, but are united in participating in the tradition of the Church and in making the Church's faith their own. The faith and life of the Church served them as the guiding principle in selecting and arranging their material."[9]

In his book, *The Gospel Image of Christ,* Prof. Veselin Kesich describes "three stages in the growth of the Gospels":

> First came the events of Christ's life and works, "the things which have been accomplished among us." The second stage was characterized by the delivery and transmission of these "things" by their "eyewitnesses and ministers of the word." This is the work of the apostles after Christ's resurrection. . . . Finally, the third stage was the writing of the Gospels by the evangelists.[10]

Kesich goes on to point out that the ancient Church regarded the first and fourth gospels as the work of the apostles Matthew and John; whereas the second and third gospels were attributed respectively to Mark, a disciple of St. Peter, and to Luke, a Greek-speaking physician who was a close companion of St. Paul.[11] According to St. Irenaeus of Lyons (d. c. 200), the Gospel according to St. Mark contains the substance of St. Peter's preaching about Christ, while the Gospel according to St. Luke is an expression of the message of salvation proclaimed by St. Paul.[12] Thus, within the historic life of the Church, the apostolic origin and authority of the four gospels has never been doubted.

St. Mark's gospel was written c. 65 A.D. in Rome. It was apparently intended for an audience of Gentile Christians, although the book contains a number of allusions to the Old Testament. The major purpose of Mark's gospel was to show Jesus as the crucified Messiah, "the fulfiller of the hope of Israel."[13] The gospels of Matthew and Luke were written in the early seventies of the first century. St. Matthew's gospel was composed in Syrian Antioch, for Jewish Christians, and its central theme is the fulfilment of Israel's messianic hope in the person and work of Jesus. St. Luke wrote his gospel and the book of Acts as two volumes of a single work, describing the ministry of Jesus and the history of the early Christian community under the leadership of the apostles. Writing in southern Greece primarily for Gentile converts to Christianity, Luke emphasizes the universal significance of the Christian gospel: in Christ, salvation has been made possible not only for Jews but for all mankind. St. John's gospel was written in Ephesus (in Asia Minor) during the late first century (c. 85-90 A.D.). In his gospel, John "tells us who Christ is and what His meaning is for the world, the Church, and the individual."[14]

The gospels, then, are written expressions of the apostolic message of salvation through Christ. Several distinct strands of the apostolic tradition are present in the four gospels. The first, second and third gospels seem to be based upon common sources, whereas the Gospel according to St. John is built upon sources not employed by Matthew, Mark and Luke and is rather different from them in structure and content. The latter are known as the "synoptic" gospels, for "when we put their material side by side in three columns, we notice that the material is arranged in a similar manner, and very often they use the same words to describe events or to record the sayings of Jesus."[15] In the present chapter, we shall discuss the content and theological significance of the three synoptic gospels; and in chapter 6, the theology of the Gospel according to St. John will be examined.

THE GENERAL STRUCTURE OF THE
SYNOPTIC GOSPELS

The majority of contemporary biblical scholars are agreed that the earliest of the New Testament gospels is that of St. Mark. It is also widely believed that Mark's gospel was one of the sources utilized in the composition of the gospels of Matthew and Luke. Matthew's gospel contains 1,068 verses, and 500 of these are parallel to 606 out of the 673 verses of Mark. Of the 1,149 verses in Luke, 380 are taken over verbatim from Mark's gospel. Mark contains only 31 verses not duplicated in either Matthew or Luke.

Matthew and Luke also share approximately 250 verses of material not paralleled in Mark; and "sometimes this common material appears in . . . practically identical language, while sometimes the verbal divergence is considerable."[16] Most biblical researchers have concluded that the non-Markan material common to Matthew and Luke derives from an early written (but no longer extant) source called "Q" (after the German word *Quelle,* which means "source"). Possibly compiled by St. Matthew prior to the composition of his gospel, Q was a collection of the sayings of Jesus which apparently circulated among Christian communities in ancient Judea, Syria, Asia Minor and Greece.[17] Matthew and Luke, working independently of one another, incorporated the material contained in Q into their respective gospels.

Furthermore, the Gospel of Matthew contains approximately 300 verses not paralleled in the other gospels, while Luke contains some 520 verses peculiar to itself. These blocks of unique material are known as "M" and "L," respectively. The origins of these materials are not known, but many scholars have speculated that M represents traditions about Jesus which were preserved in the churches of Judea, while L is derived from traditions maintained in the church of Caesarea. Whether the traditions behind M and L were oral or written is, at present, an unresolved issue in biblical scholarship.

The synoptic gospels are constructed in biographical form— that is, they present the apostolic message of salvation through an apparently chronological account of the major events in the life of Jesus. But they are not, in fact, complete or scientific biographies of Christ. They tell us very little of the first thirty years of our Lord's life; they do not describe his appearance, education or psychological development. Instead, the synoptics concentrate exclusively upon those aspects of Christ's earthly life that are crucial to the salvation of mankind and the world. They tell us who Jesus was, what he said and what he did—and they seek to explain the sense in which his identity, teachings and works have made our salvation from evil and death a real possibility. As Prof. Kesich puts it:

> The Gospels were not meant to provide a literal description, but an image of Jesus, not a photograph, but a portrait of Him. . . . The Gospels have often been compared to an icon, and been called the verbal icon of Christ. This icon or image is not a product of the extraordinary creative talents of the evangelists, but it comes from the tradition with which they were acquainted, in which they participated, and from which they drew their material.[18]

The synoptic gospels, then, are theological interpretations of the earthly ministry of Jesus, written expressions of the apostolic proclamation of salvation. Their ultimate aim is not to present a biographical study of the Lord's life, but to witness to the fulfilment of God's redemptive purpose in the person and work of Jesus Christ.

The synoptic gospels describe only two periods in the life of Jesus. Matthew and Luke present substantial blocks of material on the Lord's birth and childhood; and all three synoptics contain extensive accounts of the public ministry of Christ, which, according to tradition, took place during the last three years of his earthly life. Matthew, Mark and Luke are virtually silent concerning the years between the Lord's early childhood and the commencement of his public ministry. The only exception is found in Luke 2:41-51 (telling of the twelve-year-old Jesus' discussions with the rabbis in the Jerusalem Temple). Apart from this story, all we are told is that, as a child, Jesus was strong, filled with wisdom and blessed by the grace of God (Lk 2:40); and that as a young man he advanced in wisdom, grew in physical stature and lived in spiritual harmony with God and in favor with his fellow man (Lk 2:52).

Thus, assuming that Christ was thirty-three years old when he was crucified, as tradition suggests, the synoptics tell us practically nothing of nearly thirty years of our Lord's life. During these "silent years," or "years of preparation," no doubt, the Son of God, in communion with the Father and the Holy Spirit, was made ready for his public ministry; but what exactly went on during that time has not been revealed to the world. There are, to be sure, ancient apocryphal writings containing speculations upon the hidden events of Christ's youth and early manhood,[19] but the historic Church has repeatedly condemned such writings as spiritually dangerous and heretical. From an Orthodox Christian point of view, detailed knowledge of the "silent years" belongs to God alone, and for the purposes of our salvation from the bondage of sin and death, the gospels of Matthew and Luke tell us all we need to know of the early life of Christ.

The Birth and Childhood of Christ

The Roman empire was in effective control of the Middle East after 63 B.C. By permission of the Romans, Herod the Great (a nominal Jew of Idumaean descent)[20] reigned as "King of the Jews" in Palestine from 37 B.C. until his death in 4 B.C. Jesus was born in Bethlehem of Judea, "the city of David," during the latter days of Herod's kingship[21] (see Mt 2:1, 19).

Two complementary accounts of the miraculous birth of Christ are contained in Matthew 1-2 and Luke 1-2. Both Matthew and Luke attest to the virgin birth of Christ. The annunciation of the advent of Christ by the angel Gabriel to Mary, the mother of Jesus, is recorded in Luke 1:26-38; and the Orthodox Church teaches that Mary's voluntary submission to the will of God— her freely willed agreement with the divine plan announced by the angel—was a fundamental and necessary condition of the union of God and man in Christ. "The Incarnation was not only the work of the Father, of His Power and His Spirit; it was also the work of the will and the faith of the Virgin."[22] Because of Mary's positive response to the annunciation, our salvation through her Son, Jesus Christ, has become possible. Thus, when the Orthodox Church "shows honor to the Mother of God, it is not just because God chose her but also because she herself chose aright."[23]

In the course of time, then, the Virgin Mary "was found to be with child of the Holy Spirit" (Mt 1:18). When Joseph, to whom Mary was engaged, discovered her pregnancy, he "resolved to divorce her quietly."[24] But an angel of the Lord appeared to Joseph in a dream and told him to take Mary for his wife, "for that which is conceived in her is of the Holy Spirit." The angel also told Joseph that Mary's child would be a son who was to be named "Jesus" (which means "the Lord saves"), "for he will save his people from their sins" (Mt 1:20-21).

Thus, Joseph and Mary were married according to Jewish law. And while the couple was on a journey to Bethlehem (to enroll their names in a census that had been ordered by the Emperor Augustus Caesar), Mary gave birth there to her divinely conceived son (see Lk 2:1-7). Matthew interprets the miraculous conception and birth of Christ as a fulfilment of the words of the prophet Isaiah: " 'Behold, a virgin shall conceive and bear a son, and his name shall be called Emmanuel' (which means, God with us)" (Mt 1:22-23; see also Is 7:14).

Matthew and Luke represent two different traditions concerning the immediate aftermath of Christ's nativity. According to Luke, the birth of the Savior was announced by angels to shepherds tending their flocks "out in the field"; and the shepherds, hearing the joyful tidings of the advent of the Messiah, visited the holy family in Bethlehem in order to "see this thing that has happened, which the Lord has made known to us" (Lk 2:8-20). Luke goes on to tell us that, at the age of eight days, Christ was circumcised and given the name Jesus, and that, thirty-three days after his circumcision, at a service of purification in the Jerusalem Temple, he was presented to God "according to the custom of the law" (Lk 2:21-27; see also Lv 12; Ex 13:2, 12; Nb 3:13).

The Roman Catholic Church and some Protestant churches hold a yearly festival commemorating the "Presentation of Christ in the Temple" or the "Purification of the Blessed Virgin Mary." But in the Orthodox Church, this festival (celebrated on February 2) is known as the "Meeting of Our Lord"—"the meeting, that is, of Christ with his people."[25] For at his presentation, as Luke tells us, Jesus' messianic identity was recognized and proclaimed by the holy man Simeon and the prophetess Anna (Lk 2:25-38). "Our Lord, brought to the Temple by His mother and by Joseph, now meets His chosen people in the persons of Simeon the Elder and Ann [or Anna] the Prophetess."[26] The Holy Spirit had revealed to Simeon "that he should not see death before he had seen the Lord's Christ" (Lk 2:26). And upon seeing the baby Jesus, Simeon was prompted by the Spirit to cry out, "Lord, now lettest thou thy servant depart in peace . . ."—the famous "Song of Simeon" (Lk 2:29-32), which is sung in the Vespers services of Orthodox churches throughout the world. Simeon also said to Mary, "Behold, this child is set for the fall and rising of many in Israel, and for a sign that is spoken against (and a sword will pierce through your own soul also)" (2:34-35). Supporting the witness of Simeon, the prophetess Anna "gave thanks to God, and spoke of . . . [Jesus] to all who were looking for the redemption of Jerusalem" (2:38).

After his account of the Meeting of Our Lord, Luke states that Joseph and Mary took the child Jesus and "returned into Galilee, to their own city, Nazareth" (2:39).

Matthew's post-nativity narrative stands in significant contrast to the account presented in Luke. Following his description of Christ's birth, Matthew tells us that "wise men" (Magi, or *magoi*, seers, astrologers, magicians) from the "East" (probably Persia) came to Jerusalem, saying, "Where is he who has been born king of the Jews? For we have seen his star in the East, and have come to worship him" (Mt 2:1-2). According to a popular Christian tradition, there were three Magi, and they were not only visionaries but also kings. Herod, who thought of himself as "King of the Jews," and knowing that the Messiah was to be born in Bethlehem, sent the Magi to that city, encouraging them to seek out the newborn child, "that I too may come and worship him" (Mt 2:3-8). Herod's real intention, of course, was to find the Christ and have him killed. Guided by the "Star of Bethlehem," the Magi found the holy family, "and they fell down and worshiped" the Christ-child, offering him gifts of "gold and frankincense and myrrh" (Mt 2:9-11). These gifts, it has been said, symbolize the kingship, the deity and the humanity of Jesus; for in ancient Middle Eastern thought, gold was the substance of kings, incense was an offering to God and myrrh—a cosmetic and medicinal spice—was associated with the human body.

After venerating the infant Jesus, the Magi, warned by God of the dark purposes of Herod, returned to their own country without informing the evil king of the whereabouts of the Messiah. Joseph, too, was warned of Herod's plan, and he fled with Mary and Jesus into Egypt. Herod, "in a furious rage" at having been "tricked by the wise men," had all the male children in the region of Bethlehem "who were two years old or younger" killed. Shortly after this "Massacre of the Innocents,"[27] Herod died (in 4 B.C.), and the holy family, like ancient Israel, returned from Egypt to Palestine. Joseph, his wife and his foster child went to live in Nazareth, a small city in the northern district of Galilee (see Mt 2:13-23).

Although the post-nativity accounts of Matthew and Luke are different, they are not necessarily contradictory. It is quite possible that the traditions incorporated in Matthew and Luke have preserved true but partial recollections of the Lord's infancy. It is unlikely that the visit of the Magi took place immediately following the birth of Christ, for the text of Matthew implies that the wise men themselves had calculated the nativity as occurring up to a year or two prior to their visit (2:7, 16). Thus, these events may well have taken place subsequent to the Meeting of Our Lord in the Temple (Lk 2:21-38), but prior to the holy family's "return to Nazareth," spoken of in Luke 2:39. It is then possible to see the post-nativity accounts of Matthew and Luke as together constituting an icon of Christ's saving mission to both Jews and Gentiles. For the Lukan account stresses that the advent of the Messiah was revealed first to Jews (the shepherds in the field), and in his description of the circumcision and meeting, Luke emphasizes that everything was performed according to the Mosaic law (see Lk 2:39). In contrast to Luke, Matthew's story of the Magi represents Christ's relationship with the Gentile world; and the Magi's worship and adoration of the Lord is a symbol of the Church, the new Israel, in which membership is determined by faith and not by ethnic lineage. Thus, on Christmas Day, the Orthodox Church sings: "O Master who hast risen as a Star out of Jacob, Thou hast filled with joy the watchers of stars [the Magi] . . . As the first fruits of the Gentiles were they led unto Thee, and Thou hast openly received them, as they brought Thee acceptable gifts."[28]

The Gospel of Matthew begins with a detailed genealogy tracing the ancestry of Jesus (1:1-18); and there is also a genealogy of Jesus in the Gospel of Luke (3:23-38). These two genealogies differ in many respects, and the divergences between them have never been adequately explained.[29] But it is possible to discern the major theological point of these difficult texts. Both genealogies seek to establish the fact that Jesus, through his legal relationship with his foster-father Joseph, was a descendant of King David, upon whom Israel's messianic ideal was in part based.[30] The Messiah, according to the Old Testament prophets, was to be a member of the house of David.

Matthew's genealogy traces the ancestry of Jesus back to Abraham, the father of the nation of Israel, thereby emphasizing Christ's relationship with God's chosen people of the old covenant. By contrast, Luke goes back beyond Abraham to Adam, who was, originally, "the son of God" (Lk 3:38). St. Paul, the apostle to whom Luke was a disciple, thought of Christ as the new Adam (see 1 Co 15:22, 45-49) in whom we may be adopted as "sons of God" (see Rm 8:14-17). It is likely that this Pauline teaching lies behind Luke's genealogy, and that Luke's purpose in tracing the ancestry of Christ to Adam is to emphasize the Lord's solidarity with the entire human race and to underline the divine sonship, which is offered to all in Christ.[31]

The genealogies of Christ, then, which are presented in the gospels of Matthew and Luke, proclaim that Jesus is "the Son of David," "the Son of Abraham" and, indeed, "the Son of God."

The Ministry of St. John the Baptist

While only Matthew and Luke contain narratives dealing with the ancestry, birth and childhood of Jesus, all three synoptic gospels present detailed accounts of the Lord's public ministry. And each account begins with a description of the relationship between the ministry of St. John the Baptist and the mission of Christ.

John the Baptist was a transitional figure in the "salvation history" revealed in the Bible—the last of the old and the first of the new covenant prophets. An ascetic who lived in the wilderness of Judea for many years prior to his public ministry, the synoptics depict him as the prophetic forerunner of Christ, sent by God to prepare the way for the work of Jesus (see Mt 3:1-6; Mk 1:1-6; and Lk 3:1-6). The Jews of Jesus' time expected the prophet Elijah to return to the world prior to the coming of the Messiah, and to announce the advent of "the great and terrible day of the Lord" (see Ml 4:4-6). Thus, in the synoptic gospels, the work of John the Baptist is associated with the end-time mission of Elijah. According to Matthew 3:4 and Mark 3:6, John wore a garment made of camel's hair and a leather belt around his waist—the manner of dress attributed to Elijah in 2 Kings 1:8. And Luke tells us that John was sent before Jesus "in the spirit and power of Elijah" (Lk 1:17; see also Mt 11:14).

In his preaching (which began in the late twenties of the first century A.D.), John warned of the day of judgment which would precede the advent of the kingdom of God, and he called upon his fellow Jews to repent—that is, to turn away from evil and toward God (see Mt 1:2, 7-10; Mk 1:4; and Lk 3:3, 7-9). In accord with his insistence upon the coming judgment and the need for repentance, John baptized those who were seeking God's forgiveness of their sins (Mt 1:5-6; Mk 1:4-5; and Lk 1:3, 7-14). The gospels do not describe the exact manner of baptism that John used, nor how it arose. It quite likely "was not introduced by John but was already a familiar custom," and "probably signified a cleansing or purification."[32]

John also heralded the coming of the Messiah: "After me comes he who is mightier than I, the thong of whose sandals I

am not worthy to stoop down and untie. I have baptized you with
water; but he will baptize you with the Holy Spirit" (Mk 1:7-8;
see also Mt 1:11-12 and Lk 3:15-18). And the synoptics proclaim that Jesus of Nazareth was the divinely promised Messiah
expected by John and other pious Jews of those days (see Mt
11:2-19 and 7:8-35).

After the beginning of the public ministry of Christ, John the
Baptist was arrested and subsequently executed by order of the
son and successor of Herod the Great, Herod Antipas (d. c. 40
A.D.), a grossly immoral man whose evil ways had been publicly
denounced by John (see Lk 3:19-20 and Mt 14:1-12).

The Baptism and Temptation of Christ

Jesus began his public ministry by submitting to baptism at
the hands of John the Baptist.

> In those days Jesus came from Nazareth of Galilee and
> was baptized by John in the Jordan. And when he came
> up out of the water, immediately he saw the heavens
> opened and the Spirit descending upon him like a dove;
> and a voice came from heaven, "Thou art my beloved Son;
> with thee I am well pleased." (Mk 1:9-11; see also Mt
> 3:13-17 and Lk 3:21-22)

The baptism of Christ is celebrated by the Orthodox as the Feast
of Theophany (January 6). "Theophany" means "manifestation
of God," and Christ's baptism truly is a "manifestation of God"
to the world, both in the sense that it marks the beginning of his
public ministry, and in a more profound sense, because it represents a revelation of the Holy Trinity. "All three Persons were
made manifest together: the Father testified from on high to
the divine Sonship of Jesus; the Son received His Father's testimony; and the Spirit was seen in the form of a dove, descending
from the Father and resting upon the Son."[33]

The baptism of John was, as we have seen, a baptism of
repentance. Why, then, was Christ, who is sinless, baptized by
John? To this question, the Orthodox Church replies that in

becoming human at his incarnation, our Lord "became the New Adam, summing up the whole human race in Himself, just as the first Adam summed up and contained all mankind in himself at the Fall."[34] At his baptism, he was cleansed for all men's sins. Identifying himself with our sinful condition and, indeed, with the fallenness of the whole world, Christ has redeemed mankind and the world from the bondage of evil; and his baptism is a sign of that glorious redemption. Christ, then, was baptized not for his own sake but for ours, and for that of the whole cosmic order.[35]

Following his baptism, Jesus "was led up by the Spirit into the wilderness to be tempted by the devil" (Mt 4:1-11; Mk 1:12-13; Lk 4:1-13). The biblical account of the temptation implies that the Exodus imagery of the Old Testament has received its spiritual recapitulation and fulfilment in the person and work of Jesus. Following her "baptism" in the Red Sea and prior to her entry into the land of Canaan, ancient Israel underwent a forty-year period of testing in the wilderness of Sinai.[36] Similarly, after his baptism in the Jordan and before the culmination of his redemptive mission, Jesus spent forty days and nights in the wilderness of Judea and was tempted by the devil. Christ, then, and those who are one with him through faith and obedience, constitute the new Israel. And as the old Israel entered into the promised land of Canaan, so would the new Israel enter into the true land of promise—the kingdom of God. The exodus in Christ is "the new Exodus of salvation."[37]

The temptation of Christ is also a recapitulation of the temptation of Adam and Eve as depicted in Genesis 3. Christ's submission to satanic temptation is a further sign of his assumption of the human condition, of his identification with the sons of Adam and the daughters of Eve. And in defeating the devil in the wilderness of Judea, Christ did what Adam had failed to do in the garden of Eden. In the first Adam, mankind was led away from God by the deceptions of Satan; but in Christ, the new Adam, mankind's bondage to the devil is broken and reconciliation with God is made possible.

The three satanic temptations of Christ[38] were attempts to exploit the Lord's humanity and, on that basis, to induce him to either doubt or renounce his divine sonship. Human beings are continually tempted to place their physical needs above their spiritual needs, and to seek miraculous signs that will ease their doubts concerning the existence and goodness of God. Following his fast, the Bible tells us, Jesus was hungry—yet another indication of his true humanity. Approaching the Lord in his hunger, the devil sought to direct Christ's attention to his need for "bread"—that is, to his physical needs—and thus to divert him from his spiritual purpose. Christ, however, proclaimed that the fulness of life sought by mankind is contained not in physical satisfaction but in the revealed Word of God. Thus, the first temptation of Christ teaches us to beware of the spiritual dangers following from "the incontinence of the belly" and other fleshly desires.[39]

The phrase, "*If* you are the Son of God," which appears in the first and second temptations, is also significant, for it shows that the devil was trying to generate doubt in the mind of Christ concerning his relationship with God the Father. Satan, quoting Psalm 91, challenged the Lord to quell all doubt by providing miraculous demonstrations of his divine sonship. In refusing to do this, Christ overcame the temptation of doubt, of "tempting" his Father into a spectacular and vain display of supernatural power.[40] Following the temptation, however, and without Christ asking for it, the Father's abiding love for his Son *was* manifested supernaturally in the attending angels who were sent to minister to the Savior. This too, according to St. John Chrysostom, is a lesson for those of us who are seeking reconciliation with God: "... we must overcome the devil, not by miracles, but by forbearance and long-suffering, and . . . we should do nothing at all for display and vainglory."[41]

In the third temptation, the devil made himself out to be God, and he endeavored to use the human desire for wealth, status and power to turn Christ away from his Father. But Christ, commanding the devil to depart, declared that man is to worship and serve God alone. Membership in the kingdom of God rather than the possession and enjoyment of worldly glory should be our primary concern.

Christ's Ministry in Galilee

After his temptation, Jesus entered fully into the work of his public ministry. The synoptic gospels offer a roughly chronological account of Christ's ministry. The materials on the major teachings and miracles of Christ, however, are arranged in topical rather than chronological order—probably a reflection of the manner in which these materials had been preserved in the oral tradition of the early apostolic community. And furthermore, the synoptics concentrate upon only two phases of the Lord's public ministry: his activity in the region of Galilee, and his final journey through Judea to Jerusalem. But it must be kept in mind, as the Gospel of John makes clear, that during his earthly life, Christ traveled frequently between Galilee and Jerusalem, spending a good deal of time in Judea.[42]

The Galilean ministry of Christ is described in Matthew 3-18, in Mark 1-9 and in Luke 3-9. Following his baptism and temptation, and some early preaching in Judea and Samaria, Jesus began to attract a following (see Jn 1-4). Indeed, the "Jesus movement" soon overshadowed the ministry of John the Baptist, a fact which the latter humbly accepted as a necessary dimension of the divine plan of redemption (see Jn 3:25-30). After the arrest of John the Baptist, Jesus and a number of his disciples returned from Judea to Galilee. He established his headquarters in the city of Capernaum, which was situated on the northwestern shore of the Sea of Galilee. As his following continued to grow, Jesus began to travel throughout the region of Galilee, "teaching in their synagogues and preaching the gospel of the kingdom, and healing every disease and every infirmity among the people" (Mt 4:23).

At some point in the Galilean ministry, Jesus chose twelve of his disciples to be his special agents in the propagation of his message. The twelve apostles (from the Greek *apostolos,* meaning "one sent forth") were Christ's closest associates, his personal representatives, upon whom he conferred authority to speak and heal in his name (see Mt 10:1-15; Mk 6:7-13; and Lk 9:1-6). As the twelve sons of Jacob had been the fathers of the old Israel, so the twelve apostles were to be the fathers of the new

Israel, the Church.[43] And during the time of Christ's earthly
ministry, as his co-workers, they were made ready for the service
they were to perform after the Lord's saving mission had been
carried out.

Mark summarizes Jesus' preaching on "the gospel of the
kingdom" as follows: "The time is fulfilled, and the kingdom of
God is at hand; repent and believe in the gospel" (Mk 1:15).
And in his sermons, parables and conversations on the kingdom
of God, Jesus taught what John the Baptist and the other prophets of Israel had taught: that to enter the kingdom of God, one
must repent—that is, renounce the world, the flesh and the devil
and turn toward God in faith, love and obedience. But unlike the
prophets, who proclaimed the divine Word in the name of God,
Jesus spoke with authority in his own name: "Truly, truly, I say
to you."

Each of the synoptic gospels contains compilations of Christ's
teachings on the kingdom of God (see Mt 5-7, 13, 24-25; Mk 4,
13; and Lk 6, 8, 10-19). The teachings of the Lord during his
Galilean ministry are summarized in detail in Matthew 13, in
a series of parables on the nature and growth of the heavenly
kingdom. In these parables, Jesus taught that the kingdom of
God is of absolute value and ought to be the object of every
man's ultimate concern (Mt 13:44-46); that the kingdom is,
even now, present and growing in the world (that is, in the person
of Christ and in the historic life of his Church—Mt 13:31-33);
that, in order to enter into the growing kingdom, we must live
faithfully and obediently in the light of God's revealed Word
(Jesus himself—Mt 13:1-23); and that, at the last judgment,
those who have not lived according to God's Word will be
eternally separated from the abundant life of the Lord's kingdom
(Mt 13:24-30, 36-43, 47-52).

Jesus also delivered a number of sermons on the kingdom
of God. The so-called "Sermon on the Mount" in Matthew 5-7
is actually a compilation of sermons which the Lord delivered
on various occasions, mainly during his ministry in Galilee. The
sermon is much too complex to be explained in detail here, and
we shall content ourselves with a brief discussion of its overall
content and meaning. The sermon begins with the Beatitudes
(*beatitudo* is a Latin word meaning "blessing"), a description

of the way of true discipleship, of the character of those who are worthy to be called the people of God (5:1-16). A child of God must be "poor in spirit," that is, aware of his total dependence upon God; he must be "mournful" concerning the sins and sufferings of mankind; he must be "meek" (or humble) before God and before his fellow man; he must "hunger and thirst after righteousness," after the kingdom of God, with his whole being; he must be "merciful" toward others because he knows that God has been merciful to him; he must be "pure in heart," seeking God without submitting to the distractions of the flesh; he must be a "peacemaker," at peace with God and sharing that peace with those around him; and he must be willing to be "persecuted for righteousness' sake," always upholding God's truth and refusing to compromise with the ways of the world. Such a person, Jesus taught, will be "the salt of the earth" and "the light of the world" in his living witness to the glory of God.

Following the Beatitudes, Christ goes on to interpret and apply the divine law revealed to Moses and recorded in the Old Testament (5:17-48). He also describes the nature of true religious piety (6:1-8), and proclaims that the key to human fulfilment is a singleminded concern for and devotion to God (6:19-34). He concludes the sermon with instructions on how to live in harmony with God and righteously with mankind, and with warnings concerning the spiritual distractions that can keep us from entering into the kingdom of heaven (7:1-29).

The "Sermon on the Mount" describes the nature of true righteousness and true justice. It reveals the law of the kingdom of God, the principles of order which govern the heavenly city, and reveals how through faith in Christ, and with the cooperation of the Holy Spirit, we can strive to live according to that law and grow in grace toward our ultimate union with God. Thus, the "Sermon on the Mount" is a message of inspiration and liberation. But for he who rejects Christ it is also a message of conviction, for only in Christ can we hope to gain access to the kingdom of God. Indeed, it has been said that Christ *is* our promised land; that he is, in himself, the inauguration of the kingdom of God; that he is "the kingdom in person" (*autobasileia*).[44]

The synoptic gospels also report that, during his Galilean

ministry (and at other times), Christ performed many healings and other miracles. These spectacular acts were performed as a fulfilment of the messianic prophecies of the Old Testament (see Mt 11:2-7; Lk 7:18-23). Thus, Christ healed the sick; he exorcised demons; he walked upon the Sea of Galilee (see 14:22-36); he miraculously fed multitudes of people (see Lk 9:10-17); he resuscitated the dead (see Mt 9:18-26; Mk 5:21-43; Lk 7:11-17, 8:40-56). All of these acts were "signs" of the advent of the kingdom of God in Christ.

During the early days of his ministry, Jesus did not declare himself to be the Messiah, nor did he proclaim his divine sonship. But his threefold work of preaching, teaching and miracle-working was, in effect, an enacted or performative announcement of his identity. In time, his followers and many of the people of Galilee and Judea began to see in Jesus the fulfilment of Israel's messianic expectations; and they began to hope that, through him, God's people would finally be delivered from the bondage of evil.

But the nature of Jesus' messiahship was misunderstood, even by his apostles. On a journey to the city of Caesarea Philippi,[45] Jesus asked the twelve, ". . . who do you say that I am?" And Peter, speaking for the apostles, replied, "You are the Christ, the Son of the living God." But when, in response to this correct identification, the Lord went on "to show his disciples that he must go to Jerusalem and suffer . . . and be killed, and on the third day be raised," Peter declared, "God forbid, Lord! This shall not happen to you." The Lord then chastised Peter, saying, "Get behind me, Satan! You are a hindrance to me; for you are not on the side of God, but of men" (see Mt 16:13-28).

Most of the Jews of those days thought of the Messiah as a divinely guided political-military hero who would liberate Israel from Roman domination and restore her earthly power. This political liberation of Israel, it was believed, would set the stage for the conversion of the nations, the final resurrection of the dead, the last judgment and the ultimate redemption of all creation in the kingdom of God. But the prophetic conception of the Messiah as a divine king who would have to suffer and die in order to redeem his people and the world[46] was, by Jesus' time, repugnant to the Jewish mind. For this reason, and until the final stages of his ministry, Jesus sought to keep his divine and messianic identity secret.[47]

As his public ministry progressed, Jesus inevitably came into conflict with the dominant religious sects of ancient Judaism. The gospels mention two such sects: the Pharisees and the Sadducees. The Pharisees (or "separated ones") followed the oral law of the Scribes, a school of teachers who sought to apply the general principles of the Torah (or Mosaic code) to every detail of life.[48] By the time of Christ, this scribal law, which had been developing for several centuries, had grown into a huge body of complicated rules and regulations governing almost every facet of daily existence. The Pharisees, like most of the Jews of that age, were looking for the Messiah and believed in the resurrection of the dead. The Sadducees were a small aristocratic and wealthy sect, holding most of the priestly offices and dominating the Sanhedrin (the governing body of the Jews during the second century B.C. through the first century A.D.). Unlike the Pharisees, the Sadducees rejected scribal law, did not believe in the coming of the Messiah and denied the doctrine of the resurrection of the dead. Both the Pharisees and the Sadducees were elitists, contemptuous of the "ignorant and illiterate masses" (the *am-ha-arez*), the "hated mixed race" of the Samaritans and all Gentiles.[49] The Pharisees and the Sadducees also had a common interest in preserving the social and political status quo in Palestine, for under Roman rule each of these powerful sects enjoyed prosperity and relative autonomy.

Jesus drew many of his followers from the common people of Galilee and Judea, and while he worked mainly among the Jews, he ministered also to Samaritans and Gentiles (see Lk 17:11-19 and Mt 8:5-13). He frequently criticized the legalism of the Pharisees, and he and his disciples repeatedly violated the scribal law itself (see, for example, Mk 2:1-3:6). The Lord also publicly rebuked the Sadducees for their ignorance of scripture and of the power of God (see Mk 12:18-27). Thus, both the Pharisees and the Sadducees, for their own reasons, came to regard Jesus as a "false Messiah," and both feared that his movement might provoke the Romans into instituting more stringent control over Jewish affairs. This conflict between Jesus and the

Jewish religious authorities would reach its climax during his final week in Jerusalem, with his arrest, trial and execution.

The Transfiguration of Christ

After the beheading of John the Baptist, and following Peter's confession at Caesarea Philippi that Jesus was "the Christ, the Son of the living God," the Lord began to prepare himself and his apostles for the culminating events of his earthly life. Taking the apostles Peter, James and John with him, Jesus went to the top of a high mountain (according to tradition, Mount Tabor in Galilee).

> And he was transfigured before them, and his face shone like the sun, and his garments became white as light. And behold, there appeared to them Moses and Elijah, talking with him. . . . He was still speaking, when lo, a bright cloud overshadowed them, and a voice from the cloud said, "This is my beloved Son, with whom I am well pleased; listen to him." When the disciples heard this, they fell on their faces, and were filled with awe. (Mt 17:1-9; see also Mk 9:2-13 and Lk 9:28-36)

The Orthodox Church celebrates the Transfiguration of Our Lord, one of the twelve great feasts of the Church year, on August 6. From an Orthodox point of view, the transfiguration was "another Theophany"[50]—a manifestation of Christ's divine sonship and of the trinitarian nature of God. "On Tabor, as at the baptism in the Jordan, the Father speaks from heaven, testifying to the divine Sonship of Christ: and the Spirit is also present, on this occasion not in the likeness of a dove, but under the form of dazzling light, surrounding Christ's person and overshadowing the whole mountain. This dazzling light is the light of the Spirit."[51]

The transfiguration of Christ has also played a significant role in the development of the Orthodox doctrine of the deification of man.

The glory which shone from Jesus on Tabor is a glory in which all mankind is called to share. On Mount Tabor we see Christ's human nature . . . filled with splendor, "made godlike" or "deified." What has happened to human nature in Christ can happen also to the humanity of Christ's followers. The Transfiguration, then, reveals to us the full potentiality of our human nature: it shows us the glory which our manhood once possessed and the glory which, by God's grace, it will again recover at the Last Day.[52]

In revealing his divine glory to Peter, James and John, the Lord was seeking to prepare them for his crucifixion and for "the glory of the resurrection" which lay beyond the cross. The presence of Moses and Elijah, "who both conversed with God on Mount Sinai,"[53] was a sign to the apostles that Jesus was the fulfilment of the law and prophecy of the Old Testament. And according to the Lukan account of the transfiguration, Moses and Elijah, as representatives of the law and the prophets, spoke of the Lord's "departure," which was to be accomplished in Jerusalem (Lk 9:30-31). Following the transfiguration, Jesus once again told his apostles of his coming passion, that he was "to be delivered into the hands of men . . . [who would] kill him," but that "on the third day" he would rise from the dead (Mt 17:22-23). But still, the apostles were "greatly distressed" and did not understand him. Only after his resurrection did they begin to grasp the true nature of God's plan of salvation through Christ.

Christ's Journey through Judea to Jerusalem

Shortly after his transfiguration, Jesus "set his face to go to Jerusalem" (Lk 9:51). Matthew and Mark give the impression that the Lord's final journey through Judea to Jerusalem was a brief one (see Mt 19-20 and Mk 10). But Luke's detailed account of the teachings delivered by the Lord on that journey makes it likely that the Judean ministry covered a substantial period of time. And the Gospel of John indicates that the Lord spent at least a few months in Judea prior to his final days in Jerusalem, and that he made more than one visit to the holy city during that time (see Jn 7:1-12:11). During the Judean ministry, as Luke reports, Jesus did some of his most memorable teaching on the nature of true spirituality, on the way of salvation and on the coming of the kingdom of God (see, for example, Lk 10:25-37, 11:1-13, 12:49-59, 13:22-30, 14:7-24, 15:3-32, 16:1-31, 17:20-37 and 18:1-30). Luke also tells us that Jesus' conflict with the Pharisees became more pronounced and heated during the Judean ministry (see 11:14-28, 12:1-12 and 16:14-18).

The last week of Christ's mission to the world began with his triumphal entry into Jerusalem (on the first of all Palm Sundays). He rode into Jerusalem on a donkey (Mt 21:1-9), thereby fulfilling the prophecy of Zechariah that the Messiah of Israel would reveal himself to be a king, not of war but of peace, by humbly entering the holy city "mounted on an ass" (Zc 9:9). The crowds who welcomed him by spreading their garments and palm branches before him, shouting "Hosanna!" (which means "save now" in Hebrew), expected this "Son of David" to lead them to victory over their enemies and to reestablish the kingdom of Israel. When, by the end of the week, it was apparent that Jesus was not the kind of Messiah they had expected, the crowds joined the Jewish authorities and the Romans in condemning him to death. It was the time of the yearly Passover festival.

On the Sunday, Monday, Tuesday and Wednesday nights of that last week, Jesus and his entourage stayed with friends in the town of Bethany on the Mount of Olives, just outside Jerusalem (Lk 21:37-38). On those nights, the Lord instructed his apostles and disciples concerning the time that would intervene between his death and his second coming. These teachings on the movement of history toward "the last days" are compiled in "the Olivet discourse," which appears in Matthew 24-25, Mark 13 and Luke 21. In this discourse, Jesus speaks of the destruction of Jerusalem by the Romans (which took place in 70 A.D.), the period of chaos and "great tribulation" that will precede the second coming of the Son of Man (the *parousia*), the last judgment and the final establishment of the kingdom of God.[54]

During the last week, Jesus spent each day, from Sunday through Wednesday, in the Jerusalem Temple, teaching the people, healing infirmities and debating with his opponents, the Pharisees and the Sadducees (see, for example, Mt 21-23). He even went so far as to drive the money-changers and the sellers of sacrificial pigeons out of the vestibule of the Temple, declaring that this mercantile activity was depriving the religious services of their spiritual significance (Mk 11:15-9). The Sanhedrin—"the chief priests, the scribes, and the elders"—took the "cleansing of the Temple" as a direct attack upon their leadership, and they became increasingly alarmed at Christ's popularity for fear that their own authority with the people might be undermined. They were also concerned that the excitement generated by Jesus' activities might lead to trouble with the Romans. And thus, the leaders of the Sanhedrin began to seek "a way to destroy him" (Mk 11:18).

The Trial and Death of Christ

The gospel account of the conspiracy against Jesus and of his eventual arrest, trial and execution is commonly called the "passion narrative" (from the Greek *pathein,* used in Acts 1:3 to refer to the suffering of Christ). The synoptic passion narrative (Mt 26-27; Mk 14-15; Lk 22-23) begins with a report of the plot to kill Jesus, hatched by leading members of the Sanhedrin and abetted by the treason of Judas Iscariot, one of the original twelve apostles (see Mt 26:1-5, 14-16). Judas' motives for joining Christ's enemies are not explained fully in any of the four gospels. But it is most probable that Judas' inordinate love of money together with his disillusionment at realizing that Jesus was serious in refusing to be a political-military Messiah left the apostle open to demonic possession. In yielding to the temptations of Satan, Judas became the instrument by which Christ's arrest out of public view was made possible.[55]

The passion narrative continues with a description of the anointing of Christ by a woman of Bethany (see Mt 26:6-13), which is portrayed as a foreshadowing of Christ's impending death and burial. The conspiracy against Jesus and his anointing at Bethany took place on Wednesday during that first Holy Week. On Thursday evening, Christ and his apostles celebrated Passover together for the last time, gathering in the guest-room of a house in Jerusalem (see Mk 14:12-16).[56] During the meal,

Christ predicted that one of the apostles would betray him (see Mt 26:20-25). Judas asked him, "Is it I, Master?" and Jesus responded, "You have said so" (Mt 26:25). The other apostles, apparently not comprehending the meaning of this exchange, were perplexed and "began to question one another, which of them it was that would do this" (Lk 22:23). Although the synoptics do not say so, the Gospel of John implies that Judas left the Passover celebration shortly after Christ's words concerning the impending betrayal (Jn 13:21-30).

As the Passover was ending, Jesus performed a set of actions that marked the transcendence of the Jewish Passover celebration by the Christian sacrament of the holy eucharist. Taking bread, Jesus blessed it, broke it and gave it to the apostles, saying, "Take, eat; this is my body" (Mt 26:26). Then he took a cup of wine, blessed it and gave it to them, saying, "Drink of it, all of you; for this is my blood of the new covenant, which is poured out for many for the forgiveness of sins" (Mt 26:27-28). The institution of the eucharist, or Lord's supper, is described in all three synoptic gospels (see Mt 26:26-29; Mk 14:22-25; Lk 22:19-20), and it is presupposed in the Gospel of John.[57] But the earliest New Testament record of the first holy communion is contained in St. Paul's first letter to the Corinthians (11:23-25), written c. 55 A.D.

Christ's pronouncement to the apostles that his body and blood were given "for you" or "for many" was a Hebraic way of saying "for all."[58] Christ died for the sins of all, and in his sacrificial death there is forgiveness for all who acknowledge him as Savior and Lord. Just as ancient Israel was delivered from Egypt and from destruction by the body and blood of the Passover lamb, so mankind is delivered from the bondage of sin and death by the body and blood of Christ. For Christ is the true Passover lamb whose death on the cross has taken away the sin of the world. In Christ, and in his eucharistic action, the Passover imagery of the Old Testament is both fulfilled and transcended. With the breaking of Christ's body, and with the pouring out of his blood, a new covenant has been established between God and mankind. As the old covenant was "dedicated with the blood of sacrificed animals," so the new covenant in Christ has been "dedicated with the blood of the beloved Son."[59]

In eating and drinking the consecrated bread and wine of the holy eucharist, Christians partake of the very body and blood of Christ (1 Co 10:16), and both commemorate and participate in the death of the Lord. In this way, Christians become one with Christ, entering into his atoning death and thence into his divine life, which was made manifest in his resurrection. The sacrament of the holy eucharist is the life of the Church, for in the eucharist, the Church is united with Christ, who is one with the Father and the Holy Spirit, and thus the members of his Church enter into the eternal life of the Holy Trinity—they become one with God.

The Trial of Christ. The synoptic passion narrative goes on to tell us that, after the last supper, Christ led his apostles out of Jerusalem to "a place called Gethsemane," a garden or park located on the Mount of Olives (Mt 26:36). On the way, Christ predicted that all the apostles would soon fall away from him. And when Peter protested that he would "never fall away," the Lord said to him, "Truly, I say to you, this very night before the cock crows, you will deny me three times" (see Mt 26:30-35).

Upon reaching Gethsemane, Jesus "took Peter, James, and John, the three who saw His glory on the Mount of Transfiguration, to be witnesses of another glory, the glory of His obedience, manifested at the moment He was facing death."[60]

And he said to them, "My soul is very sorrowful, even to death; remain here, and watch with me." And going a little farther he fell on his face and prayed, "My Father, if it be possible, let this cup [of agony] pass from me; nevertheless, not as I will, but as thou wilt." And he came to the disciples and found them sleeping; and he said to Peter, "So, could you not watch with me one hour? Watch and pray that you may not enter into temptation; the spirit indeed is willing, but the flesh is weak." Again, for the second time, he went away and prayed, "My Father, if this cannot pass unless I drink it, thy will be done." And again he came and found them sleeping, for their eyes were heavy. So, leaving them again, he went away and prayed for the third time, saying the same words. Then he came to the disciples and said to them, "Are you still sleeping and taking your rest? Behold, the hour is at hand, and the Son of Man is betrayed into the hands of sinners. Rise, let us be going; see, my betrayer is at hand. (Mt 26:36-46; see also Mk 14:32-42 and Lk 22:40-46)

In this passage, Christ's unique relationship with and perfect obedience to his Father is made manifest, as is the inconstancy of his apostles, who were unable to pray and keep watch with the Lord for a single hour.

The account of Christ's agony in Gethsemane sets the stage for his arrest, which is described in Matthew 26:47-56, Mark 14:43-52 and Luke 22:47-53. While the Lord was still speaking to his apostles, Judas arrived, accompanied by Temple police sent by the Sanhedrin. "Now the betrayer had given them a sign, saying, 'The one I shall kiss is the man. . . .' And when he came, he went up to him at once, and said, 'Master!' And he kissed him. And they laid hands on him and seized him" (Mk 14:44-46). Thus, with Judas' help, Christ was arrested on Thursday night, at a time when "everybody was busy with the celebration of the Passover." The enemies of Christ were therefore enabled to lay hands upon him without arousing public unrest.[61]

Following his arrest, Christ was put on trial before the Sanhedrin and was accused by the high priest, Caiaphas, of the religious crime of blasphemy. Christ's trial before the Sanhedrin was apparently held late Thursday night or during the early hours of Friday morning. After the testimony of several false witnesses failed to convince the assembled priests, scribes and elders that Jesus was guilty of any serious offense (see Mk 14:55-61), Caiaphas stepped forward and asked him, "Are you the Christ, the Son of the Blessed?" (Mk 14:61) Jesus, who had remained silent when accused by false witnesses, now responded to the question of the high priest, boldly admitting that he was both the Christ and the Son of God (see Mk 14:62). For the Jews of Jesus' time, as Prof. Kesich points out, "the Messiah was to be a human being and was below God. That God has a Son and that Jesus claimed to be this Son of God, for Caiaphas, was 'ultimate impiety.' "[62] Thus, "the high priest tore his [own] garments [an act signifying the crime of blasphemy], and said,

'Why do we still need witnesses? You have heard his blasphemy. What is your decision?' " On this basis, in accordance with the Mosaic code (see Lv 24:16), the Sanhedrin voted to condemn Jesus to death (see Mk 14:63-65).

While the trial before the Sanhedrin was going on, the apostle Peter, as Jesus had prophesied, was in the process of denying his relationship with Christ (see Mt 26:69-75; Mk 14:66-72; Lk 22:54-62). And Judas, apparently appalled by what he had done, committed suicide (Mt 27:3-10).

Some hours after his religious trial (at about 6:00 a.m.), Jesus was taken to Pontius Pilate, the Roman governor of Judea. For although under Jewish law Christ had been condemned to death, the Romans did not allow the Sanhedrin to execute criminals. The Romans would carry out death sentences passed by the Sanhedrin, but only after such sentences were reviewed and confirmed by the Roman authorities themselves. And since the Romans did not consider blasphemy against the God of the Jews to be a crime, the Sanhedrin, to have its way with Jesus, had to convince Pilate that this "blasphemer" was a threat to Roman political power. Thus, before the governor, the enemies of Jesus accused him of "perverting our nation, and forbidding us to give tribute [pay taxes] to Caesar, and saying that he himself is Christ a King" (Lk 23:2).

Pilate, however, after speaking briefly with Jesus, was unconvinced that the accused was, in fact, a dangerous criminal (Lk 23:3-4). Learning that the "criminal" was a Galilean, and hoping to avoid trouble with the Jewish authorities, Pilate sent Jesus to be examined by Herod Antipas, the Tetrarch of Galilee, who was visiting Jerusalem for the Passover (Lk 23:5-7). Although Herod treated Jesus with contempt, he, like Pilate, could find no crime in the man (Lk 22:8-12). Thus, when Jesus was brought back to Pilate, the governor announced that he and Herod had concurred in the judgment that Jesus was not guilty of any crimes against the Roman state (Lk 22:13-16).

By that time (early Friday morning), word of Jesus' trial had spread throughout the city, and a crowd began to gather at the governor's residence. Seeking a way to release Jesus over the protests of the Jewish authorities, Pilate appealed to the crowd. It had become customary for the Roman governor to release a prisoner each year at Passover. Pilate offered the crowd a choice between Jesus and Barabbas, an anti-Roman revolutionist who was guilty of murder. But the leaders of the Sanhedrin "stirred up the crowd" against Jesus (perhaps suggesting that his "defeat" was proof that he was a false Messiah), and the crowd, contrary to Pilate's expectations, cried out for the release of Barabbas (see Mt 27:15-21). They also demanded that Jesus be crucified, cruci-fixion being the method employed by the Romans in the execution of the worst criminals. Seeing that a riot was likely if he resisted the will of the crowd, Pilate gave in and ordered that Barabbas be released and that Christ be scourged and crucified (see Mt 27:22-26). The Gospel of John states that Pilate was also moti-vated to allow Christ's execution by his fear that the Jewish leaders would depict any leniency to this "King of the Jews" as disloyalty to Caesar (see Jn 19:12-16).

The Crucifixion, Death and Entombment of Christ. Condemned to death, Jesus was then taken away by Pilate's soldiers— along with two criminals who had also been sentenced to death— to "the place called Golgotha (which means the place of the Skull)" (Mk 15:17-22). The Lord was offered "wine mingled with myrrh," but he declined to drink it (Mk 15:23). "It was the custom to give this drink to a condemned man in order to make him less sensitive to pain, for crucifixion caused unbearable pain and suffering. Jesus refused the drink and thus passed through all the suffering while fully conscious."[63]

Mark tells us that Jesus was crucified at 9:00 a.m. on Good Friday (Mk 15:25). An inscription was placed above his head which read, "This is Jesus the King of the Jews" (Mt 27:37; Mk 15:26; Lk 23:38). The two criminals were crucified along with him, "one on his right and one on his left" (Mk 15:27). Having stripped him of his clothes, Pilate's soldiers "divided his garments among them by casting lots" (see Mt 27:35). And the soldiers, along with the watching crowd and the leaders of the Sanhedrin, taunted and mocked the crucified Christ, challenging him to show his divine powers by miraculously coming down from the cross (Mt 27:39-43; Mk 15:29-32; Lk 23:35-37). In response to this abuse, Christ prayed, "Father, forgive them; for they know not what they do" (Lk 23:34). The criminals who were crucified with him "also reviled him" (Mk 15:32); but one of them, whether from pity or an awakened sense of Christ's true identity, ceased his mocking and said, "Jesus, remember me when you come into your kingdom" (Lk 23:42). And to the penitent criminal Jesus said, "Truly, I say to you, today you will be with me in Paradise" (Lk 23:43).

Jesus suffered on the cross for six hours, from 9:00 a.m. until 3:00 p.m. From 12:00 noon until 3:00 p.m., "there was darkness over all the land" (Mt 27:45; Mk 15:33; Lk 23:44). Shortly before 3:00 p.m., Jesus cried out, "My God, my God, why hast thou forsaken me?" (Mt 27:46 and Mk 15:34). These words constitute the first verse of Psalm 22, which seems to prophesy the death of the Messiah. This psalm, from a Christian point of view, "sets forth Christ's emotions on the cross" and represents "the suffering He endured through crucifixion."[64] The psalm speaks of his being scorned, despised and mocked; of his physical sufferings on the cross; and of those who cast lots for his garments during the time of his crucifixion (Ps 22:1, 6-8, 14-18). It then goes on to say that through the suffering of the Messiah, God will deliver the world from evil:

> You who fear the Lord, praise him! . . . For he has not despised or abhorred the affliction of the afflicted; and he has not hid his face from him, but has heard, when he cried to him. . . . The afflicted shall eat and be satisfied. . . . All the ends of the earth shall remember and turn to the Lord; and all the families of the nations shall worship before him. For dominion belongs to the Lord, and he rules over the nations. (Ps 22:23-24, 26, 27-28)

In his crucifixion, Christ identified himself with our sinful condition and experienced the absolute abandonment by God which is the ultimate consequence of sin. But in beginning to recite Psalm 22, the Lord was declaring that the promise of redemption contained in the Old Testament song has been fulfilled in him. Summing up the patristic interpretation, Prof. Kesich comments:

> . . . Christ had passed through all the sufferings of human

beings whose sin separates them from God. The sinner has abandoned God and "loved darkness rather than light" (Jn 3:19). The climax of this estrangement of man from God finds its full expression when Christ cries out "My God, my God, why have you forsaken me?" He speaks these words in the name of humanity, to bring an end to alienation and to turn the face of man toward God, who has been searching for him. In union with God and solidarity with man, Christ turns man toward his God. . . . In his person he represents us, and is praying on our behalf.[65]

Following his quotation of Psalm 22, Jesus exclaimed, "Father, into thy hands I commit my spirit!" "And having said this he breathed his last" (Lk 23:46). At Christ's death, "the curtain of the temple was torn in two, from top to bottom" (Mk 15:38). The curtain referred to here was a veil separating the Temple sanctuary from the "Holy of Holies," a place beyond the altar symbolizing God's invisible presence. This veil or curtain was a sign of sinful man's alienation from God. By Christ's death, the gospels tell us, this alienation was overcome. Through faith in Christ, we can enter into the very presence of God.[66]

On the evening of Good Friday, with Pilate's permission, a disciple of Jesus by the name of Joseph of Arimathea, a well-to-do and respected member of the Sanhedrin, came and claimed Christ's body. Taking the body down from the cross, Joseph (and other friends of Christ) wrapped the Lord in a linen shroud "and laid him in a tomb which had been hewn out of the rock" (Mk 15:46). A great stone was rolled against the entrance to the tomb and, at the insistence of the Jewish authorities, the Temple police were sent to guard the burial site "lest his disciples go and steal him away, and tell the people, 'He has risen from the dead'" (see Mt 27:57-66). With his entombment, the passion of our Lord Jesus Christ had come to an end.

The Resurrection and Ascension of Christ

The synoptic accounts of the Lord's resurrection are contained in Matthew 28, Mark 16 and Luke 24. Jesus' followers had to postpone his burial rites until after the Sabbath observance (which begins on Friday evening and ends twenty-four hours later). At dawn on the Sunday following Christ's death, Mary Magdalene and a few other women disciples went to his tomb to anoint his body with embalming spices. They were wondering who would roll away the stone at the entrance to the tomb in order that they might go in and minister to their Lord (see Mk 16:1-3).

> And behold, there was a great earthquake; for an angel of the Lord descended from heaven and came and rolled back the stone, and sat upon it. His appearance was like lightning, and his raiment white as snow. And for fear of him the guards trembled and became like dead men. But the angel said to the women, "Do not be afraid; for I know you seek Jesus who was crucified. He is not here; for he has risen, as he said. Come, see the place where he lay. Then go quickly and tell his disciples that he has risen from the dead." (Mt 28:2-7)

Astonished and awestricken at what they had seen and heard, the women ran from the sepulchre to tell the bereaved apostles and other disciples that "Christ is risen from the dead!"

But it was not only the testimony of angels and of the myrrhbearing women that convinced the apostles and disciples that Jesus' resurrection prophecies had been fulfilled. For the risen Lord himself appeared to many of them during the forty-day period between his resurrection and ascension.[67] For example, Jesus met the myrrhbearing women as they were leaving his tomb (Mt 28:9-10); and Mary Magdalene was the first of these women to realize that the person before them was indeed the Lord (Mk 16:9). After appearing to the myrrhbearers, on the morning of that first Pascha, Christ manifested himself to the apostle Peter (Lk 24:34). Later on that same day, the Lord appeared to two of his disciples as they walked from Jerusalem to Emmaus, a village about seven miles from the holy city (Lk 24:13-35). On the evening of resurrection day, Christ appeared to the apostles, ate with them, taught them the meaning of his mission and commissioned them to preach his gospel to all nations (Lk 24:36-49; see also Mk 16:14-18). Then, when the apostles returned to

Galilee some weeks after the resurrection, Christ met them on a mountain (Mount Tabor?) and proclaimed to them the "great commission" of all true Christians: "All authority in heaven and on earth has been given to me. Go therefore and make disciples of all nations, baptizing them in the name of the Father and of the Son and of the Holy Spirit, teaching them to observe all that I have commanded you" (Mt 28:16-20). And forty days after his resurrection, Christ appeared to his apostles in Bethany (near Jerusalem) and, after promising them that they were soon to receive the gift and power of the Holy Spirit (Ac 1:1-11), he ascended into heaven and was exalted to the right hand of God (see Mk 16:19; Lk 24:50-51; Ac 1:9-11).[68]

Prior to his ascension, Christ had told the apostles that he would be with them always (Mt 28:20), and he had promised them that the Holy Spirit would shortly come upon them (Ac 1:1-11). Ten days after the ascension of the Lord, on the Jewish feast of Pentecost,[69] the apostles and disciples of Christ were "filled with the Holy Spirit" (see Ac 2). Through the power of the Holy Spirit, the followers of Christ were transformed into the Church, the body of Christ, the apostolic community which was to spread the "good news" of salvation throughout the world. Thus, it has been well said that the day of Pentecost was the birthday of the Christian Church.

According to the synoptic gospels, Jesus of Nazareth was the "Son of David," the Messiah, the Christ. But he was not the Christ expected by the Jews of his time. His purpose was not to reestablish the earthly kingdom of Israel, but to inaugurate (in himself and in his Church) the heavenly kingdom of God. Jesus quite often referred to himself as the "Son of Man." As pointed out in chapter 4, the ancient Jews thought of the Son of Man as a transcendent being whose origin is heavenly rather than earthly.[70] In applying this title to himself, therefore, Jesus was claiming to be a divine being. The synoptics also speak of Jesus as the "Son of God" and as "Lord," thus underlining the radical theological implications of Christ's "Son of Man" sayings. The divine sonship and lordship of the Son of Man are revealed in the synoptic accounts of Christ's virgin birth, of the theophany at Christ's baptism, of the transfiguration of Christ, and of Christ's glorious resurrection and ascension. Matthew, Mark and Luke also stress the true humanity of Jesus (for example, in their depictions of his temptation and his passion); but it was Christ's claim to divine sonship that so shocked and scandalized the Sanhedrin at his trial. From a Jewish point of view, the Messiah is a divinely ordained, but not divine, human being.

Another dimension of Jesus' messiahship that was unacceptable to most of his fellow Jews was his submission of himself to suffering and death—to apparent defeat in the eyes of the world. In his predictions of his passion (see Mt 16:21-28, 17:22-23, 20:17-19), and in his undergoing of that passion, Christ the Lord—the divine Son of Man—was revealed to be the "Suffering Servant" of God spoken of by the prophet Isaiah.[1] But again, from a Jewish point of view, the idea that the Messiah should be a sufferer even unto death was outrageous and unacceptable. The Jews of the Hellenistic age expected the Messiah to be a warlike king, a national liberator, a world leader.

The synoptic gospels, then, proclaim a Messiah who is both divine and human and who has suffered and died for the sins of the world. The synoptics also proclaim that this divine-human Christ has, through his death and resurrection, liberated mankind and the world from the tyranny of sin and death. Through faith in Christ as Savior and Lord, and through the gift of the Holy Spirit which comes to all who are "in Christ," man can be reconciled with God and thus restored to a condition of "divine sonship." For through Christ, in whom human nature has been deified, mankind can "ascend" into the very life and being of the Holy Trinity, into full fellowship and communion with the triune God. Such is the central message of the synoptic gospels. And while this message may constitute a stumbling-block for Jews and many others, it is, for the Christian, the very power and wisdom of God (1 Co 1:24).

CHAPTER 6

The Theology of the Gospel according to St. John

The fourth gospel[1] was written in Ephesus (in present-day Turkey) during the late first century (c. 85-90 A.D.). According to tradition, the author of this book was St. John, one of the original twelve apostles (Mt 10:1-15). Many modern scholars, however, believe that the text was put into its present written form not by John himself but by one of his close and trusted disciples.[2] But whether he penned the book himself or dictated it to an amanuensis, there is little doubt that the fourth gospel contains the recollections of John the apostle concerning the ministry of Christ—that it is, indeed, the "Gospel according to St. John."[3]

John had been one of Jesus' closest friends (see Mt 12:1-9, 26:36-46; Jn 13:23-25, 19:25-27), and he was one of the chief pillars of the early Church (see Ga 2:9-10). In his later years (c. 85-100 A.D.), John served as the bishop of Asia Minor, with his central residence in the city of Ephesus.[4] Urged on by his friends and disciples, the aged apostle composed (or dictated) his version of the gospel. In addition to his gospel, the New Testament contains four other documents that have been attributed to John: three of his letters (1, 2 and 3 John) which were written c. 90 A.D.; and the book of Revelation (or the Apocalypse), written c. 95 A.D. St. John the Apostle was almost one hundred years old when he died (c. 95-100 A.D.).

There are many differences between the Gospel of John and the synoptic gospels. John does not tell of the birth, childhood, baptism, temptation, transfiguration or ascension of Christ. And

157

instead of cataloging the many miracles performed by the Lord, as do the synoptic writers, he recounts only seven of those works. The synoptics contain compilations of Christ's sermons, parables, stories and short sayings; but in the Gospel of John, the teachings of the Lord are presented almost exclusively in the form of long and rather complicated theological discourses (see Jn 3, 4, 5, 6, 7-8, 10 and 14-16). It has further been pointed out by many scholars that the language and thought-forms employed by John are more mystical and philosophical than those of the synoptics. And while he omits a good deal of the material contained in Matthew, Mark and Luke, John also tells us much that is not mentioned by them. Among the events described only by John are Christ's first miracle at the marriage feast at Cana in Galilee (2:1-11); the dialogue between Nicodemus and Jesus (3:1-21); Jesus' revelation of himself as the Messiah to the Samaritan woman (4:1-42); his raising of Lazarus from the dead (11:1-57); and his washing the feet of the apostles at the last supper (13:1-20).[5]

There is also a contrast between the ways in which John and the synoptics depict the chronological and geographical scope of Christ's public ministry. As indicated in chapter 5, the synoptic gospels concentrate exclusively upon the Lord's Galilean ministry and his final journey through Judea to Jerusalem, giving the impression that Christ's public ministry was quite brief, only one year in duration. But John tells us that, during the public ministry, there were at least three Passover festivals (2:13, 6:4, 12:1), and that during that approximately three-year period Jesus worked extensively in Judea as well as in Galilee. His final sojourn in Judea, moreover, lasted a number of months; and he made more than one visit to Jerusalem during that time (7:1-12:11).

These differences between John and the synoptics can be rather easily explained. The Gospel of John was written between ten and twenty-five years later than the synoptic gospels. John presupposes that his readers are familiar with the tradition represented by Matthew, Mark and Luke[6] and that there is, by and large, no need to cover the ground already covered by those earlier writers. Thus, John seeks to supplement the synoptic tradition both historically and theologically. That is, he provides us with much information concerning phases of Christ's public ministry not recorded in the synoptics, and he emphasizes the deity of the Lord more starkly and more vividly. His predominant theological aim is to explain "the mystery of the person of Jesus," to proclaim "the eternal origin and divine nature of this Man who was more than man."[7] This theological purpose is the determining factor in John's selection of only seven of the miracles performed by Christ and in his presentation of the Lord's teachings in discourse form. The seven miracles are depicted as "signs" of Christ's full deity, and the discourses are intended to make it clear that Jesus the man was also God the Son. The mystical and philosophical character of the fourth gospel was apparently derived from the esoteric Judaism of the Hellenistic age, a tradition rooted in the wisdom literature of the Old Testament and very well suited to John's theological intentions.[8] Because of the theological character of his work, the fathers of the Church spoke of the author of the fourth gospel as "St. John the Theologian."

Other differences between John and the other three gospels have to do with several matters of historical fact. For example, John places Christ's cleansing of the Temple at the beginning of the public ministry (Jn 2:13-25), while the synoptics describe this event as taking place during the last week of the Lord's earthly life (Mt 21:12-17; Mk 11:15-19; Lk 19:45-48). For another example, the synoptics tell us that the anointing of Christ by a woman of Bethany took place after his triumphal entry into Jerusalem (Mt 26:6-13; Mk 14:3-9), but according to John, it occurred prior to the triumphal entry, and the "woman of Bethany" was Mary, the sister of Martha and Lazarus (Jn 12:1-11). For still another example, the synoptics date the crucifixion of Jesus on the day of the Passover, while John dates it on the day *before* Passover; for according to John, "the Passover in the year in which Jesus was crucified [c. 30 A.D.] fell on a Saturday and not on a Friday." Thus, while the four gospels agree "that the Last Supper took place on Thursday evening, and the crucifixion on the following Friday . . . they disagree as to whether or not the Last Supper was a Passover meal."[9]

These factual discrepancies between John and the synoptics are difficult to resolve. Some have suggested that Jesus drove the money-changers from the Jerusalem Temple on more than one

occasion.[10] But it is more likely that John deliberately took the
cleansing of the Temple out of historical context in order to
make a theological point: "He may have chosen the cleansing of
the Temple as a major symbolic act, indicating that the life of
Jesus was in danger from the start, that the shadow of the cross
lay over His whole ministry." Furthermore, Jesus here "revealed
Who He was, and this in turn led to His death. He claimed divine
prerogatives for Himself. He came to His own home as the Lord
of the Temple, but His own rejected Him."[11] It is also likely that
John chose to place the anointing of Jesus by Mary of Bethany,
which was a foreshadowing of Christ's death, prior to the triumphal entry in order to stress the significance of the Lord's
final visit to Jerusalem. On the question of whether the last
supper was a Passover meal or not, most contemporary biblical
scholars agree with John rather than with the synoptic evangelists.[12] But this should not lead us to conclude that the synoptic
gospels are entirely wrong on this matter, for although the last
supper was held a day earlier than the Jewish Passover, it *was*
the paschal rite for Jesus and the apostles, "and during it the new
rite, the Eucharist, was instituted."[13]

Thus, while there are differences, and even a few factual discrepancies, between John and the synoptics, these differences and
discrepancies are by no means fundamental contradictions. The
synoptic gospels, drawing from common sources in the early
apostolic tradition, represent one dimension of the early Church's
understanding of who Jesus was, what he said and what he did.
And the fourth gospel, drawing mainly from the mind and
memory of the apostle John, represents another and more deeply
theological perspective on the person and work of Christ. John's
gospel supplements and completes the synoptic account of Christ's
earthly life and is thus "the key to the proper understanding of
the synoptic gospels."[14] Through the work of John and his fellow
evangelists, the apostolic Church passed on to posterity her
"Gospel Image of Christ."

JOHN 1-11: THE DIVINE SONSHIP
OF JESUS CHRIST

The major purpose of John 1-11 is to define the identity of Jesus of Nazareth—to proclaim that Jesus was both the Messiah of Israel and the incarnation of Gon the Son. In accordance with his purpose, John begins his gospel with his well-known "Prologue" (1:1-18), a dramatic and beautiful proclamation of the deity of Christ: "In the beginning was the Word, and the Word was with God, and the Word was God."

The Gospel of John, of course, like the other books of the New Testament, was written in Greek. And the English term "Word" is a translation of *Logos,* a Greek expression signifying "wisdom" (or "reason") as well as "Word." In presenting Jesus as the incarnation (or "enfleshment") of the divine Logos, John is telling us that the Wisdom and Word of God has entered into union with human nature. In the wisdom literature of the Old Testament, the principle of wisdom is often personified and spoken of as a manifestation of God which has been *with* God from all eternity (see Pr 8:22-36; Ws 7:22-8:1). And the Old Testament prophets thought of the Word of God as in some sense the presence of the Lord himself, a revelation of the very being of God. The Old Testament also teaches that the cosmos was created by the power of God's Word and Wisdom (see Gn 1 and Ps 33:6, 9). John speaks of the creative Wisdom and Word of God as a distinct person within the divine nature, as "the only Son from the Father" (1:14). And in the incarnation, the eternal and preexistent Logos, being himself divine and of one essence with God the Father, "nevertheless condescended to assume human nature for the purpose of man's redemption and restoration."[15]

As the divine Word incarnate, Christ is also the source of life and enlightenment (Jn 1:4). Through the "true light" of the incarnate Lord, the darkness of spiritual blindness and of evil can be overcome (Jn 1:5, 9). But to be delivered from spiritual darkness—to enter into the grace, truth and eternal life of the divine Logos, to be reconciled with God—we must receive Christ into our hearts and believe in him. Speaking to those Jews of his time who believed that to be a physical descendant of Abraham was to be a child of God, John asserts that divine sonship is not dependent upon ethnic identity but upon faith in Jesus (1:12-14). Christ alone, the Word made flesh, makes God the Father known to us (1:18); and only through faith in Christ may we receive "power to become children of God" (1:12). We are not born into the family of God by being born into a Jewish family—or into a Christian family, for that matter. We are not saved by "the faith of our fathers," but by our own faith.

Throughout the Gospel of John, there is an insistent emphasis upon what might be called the physical or material dimension of God's work of salvation. Salvation is not deliverance from, but deliverance in and through, the material world. The true deity of God the Son is embodied in the true humanity of Jesus Christ. In Christ, the Word "became flesh and dwelt among us" (Jn 1:14). And in him, the spiritual glory of God has been made visible (1:14, 18). As we shall see, the public ministry of Christ was itself a physically real manifestation of the spiritual power of God. The discourses recorded by John were spoken by Jesus; they were physically audible and full of references to such material realities as water, bread, light, darkness, the human body, flesh and blood. The miracles of Christ described in the fourth gospel are also physical acts filled with spiritual significance: water is transformed into wine (2:1-11); bodily infirmities are healed (4:43-54, 5:1-9, 9:1-41); the hungry are miraculously fed (6:1-14); Jesus walks upon the sea (6:15-21); and Lazarus is literally raised from the dead (11:1-57). The teachings and miracles of the Lord, moreover, were presented and performed in specific places at specific times in the region of ancient Palestine.[16] It was, furthermore, the genuinely human and fully divine Christ who suffered and died upon the cross and who was resurrected bodily from the dead. And it is through his broken body and shed blood that mankind may be delivered from the powers of sin and death.

John's theology, then, is a "sacramental" theology. A sacrament, in the broad sense, is a "visible means of grace," an event or act in the world which makes the grace of God present and available to mankind. *Sacramentum* is a Latin word meaning "pledge." A sacrament, in this sense, is a "pledge of salvation" made by God to all who live in a spirit of faith and obedience. In Orthodox theology, the sacraments are called "mysteries" (from the Greek, *mysterion*) to emphasize the mystical and supernatural significance of the saving acts of God. Writing late in the first century A.D., at a time when the liturgical life of the Church had reached a rather high level of development, John stresses the mysterious but very real and physical presence and activity of God in the world, the ultimate sacrament, linking the saving work of Christ to the sacramental works of the Church (baptism, chrismation, the eucharist, and so on). The salvation of God was made "really present" in Christ, and through the power of the Holy Spirit that salvation remains "really present" in the Church, the sacramental and mystical body of Christ.

John's purpose in emphasizing so strongly the material, incarnational and sacramental dimensions of God's redemptive work was to counteract a heresy known as *gnosticism*. Gnosticism was a religious and philosophical perspective derived from the mystery religions of Greece, Persia and Egypt. Before and during the time of Christ, certain sects within Judaism had adopted the gnostic view of the world; and later, as the Christian movement spread from Palestine throughout the Mediterranean and the Middle East, many Christians came to be influenced by gnosticism.[17]

The gnostics (whether pagan, Jewish or "Christian") taught that salvation from suffering and death depends upon the acquisition of certain secret (esoteric, occult) "knowledge" (from the Greek *gnosis*: "knowledge" or "wisdom"). To be saved, one must overcome one's spiritual ignorance and delusions by learning the "truth" about reality. The "truth," according to the gnostics, is that spirit, which is essentially good, and matter, which is essentially evil, are absolutely opposed to one another. In the beginning, spirit (the realm of God) and matter (the realm of darkness and chaos) were absolutely separate and unmixed. From God, there emerged a multitude of angels (or "aeons"), and some of these angels became hostile to God. It was the leader of these rebellious angels (the devil) who, in opposition to God's will, created the space-time world in which spirit and matter are mingled. Man is a product of this unholy union of spirit and matter and can be delivered from the corruption of the physical world only through the absolute negation of the flesh. Through the special wisdom of gnosticism, which had been sent by God through a series of good angels, spiritual illumination and liberation from the material order are possible.

Jewish and Christian gnostics maintained that "the God of the Old Testament" was actually the devil; for the true God would not have anything to do with the realm of matter, darkness and evil. And the Christian gnostics thought of Jesus as one of God's good angels, who had taken on the form or appearance (but not the real nature and body) of a man, in order to reveal the "secret knowledge" which leads to deliverance from the world. For the gnostics, Jesus was not genuinely human, nor was he fully divine; he was not actually "born of woman," nor did he live, suffer and die in the flesh; and he was resurrected not "in the body" but in spirit only.

Such were the teachings of gnosticism, which threatened the Orthodoxy of the Church during the first three centuries of her historic life.[18] John wrote his gospel in deliberate opposition to the heresies of the gnostics. He saw that gnosticism required the rejection of the doctrines of God's creation of the world; the union of God and man in the incarnation; the bodily life, death, resurrection, ascension and exaltation of the Lord Jesus Christ; the general resurrection of the dead at the end of days; and the inherent goodness of the material universe. Thus, John proclaimed that the Logos "became flesh" in Jesus Christ (1:14); that in and through the divine Logos, God made "all things" (1:3); and that *"God so loved the world* that he gave his only begotten Son, that whoever believes in him should not perish but have eternal life" (3:16). In opposition to the hyperspiritualism of the gnostics, John gives his apostolic certification to the Orthodox doctrine of the creator-God who is continually present and active in the world which he has created.

The Messiah of Israel

John, like the other writers of the New Testament, proclaims Jesus of Nazareth as the Christ, the messiah or Savior-king promised to Israel by God through the prophets of the Old

Testament. In our earlier discussion of the Old Testament prophets, we saw that the Messiah was to be a king in the tradition of
David, who was to suffer and die for the sins of the world and
who would be a manifestation of God himself (the "Son of
Man").[19] And in our analysis of the synoptic gospels, it was
pointed out that most Jews of Jesus' time, while still hoping for
deliverance through a messianic king, had lost touch with the
prophetic view that the Messiah was to be a divine being who was
to save the world through his own death.[20] The New Testament
tells us that even the disciples of Jesus, who recognized him as
the Christ, did not understand the true nature of his messiahship
until after his resurrection (see Mt 28; Mk 16; Lk 24; Jn 2:22,
12:16; Ac 1-2). But John, reflecting upon the ministry of Jesus
nearly seventy years after the crucifixion, portrays the messiahship
of the Lord as an almost perfect fulfilment of Old Testament
prophecy. And, as we might expect, he places special emphasis
upon the divine sonship of the Christ.

Christ's identity as the divine Son of Man was revealed in his
teachings and also in his miraculous works. John speaks of the
miracles as "signs" (from the Greek, *semeion*) which point to
the true nature of Jesus' messiahship, to the fact that the Christ
was fully human and, at the same time, fully divine. In the
broad sense of the term, all of the Lord's acts—his teachings,
miracles, passion and resurrection—are "signs" of his true identity
and of the meaning of his ministry. The fourth gospel emphasizes
that the miracles were performed "not simply to alleviate physical
suffering and need, but to bring men to the saving knowledge
of God."[21] John reports the "signs" done by Jesus in order that
we might believe that Jesus is both the Christ and the Son of
God and that, in so believing, we might have eternal life through
him (Jn 20:30-31).

According to the fourth gospel, Christ worked his first
miraculous sign at a marriage feast in the town of Cana (in
Galilee). The setting of this first sign is significant, for in ancient Jewish thought marriage feasts were symbolic of the final
union of God and Israel which was to follow the coming of the
Messiah. And there are several other notable things about this
passage (Jn 2:1-11).

Many have been puzzled by Jesus' words to his mother, "O

woman, what have you to do with me? My hour has not yet come" (Jn 2:4). The Greek text, literally translated, reads: "What to me or to you, woman? Not yet is come my hour." In calling his mother "woman," Jesus was not being disrespectful, for in his day such a title functioned much as does the English term "Lady." The mother of our Lord was distressed when the wine for the feast had run out because she feared that the parents of the bridegroom, the hosts of the party, might be humiliated before their guests. Not knowing what else to do, Mary instinctively turned to her Son, and, on behalf of her friends, petitioned him to "do something." In his mild rebuke to his mother, Jesus reminded her that the time for his full and public self-disclosure had not yet arrived, and that his "hour" would be determined by God the Father and not by the desires of men and women. The term "hour" refers both to the time of Christ's emergence as a public figure and to the time of his "glorification" (that is, his death and resurrection). But in spite of his reservations, Christ did "do something" in response to his mother's wishes. It is clear from John's text, however, that the miracle at Cana was witnessed only by a few—the Lord's mother, his disciples and some of the servants at the feast. In performing this sign, then, Jesus was honoring his mother and "saving a humble Galilean family from hurt and humiliation";[22] and in manifesting his divine glory only to a few and not to all, the Lord continued to await his "hour," and thus he was honoring his heavenly Father.

Jesus' transmutation of water into wine at Cana is symbolic of the transcendence of Judaism by Christianity. The water in question was present at the feast for the ceremonial washings before and after eating which are required by Jewish ritual law. In turning the waters of "the Jewish rites of purification" into "new wine" (see Ac 2:13), Jesus was instituting a new covenant sealed by his own blood. In the "good wine" of the holy eucharist, we receive a purification "for the remission of sins" which will enable us to attend the great marriage feast of Christ and his Church at the end of days (see Rv 19:1-10).

Jesus' Discourse with Nicodemus

At the first of three Passovers mentioned by John, Jesus engaged in a dialogue with a Pharisee by the name of Nicodemus. This is the first of eight lengthy discourses by Christ recorded in the fourth gospel. Nicodemus, we are told, was one of the Jewish leaders in Jerusalem (Jn 3:1). Visiting Jesus at night (so as to avoid being seen by his colleagues), Nicodemus said to the Lord, "Rabbi, we know that you are a teacher come from God ['Rabbi' means 'teacher' in Hebrew]; for no one can do these signs that you do, unless God is with him" (Jn 3:2). Seeing that Nicodemus was a searcher after spiritual truth, Jesus presented him with a profound but difficult pronouncement: "Truly, truly, I say to you, unless one is born anew, he cannot see the kingdom of God" (3:3). When Nicodemus wondered how a man might be born "a second time" (3:4), Jesus proclaimed:

> Truly, truly, I say to you, unless one is born of water and the Spirit, he cannot enter the kingdom of God. That which is born of the flesh is flesh, and that which is born of the Spirit is spirit. Do not marvel that I say to you, "You must be born anew." The wind blows where it wills, and you hear the sound of it, but you do not know whence it comes or whither it goes; so it is with every one who is born of the Spirit. (3:5-8)

Nicodemus was taken utterly aback by the Lord's words, saying, "How can this be?" (Jn 3:9). And Christ, going even further in his challenge to Nicodemus, concluded the dialogue by rebuking him for his ignorance of his own tradition, and then revealing to him that "as Moses lifted up the serpent in the wilderness, so must the Son of man be lifted up, that whoever believes in him may have eternal life" (3:10-16). To these words of the Lord, the author of the fourth gospel adds his own commentary:

> For God so loved the world that he gave his only Son, that

whoever believes in him should not perish but have eternal
life. For God sent the Son into the world, not to condemn
the world, but that the world might be saved through him.
He who believes in him is not condemned; but he who
does not believe is condemned already, because he has not
believed in the name of the only Son of God. (3:16-18;
see also 3:19-21 and 3:35-36)

Nicodemus was, no doubt, astounded and perhaps even overwhelmed by the Lord's teaching on "the new birth" and on the
"lifting up" of the Son of Man. The Lord's teaching on spiritual
rebirth was probably incomprehensible to many of his followers
during his earthly life. But after his resurrection and ascension,
and after the Holy Spirit had descended upon the apostles and
disciples on the day of Pentecost (see Ac 2), the Church gradually
came to understand the meaning of Christ's discourse with Nicodemus. To the Jews of his day, represented by Nicodemus, Jesus
was saying that being a physical descendant of Abraham, Isaac
and Jacob was not enough if one hoped to enter into the kingdom
of God. Only through faith in the Son of God can one receive
the gift of eternal life. And such faith is possible only on the
basis of a spiritual rebirth effected by God through the power of
the Holy Spirit. Through the waters of baptism, and through the
unpredictable agency of the Spirit of God, one may be "born
anew from above" and recognize the crucified, resurrected and
exalted Son of Man as the Savior of the world. "That which is
born of flesh is flesh, and that which is born of Spirit is spirit"
(Jn 3:6); and it is an Israel of the Spirit rather than an Israel
of the flesh which is to inherit the blessings of the heavenly
kingdom. Being a Jew is no guarantee that one will see the
kingdom of God; and being a Gentile does not exclude one from
that kingdom. Faith in and obedience to Christ is the key to the
kingdom, for Jews and Gentiles alike.

Nicodemus, a devout Jew and zealous Pharisee, had great
difficulty accepting the foregoing teaching of Christ. He must
have been especially disturbed when the Lord spoke of the "lifting up" (that is, the crucifixion, resurrection and ascension) of
the Son of Man. That salvation depends upon the Spirit rather
than upon the flesh, and that spiritual rebirth into love of the

light rather than darkness is necessary for entry into the kingdom of God, Nicodemus might have been willing to grant. But that the Messiah was to suffer and die! Such a claim, judging from John's gospel, reduced Nicodemus to a confused silence. We do not know the details of the spiritual struggle that eventually brought Nicodemus to discipleship in Christ, only that he was somehow able to respond to the promptings of the Spirit and thus to acknowledge Jesus as Lord (see Jn 7:50-51 and 19:38-42).

The water-and-Spirit baptism spoken of by Jesus was not (no doubt contrary to Nicodemus' understanding) identical with the rite performed by John the Baptist. The Baptist himself had prophesied a new baptism in the Holy Spirit which would become available in Christ (Jn 1:33). And the fourth gospel distinguishes clearly between the baptisms performed by Christ's disciples and those performed by John the Baptist (3:22-36). During the decades following the creation of the Church on Pentecost, the apostolic community came to realize the full significance of the baptismal rite which Christ had commanded his followers to perform (Jn 3:22-23; Mt 28:18-20). The rite instituted by Jesus during his public ministry was not simply a baptism symbolizing repentance, but a sign of the "new life" which was made available to the world through the saving Word of Christ and through the power of the Holy Spirit.

Christ, as we have seen, was himself baptized by John the Baptist; and in Christ, the sinless one, the sins of the world have been washed away. Identifying himself with the sins of mankind, Christ was perfectly repentant; and by identifying ourselves with him through faith, we may enter into the perfect repentance of Christ. The Lord's washing in the waters of repentance was a prelude to his immersion in death; for death is the ultimate sign of the fallenness of mankind and the world. Through his death, and through his resurrection from the dead, Christ has liberated us from the tyranny of evil and has made possible our enjoyment of eternal life in the kingdom of God. Thus, the element of repentance is both preserved and transcended in the baptismal rite of the apostolic Church. Christian baptism is a sign of man's repentance in Christ, of his deliverance from the corruption of sin and death, and of his rebirth in the life of the Spirit; it is a

baptism in water *and* in the Holy Spirit. And through the gift of
the Holy Spirit, man receives power to follow Christ faithfully
and obediently.

As the sacramental theory and practice of the Church developed, the work of spiritual regeneration came to be expressed
in two intimately related mysteries of the Church: baptism and
chrismation. It is through these two sacraments that we are "born
again," according to the teachings of the Orthodox Church.
Through immersion in the waters of baptism, we descend with
Christ into death; and upon emergence from the water, we enter
into the eternal life made possible by Christ's resurrection from
the dead. In baptism, then, we are reborn to newness of life.
And in the sacrament of chrismation, we receive "a new power
by which this life can be lived."[23] Jesus was the Anointed One
of God, "the one on whom the Holy Spirit has been poured."[24]
Through Jesus, the Church herself was anointed and born in the
Spirit on Pentecost. In chrismation, when we are anointed with
the holy oil, we receive the gift of the Holy Spirit, which enables
us (although it does not force us) to live the Christian life. As
baptism is a participation in the saving acts of Pascha—in the
death and resurrection of the Lord—so chrismation is a recapitulation of Pentecost by which we are born of the Spirit as members of the Church, the body of Christ. "Born of water and the
Spirit," we become children of God, sharing in the divine sonship
of our Lord Jesus Christ, and entering into the eternal life of the
Holy Trinity.

The Orthodox Church insists, however, that baptism and
chrismation do not automatically accomplish the salvation of the
individual. The saving grace of God is communicated to us in
the sacramental ministry of the Church; but divine grace does
not cancel out human freedom. Being baptized and chrismated
is not a sufficient condition of salvation. To make our spiritual
rebirth actual, we must respond freely to God's grace in faith and
obedience. We must accept the salvation which has been offered
to us by the Holy Trinity. We must recognize our need for salvation and, in faith, turn to Christ as our only hope of deliverance from the bondage of sin and death. We must also receive
the Holy Spirit into our hearts; for only through the power of
the Holy Spirit can we live a life of holiness under the lordship

of Christ. Only through a personal and decisive faith in Christ, and only through a life of obedience to God in the power of the Holy Spirit, can we enter into the fulness of salvation promised to us in the sacraments of baptism and chrismation. To be "born again," in Orthodox terms, we must "make a personal decision about Jesus Christ and His Church"; we must "make the faith of the Church our own" and "live each day in the profession of faith made at our baptism." We must "grow up in Christ and not allow the gift of life given us at baptism to be covered by our sin and the world." To be a "born again" Christian is "to hear the Word of God and to follow Christ."[25]

It should also be noted that the apostolic Church has never regarded the relationship between baptism-chrismation and the development of a personal Christian faith as a simple cause-and-effect relationship. From at least as early as the second century, the Church began to baptize and chrismate the children of Christian families. Thus, in the course of time, most Christians were baptized and chrismated as infants and came to conscious faith in Christ later in their lives. And, indeed, as implied above, many baptized and chrismated Christians may never develop an authentic Christian faith at all. Furthermore, during the early centuries of the Christian era, thousands upon thousands of pagans were converted to faith in Christ before being baptized and chrismated. And even today, many converts are received into the Church on the basis of their faith and then baptized and chrismated. It is clear, then, that a Christian faith may emerge both before and after baptism and chrismation. The faith of some is an actualization of sacramental grace; while the faith of others is a gracious gift of the Holy Spirit leading them into the sacramental life and fulness of the Church. The work of the Holy Spirit cannot be defined in a neat, legalistic formula.[26] For the Spirit, like the wind, "blows where it wills, and you hear the sound of it, but you do not know whence it comes or whither it goes" (Jn 3:8).

Jesus' Discourse with the Woman of Samaria

John 4:1-42 tells of Jesus' ministry to the Samaritans. The

Samaritans lived in the northern part of Judea and constituted a significant portion of the Palestinian population in Jesus' day. Descendants of Assyrian colonists of the eighth and seventh centuries B.C. who had intermarried with Jews,[27] they were regarded by "pure" Jews as both racially and religiously unclean. For Jesus to visit the Samaritans at all was a great offense to the Jews of his time, and especially to such leading sects as the Pharisees and the Sadducees.

The heart of John's account of the Lord's Samaritan ministry is contained in 4:7-38. Here, Jesus' discourse with a woman of Samaria is recorded. This, too, was a departure from the Judaism of his time; for women were not considered suitable partners in theological discussion. Even the Lord's disciples were taken aback when they learned of his conversation with the woman of Samaria (see Jn 4:27). Journeying north from Judea to Galilee, Jesus stopped by a well in Samaria (4:1-6). As he was sittting there, a Samaritan woman approached "to draw water." To the woman's surprise, Jesus engaged her in conversation, speaking of himself as "the living water of eternal life" and declaring himself to be the Messiah of Israel (4:7-26). When the woman realized what Jesus was saying, she ran into the nearby city and told the people about the man at the well (4:28-30). As a result of the woman's testimony, the Samaritans asked Jesus to stay with them for awhile. John tells us that the Lord (and his reluctant disciples) remained in Samaria for two days (4:40), explaining to his apostles that God's plan of salvation encompasses all peoples, even the accursed Samaritans (4:27, 31-38). And many Samaritans came to believe in him, declaring him to be "the Savior of the world" (4:41-42). The Messiah of Israel is the deliverer, "the fountain of immortality," not only for the Jews, but for all nations!

The Controversy with the Jewish Authorities

Christ's second miraculous sign was performed in Capernaum, a town in Galilee. A local official, or nobleman, had a young son who was sick to the point of death. Hearing that Jesus had come from Judea to Capernaum, the nobleman sought out the Lord and appealed to him for help. Once again, the Messiah, recognizing humanity's need for "signs and wonders," manifested his supernatural powers in order to reveal the truth about himself. Miraculously, the nobleman's son was cured of the disease that threatened his life (Jn 4:46-54).

Following this miracle, John details a third miracle, which includes Jesus' first full and explicit revelation of himself as the divine Son of God the Father. At a religious feast in Jerusalem, Jesus healed a lame man "who had been ill for thirty-eight years" (5:1-9). In this miraculous act, Jesus said to the lame man, "Rise, take up your pallet, and walk" (5:8). Because this took place on the Sabbath, the Jewish authorities criticized Jesus. For the healed man's carrying his pallet (the thin mattress upon which the man was lying) on the Sabbath was contrary to scribal law.[28]

When confronted by his Jewish critics (probably Pharisees), Jesus argued that God's work in the world does not cease in accordance with scribal Sabbath regulations: "My Father is working still, and I am working" (Jn 5:17). Hearing these words, the Jews were doubly offended. Jesus "not only broke the Sabbath but also called God his own Father, making himself equal with God" (5:18).

In response to the hostility of the Jewish authorities, Jesus delivered a discourse upon his relationship with God the Father and upon the implications of that relationship for the salvation of the world. He declared himself to be the Son of God, through whom newness of life has been made available to the world. And he warned that "he who does not honor the Son does not honor the Father who sent him." But those who respond to the Son in faith will receive the gift of eternal life. Speaking of the general resurrection of the dead at the end of days, the Lord proclaimed that "the hour is coming when all who are in the tombs will hear his [the Son's] voice and come forth, those who have done good, to the resurrection of life, and those who have done evil, to the resurrection of judgment" (5:19-29).

The discourse goes on to point out that John the Baptist, a man who was surely a prophet of the Most High, had borne witness to the messiahship of Jesus (5:31-35). But, even more profoundly, the heavenly Father himself has borne witness to his Son: "for the works which the Father has granted me to accomplish, these very works which I am doing bear witness that the Father has sent me" (5:36). The witness of the Father to the Son is also revealed in the sacred scriptures of the Old Testament, the scriptures of the Jews themselves. But even though the Pharisees claimed to be experts in the exegesis of the scriptures, Jesus rebuked them with the following words: "You do not have . . . [the Word of God] abiding in you, for you do not believe him whom . . . [the Father] has sent. You search the scriptures, because you think that in them you have eternal life; and it is they that bear witness to me; yet you refuse to come to me that you may have life" (5:38-40; see also 5:41-47).

Again, the fourth gospel stresses Christ's transcendence of the categories of Jewish religious thought. He was the Messiah, but not the Messiah expected by the Jews. His divine sonship constituted a stumbling-block that only a few adherents of Judaism would be able to overcome. And those few, the original apostles and disciples, represented a remnant which was to form the nucleus of a new Israel, the Church of Christ.

The Bread of Life

The theme of Christianity's transcendence of Judaism is continued in John 6, where Jesus is depicted as a new Moses leading his people, the new Israel, into the kingdom of God. The events described by John took place in Galilee on the occasion of the second Passover festival mentioned by John. The fact that the Lord and his followers celebrated this Passover in Galilee rather than in Jerusalem is significant; for Christ, and not the Temple, is the center of God's plan of salvation.

John 6 presents Christ as the fulfilment of the Old Testament's Passover imagery and as the source of the Church's eucharistic life. It begins with an account of Christ's miraculous feeding of the multitude who came to him in Galilee at Passover time in search of healing and enlightenment. From five barley loaves and two fish which were offered by "a lad," Jesus fed more than five thousand people. And the food was abundant, more than enough for all who had gathered (Jn 6:1-13).

Seeing what Jesus had done (the fourth miraculous sign reported by John), the people believed him to be "the prophet" of Deuteronomy 18:15-19, a new Moses who would lead his people out of bondage (Jn 6:14). They were, in fact, ready to proclaim him king over Israel. But, as we have seen, the Lord's messiahship was not to follow the pattern of military and political victory anticipated by the Jewish messianism of his day. Thus, he withdrew from the crowd and went off by himself (Jn 6:15).

John's account of the feeding of the multitude is followed by a description of a fifth miracle performed by Jesus. The feeding had taken place on the eastern shore of the Sea of Galilee (Jn 6:1). Jesus commanded his disciples to leave the site of the feeding and to go to Capernaum before him. Later that evening, as his disciples were rowing across the sea to Capernaum, they saw Jesus "walking on the sea and drawing near to the boat." This miraculous crossing of the water is a reenactment of ancient Israel's passage through the Red Sea. Earlier in this book it was pointed out that water is a biblical symbol of the world, which has been corrupted by sin and which is pervaded by death.[29] As Moses had led the old Israel through the sea to liberty, so Christ, the new Moses, led his disciples, the new Israel, over the sea to "the land to which they were going." Christ's walking on the sea is a sign of his victory over the world. And through Christian baptism, man may enter into that victory, being "saved through water" (1 Pt 3:20).

The climax of John 6 is Jesus' discourse on "the bread of life," in which the Lord speaks prophetically of the significance of his death and resurrection and of the sacrament of holy communion, which was to replace the Passover meal as the central feast of the people of God. Jesus delivered this discourse in response to the masses of people who continued to pursue him in the hope that he might miraculously solve all of their earthly problems. Jesus tried to turn the minds of the people from worldly to spiritual concerns, telling them not to "labor for the food which perishes, but for the food which endures to eternal life," which is available in the Son of Man (6:22-27). Speaking in the synagogue at Capernaum, the Lord reminded his audience that, during their wilderness wanderings, the hungry people of ancient Israel were fed by God with manna, a "bread from heaven." And now, through Christ, the new Moses, God has once again offered bread from heaven to his people. And in this bread, which is Jesus himself, God has given "life to the world" (6:22-34). "I am the bread of life," the Lord proclaimed to the people, and "he who comes to me shall not hunger, and he who believes in me shall never thirst" (6:35).

To those who accused him of blasphemy because of his claims to a heavenly origin (6:41-42), Jesus replied:

> No one can come to me unless the Father who sent me draws him; and I will raise him up at the last day. It is written in the prophets, "And they shall all be taught by God." . . . Truly, truly, I say to you, he who believes has eternal life. I am the bread of life. Your fathers ate the manna in the wilderness, and they died. This is the bread which comes down from heaven, that a man may eat of it and not die. I am the living bread which came down from heaven; if any one eats of this bread, he will live for ever; and the bread which I shall give for the life of the world is my flesh. (6:44-45, 47-51)

Many who heard him were perplexed and wondered what meaning the Lord's words might have. So Jesus said to them, becoming even more explicit:

> Truly, truly, I say to you, unless you eat the flesh of the Son of man and drink his blood, you have no life in you; he who eats my flesh and drinks my blood has eternal life, and I will raise him up at the last day. For my flesh is food indeed, and my blood is drink indeed. He who eats my flesh and drinks my blood abides in me, and I in him. As the living Father sent me, and I live because of the Father, so he who eats me will live because of me. This is the bread which came down from heaven, not such as the fathers ate and died; he who eats this bread will live for ever. (6:52-58)

Even his disciples took this teaching on the body and blood of Christ as "a hard saying," and many of them "drew back and no longer went about with . . . [the Lord]" (6:60-66). But the twelve apostles remained in his service. Peter spoke for the others when he said, "Lord . . . you have the words of eternal life; and we have believed, and have come to know, that you are the Holy One of God" (6:67-71).

The eucharistic significance of Jesus' discourse on the bread of life is obvious. Christ's body was broken and his blood shed on the cross. And through his death and resurrection we have been liberated from the forces of sin and death. But to realize the salvation offered to us in the "lifting up" of the Son of Man, we must eat his flesh and drink his blood. It is through the sacrament of holy communion, instituted by Jesus himself at the last supper, that we may partake of the body and blood of our crucified, risen and exalted Lord. As in baptism, so in the eucharist: through the sacramental agency of the Church, we enter into the paschal mystery of redemption, and we ascend with Christ into the eternal life and being of the Holy Trinity. For communion in the precious body and blood of Our Lord and Savior Jesus Christ is communion with God. And communion with God is the key to life eternal, the fulfilment of the human quest for perfect happiness.

The Light of the World

John 7-9 tells of Jesus' visit to Jerusalem on the occasion of a Feast of Tabernacles. Tabernacles (or *Sukkoth*) is an autumn harvest festival lasting eight days and commemorating the wanderings of ancient Israel in the wilderness of Sinai, a time when the chosen people lived in tents (or "tabernacles"). Along with Passover and Pentecost, Tabernacles was one of the three most important festivals of the ancient Jews. During the festival described by John (which probably occurred during the last year of our Lord's earthly life), Jesus taught in the Temple and attracted a great deal of public notice. Some thought him mad, others believed him to be the Messiah, and still others (Sadducees and Pharisees who were members of the Sanhedrin) considered him a threat to the religious and political status quo in Palestine (7:1-52). The Jewish authorities, alarmed at the Lord's popularity and perhaps fearful of trouble with the Romans, challenged his authority at every turn, sought to prove that he was teaching people to break the law of Moses (see 8:2-11) and plotted (unsuccessfully) to have him arrested.

In that atmosphere of religious celebration, public controversy and political maneuvering, Jesus delivered another of the great discourses in the fourth gospel. One of the ceremonies connected with the Feast of Tabernacles was the "Illumination of the Temple." On the evening of the first day of the festival, great golden lamps were lit in the center of the Temple court. This illumination was symbolic of the pillar of fire by which God led Israel during the years of her wilderness wanderings. With this ceremony in mind, Jesus spoke out in the Temple, declaring, "I am the light of the world; he who follows me will not walk in darkness, but will have the light of life" (8:12). In making this claim, Jesus was associating himself directly with the being and activity of God. The Pharisees therefore reacted to his declaration with hostility; and in response to them, the Lord spoke of his relationship with God the Father (8:13-20). But the Pharisees were either unable to understand him, or, more likely, they were simply astonished that Jesus was claiming God as his own Father (8:21-27). Others, however, were moved by the Lord's words and began to believe in him (8:28-30). To those who believed, Jesus said, "If you continue in my word, you are truly my disciples, and you will know the truth and the truth will make you free" (8:31-32).

To the prideful claim of the Pharisees that they, being "descendants of Abraham," did not need the "truth" or the "freedom" of which he spoke, Jesus responded that they were not true children of Abraham. For the father of the Pharisees is not the God of Abraham, but rather the devil! (Jn 8:33-47) Chagrined by this indictment, the Pharisees charged, in turn, that Christ was demon-possessed (8:48, 52). And when he went on to proclaim that he had the power from the Father to deliver men from the curse of death, his opponents were flabbergasted (8:49-53). "Who," they asked him, "do you claim to be?" (8:53) Jesus answered this question by asserting that he was the Messiah expected by the patriarch Abraham,[30] and by reasserting that he was the divine Son of God (8:54-56). And in response to the continuing taunts of his enemies, the Lord pronounced the final and most shocking words of his Tabernacles discourse: "Truly, truly, I say to you, before Abraham was, *I am*" (8:58). To the Jews of that time, this pronouncement by Jesus was a direct, explicit and unmistakable claim to perfect equality with God. For "I AM" was the name of God which was revealed to Moses in the revelation at the burning bush (see Ex 3:13-15). In speaking as he did, Jesus, who had declared himself to be the light and the life of the world, was asserting his oneness with the eternal being and activity of God the Father. The Jews regarded this as the most abominable form of blasphemy, and "they took up stones to throw at him," for death by stoning was the penalty for blasphemy required by the Mosaic law. But Jesus departed from them "and went out of the temple" (Jn 8:59).

Following his discourse in the Temple, Jesus miraculously healed a man who had been born blind (Jn 9:1-12). This is the sixth miracle presented in the Gospel of John, and it is a "sign" of the fact that Jesus is, indeed, "the light of the world" (9:5). John describes the miracle and its aftermath in great detail. The healing was done on the Sabbath, thus arousing still further the wrath of the Pharisees (9:13-23). The man whose eyes had been opened, however, praised Jesus as a prophet and man of God, and he refused to cooperate with the Pharisees in their attempts to incriminate and discredit the Lord. Because of this the Pharisees "cast him out" of the synagogue (9:24-34). After his excommunication, the man born blind became one of the disciples of Christ. John tells us that Jesus, having opened the man's eyes, also opened the eyes of his spirit; and the man, "seeing" the divinity of the Son of Man, worshiped the Lord (9:35-38).

It is this spiritual sight which is most important. The physical healing of the man born blind was merely a "sign" of a deeper healing. Through openness to and belief in Christ, those who are spiritually blind may come to see the truth; but those who think that they can see the truth without the Light of the world (for example, the Pharisees) are, in fact, without spiritual sight or sense (Jn 9:39-41). The brilliance of Christ's light is an illumination to some, but a blinding glare to others.

The Good Shepherd

John 10 describes another of Jesus' encounters with the Jewish authorities in Jerusalem. This encounter took place approximately three months after the Feast of Tabernacles described in the preceding section. And again, the occasion of Christ's presence in Jerusalem was a religious festival—the Feast of Dedication (*Hanukkah*), also known as the Festival of Lights (Jn 10:22). This is one of the minor feasts of historic Judaism. Instituted during the second century B.C., the Feast of Dedication commemorates one of the victories of Judas Maccabeus over the armies of the Seleucid empire in 164 B.C., his liberation of Jerusalem from Greek rule and the rededication of the Temple to the God of Israel (the Seleucid king, Antiochus Epiphanes, had desecrated the Temple in 168 B.C.—see 1 Mc 1-4). Hanukkah was an eight-day festival, celebrated in December, and included the lighting of candles in the Temple and in every Jewish home. This feast is still celebrated by the Jews of the world, but without the illumination of the Temple; for the Jerusalem Temple was destroyed by the Romans in 70 A.D. The setting of John 10, therefore, reemphasizes Jesus' identity as the light of the world, and it ironically points to the rejection of Christ by the Jews at the very time when Judaism was celebrating its rededication to God.

As was his custom during his visits to Jerusalem, Jesus preached and taught in the Temple during this feast, delivering his now-famous discourse on himself as the good shepherd (Jn 10:1-18). The Old Testament frequently speaks of both God and the Messiah as shepherds and of the people of God as members of the Lord's flock (see Ps 23:1-6, 80:1, 95:7, 100:3; Is 40:11; and the Song of Solomon 17:45). It should also be noted that, in Palestine, sheep are largely kept not for their meat but for their milk and wool. The relationship between a shepherd and his flock is a close and affectionate one, and it is common for the shepherd to give each of his sheep a name by which he calls it. The sheep, moreover, know and understand only their own shepherd's voice, and "they will never answer to the voice of a stranger."[31] In claiming to be "the shepherd of the sheep" (Jn

10:1-2), then, Jesus was, once more, identifying himself as the Messiah and associating his ministry with the activity of God. He (the shepherd) will call to the true people of God by name, and they (the flock), hearing and knowing his voice, will follow him out of the sheepfold of the world and into the green pastures of heaven (10:3-5). The Lord was also clearly implying that those who did not hear and know his voice (for example, the Pharisees) were not really members of God's flock (10:6).

When, as usual, the Pharisees did not (or would not) understand what he was saying, Jesus became more explicit: "Truly, truly, I say to you, I am the door of the sheep. . . . I am the door; if any one enters by me, he will be saved, and will go in and out and find pasture. . . . [For] I came that they [my sheep] may have life, and have it abundantly" (Jn 10:7-10). In calling himself "the door," Jesus remains "the shepherd of the sheep." For out in the pastures of Palestine, a shepherd would herd his flock at night into a wall-enclosed sheepfold. Such a sheepfold would have an opening through which the sheep could go in and out; but there was no door at the opening. The shepherd himself would lie down for the night across the opening in the wall in order to keep his flock in the sheepfold. "In the most literal sense the shepherd was the door; there was no access to the sheepfold except through him."[32] Jesus is both the shepherd and the door of God's flock. Only through him may we "go in and out"—that is, move freely and securely—in the pastures of our heavenly Father.

Continuing his discourse, Jesus proclaimed that the good shepherd would "lay down his life for the sheep." He prophesied his impending death, through which his people were to be reconciled to God the Father. Emphasizing the loving unity between himself and his Father, the Lord made it clear that his atoning death was to be voluntary on his part and that, by the power given him by his Father, he would be raised from the dead. He also made it clear that his death would be redemptively effective, not only for the remnant of Israel, but also for those Gentiles who turn to him in faith and obedience: the good shepherd's flock will include the sheep of a faithful Israel as well as "other sheep" drawn from "the nations" (Jn 10:11-18).

The climax of the good shepherd discourse came in response

to the criticisms and questions of the ever-hostile Pharisees. The Pharisees and other members of the Jewish religious establishment demanded to know in plain words whether Jesus was the Messiah or not (Jn 10:19-24). He indicated to them that he was, indeed, the Messiah (10:25-29); and then, duplicating the bold claim which he had made three months earlier at the Feast of Tabernacles, Jesus declared: "I and the Father are one" (10:30). In response to the inevitable charge of blasphemy (10:31-33), the Lord appealed to his accusers to try and view his claim to divine sonship both biblically and openmindedly (10:34-38). "If I am not doing the works of my Father," he said, "then do not believe me; but if I do them, even though you do not believe me, believe the works, that you may know and understand that the Father is in me and I am in the Father" (10:37-38). But his opponents would not listen to reason and tried, once more without success, to have him arrested (10:39).

The Resurrection and the Life

The well-known story of Christ's raising of Lazarus from the dead is told in chapter 11 of the Gospel of John. Lazarus of Bethany and his two sisters, Mary and Martha, were good friends and faithful disciples of the Lord. When Lazarus fell ill, Mary and Martha sent word to Jesus (Jn 11:1-3). The Lord knew that Lazarus must die and that, through the death of his friend, his own divine glory would be made manifest (11:4).

By the time Jesus and his disciples reached Bethany (11:5-6), Lazarus was already dead and had "been in the tomb four days" (11:17). Martha went out to meet Jesus as he approached her home. Greeting him, she said, "Lord, if you had been here, my brother would not have died. And even now I know that whatever you ask of God, God will give you" (11:21-22). Jesus responded to her, saying, "Your brother will rise again. . . . [For] I am the resurrection and the life; he who believes in me, though he die, yet he shall live, and whoever lives and believes in me shall never die" (11:23-26). Hearing these words, Martha reaffirmed her belief in the lordship of Jesus, declaring him to be both Messiah and Son of God (11:27).

When Mary heard of Jesus' arrival, she too went to greet him (11:28-32). Jesus and his disciples, together with Mary and Martha and a number of friends of the family, went to the tomb of Lazarus, a cave with a stone covering the entrance (11:33-38). The Lord commanded that the stone be removed from the entrance to the tomb (11:39-40). Having offered a prayer of thanks to his heavenly Father, Jesus "cried with a loud voice, 'Lazarus, come out!'" (11:41-43). John then testifies that "the dead man came out, his hands and feet bound with bandages, and his face wrapped with a cloth." And Jesus said, "Unbind him, and let him go" (11:44).

This astonishing occurrence is the last of the seven miraculous signs of Christ's divine sonship recorded in the fourth gospel. It was a sign of Christ's power over death itself and is thus a confirmation of the universal resurrection of the dead, which has been made possible in and through the Lord's own glorious resurrection. Strictly speaking, however, Lazarus was *raised* but not *resurrected* from the dead. For one who is resurrected will never die again, and according to tradition Lazarus did die in the flesh some years after his miraculous resuscitation by Christ. The resuscitation of Lazarus was a shadow or copy of the true resurrection of Christ himself, the final and ultimate sign of the Lord's victory over the powers of sin and death.[33]

Of all the signs performed by Jesus, the raising of Lazarus was the most shocking and alarming to the Lord's enemies in the religious establishment. It would appear that a special meeting of the Sanhedrin was then convened just to discuss the "Jesus problem" (Jn 11:45-53). One of the council members spoke as follows: "What are we to do? For this man performs many signs. If we let him go on thus, every one will believe in him, and the Romans will come out and destroy both our holy place [the Temple] and our nation" (11:47-48). The high priest Caiaphas then declared to the others, "You know nothing at all; you do not understand that it is expedient for you that one man should die for the people, and the whole nation should not perish" (11:49-50). John points out that the high priest's words were actually prophetic in that Jesus was indeed to die for the nation of Israel as well as for all of God's people among the nations of the world (11:51-52). Caiaphas, of course, did not understand the full prophetic significance of his words. But under his leadership, the growing conspiracy to have Jesus arrested and executed became both more serious and more effective (11:53).

With his description of the raising of Lazarus, the apostle John completes his portrait of the divine sonship of Christ, as the incarnate Word, the Messiah, the Son of God, the bread of life, the light of the world and the good shepherd. The episode at Bethany was a prelude to the culminating events of our Savior's earthly ministry, events which were to make manifest the profound and world-shaking sense in which Christ is truly the resurrection and the life.

JOHN 12-21: THE PASSION AND RESURRECTION OF JESUS CHRIST

The third Passover festival described in the Gospel of John brought Jesus to Jerusalem for the last time during his earthly life. The city was full of excitement because of the notoriety Jesus had attained through his escalating conflict with the Jewish establishment and through his miraculous raising of Lazarus from the dead. The crowds were hoping that he would attend the feast in order that they might hear his teaching and perhaps witness his miracle-working power. And the leaders of the Sanhedrin were also hoping that he would turn up in Jerusalem "so that they might arrest him" (Jn 11:55-57).

After he had raised Lazarus, Jesus had left Bethany, which was just outside of Jerusalem, and had gone to stay in Ephraim, some ten miles to the north of the holy city (Jn 11:54). As Passover drew near, the Lord returned to Bethany and spent the Saturday before Palm Sunday ("Lazarus Saturday") at the home of Lazarus, Mary and Martha. It was on this occasion, according to John, that Jesus was anointed by Mary of Bethany—a hospitable act interpreted by Christ as a symbol of his approaching death and burial (12:1-11). The next day, Jesus entered Jerusalem and began the final phases of his redemptive work.

John's account of the Lord's triumphal entry into Jerusalem does not differ in any major way from the parallel accounts in

Matthew 21:1-11, Mark 11:1-11 and Luke 12:28-44. But John does not report the day-to-day activities of Jesus following the triumphal entry, as do the authors of the synoptic gospels. Instead, he records a single discourse in which Christ spoke of his imminent death and resurrection, of his "glorification" (Jn 12: 20-50). "The hour has come for the Son of man to be glorified. . . . Now is the judgment of this world, now shall the ruler of the world [the devil] be cast out; and I, when I am lifted up from the earth, will draw all men to myself" (12:23, 31-32). Through his death and resurrection, the Lord declared, all mankind may be reborn to eternal life. But we must be prepared to follow Christ even unto death (12:24-26).

With the discourse recorded in John 12:20-50, the public preaching and teaching of Jesus came to an end. From that point on, the Lord concentrated upon making himself and his apostles ready for his final "glorification"—his trial, death and resurrection.

The Last Supper

John's account of the last supper is contained in chapters 13-17 of his gospel. The account does not make direct mention of the institution of the holy eucharist, for by the time John was writing (c. 85-90 A.D.), the traditions concerning the last supper which are recorded in the synoptic gospels were well known. John therefore concentrates upon "filling in" the picture drawn by the synoptics, describing events at the last supper not preserved in the traditions used by them.

John tells us that, at the last supper, Jesus washed and dried his apostles' feet (13:1-20). This act, a common form of hospitality in the ancient Middle East, was normally done by slaves or houseservants. Jesus' apostles were thus understandably shocked when their Lord stooped like a slave at their feet. When Peter tried to restrain him, Jesus said, "If I do not wash you, you have no part of me" (13:6-8). And after the foot-washing, he explained to the apostles that his act was symbolic of the mission upon which he was sending them. As he himself had been a servant of God and of mankind, so they too were to serve God and their fellow man. As Christ had made salvation available to the world, so the apostles ("sent ones") were to carry that salvation to all nations (13:12-20). Speaking of the future mission of the apostolic Church, the Lord proclaimed, "he who receives any one whom I send receives me; and he who receives me receives him who sent me" (13:20).

In saying to Peter, "If I do not wash you, you have no part of me," Jesus was, no doubt, alluding to the cleansing power of his own death and resurrection. And for the early Church, these words and the foot-washing described by John took on sacramental significance. For as we have seen, both baptism and the holy eucharist are mysteries through which we enter into the death and resurrection of Christ, into communion with our risen Lord, and thus we are made "clean all over" (Jn 13:10), both in body and in spirit. The fathers of the Church saw in the story of the foot-washing at the last supper a sign of the "lifting up" of Christ, which has been made continually present to the world in the sacraments of baptism and holy communion.

Following the foot-washing, Jesus predicted that one of the apostles would betray him, and he identified Judas Iscariot as the man. The other apostles did not understand what Jesus was talking about, nor did they realize that Judas was he of whom the Lord spoke. Jesus commanded Judas to leave the apostolic gathering and to accomplish his traitorous work without further ado (see Jn 13:21-30).

When Judas had left the group, Jesus presented to the apostles the final teachings of his earthly ministry. These teachings are compiled in John 13:31-16:33. This section of the fourth gospel is often called the "Farewell Discourse," for it is the last of the major discourses recorded by John.

Jesus began the discourse by speaking, once again, of his coming "glorification." The glory of both the Father and the Son was to be made manifest in the death of Jesus. For through that death, God was to show himself victorious over the powers of darkness, and the love of God for mankind and the world was to be confirmed. Christ's resurrection from the dead would be a sure sign of God's glory, power and love (13:31-33).

The death, resurrection and ascension of Christ would also constitute his departure from the apostles and his other followers; for where he was going, they could not go (13:33). But the separation of Christ from his followers was not to be permanent. Through his resurrection from the dead, his glorious ascension into heaven, and his exaltation to the right hand of the Father, Jesus was to make possible the entry of all faithful people into the kingdom of God. And through his second coming, which will take place at the end of days, the Lord will return to the world and lead his people into the fulness of salvation (14:1-4). Jesus is "the way, the truth, and the life": he is the *way* to salvation; in him and in his saving work we discover the *truth* about God, the world and ourselves; and by accepting that truth and following that way, we may receive the *life* of the heavenly kingdom (14:6). For in Christ, we are reconciled with God the Father. Speaking to the apostles, the Lord said, "He who has seen me has seen the Father. . . . Believe me that I am in the Father and the Father [is] in me" (14:9, 11). Because of this perfect oneness between the Father and the Son, mankind may enter into fellowship with the Father through faith in and obedience to the Son. Our relationship with Christ will determine our relationship with the Father. If we reject Christ, then we will not find the Father. But if we believe in Christ and follow him, then we ourselves will become "sons of God" (see 16:16, 20-28).

In the Old Testament, God's salvation of the world was conceived of primarily (although not exclusively) in futuristic terms: the kingdom of God *will be* established at the end of days. In contrast to the "futurist eschatology" of the Old Testament, the New Testament teaches that the kingdom of God has come *and* will come in and through the person and work of Jesus Christ. In the New Testament, we find a "realized eschatology" as well as a "futurist eschatology." In other words, the New Testament contains what has been called an "inaugurated eschatology," a doctrine of "last things" which takes into account the past, present and future dimensions of Christ's ministry.[34] Through his life, death, resurrection and ascension, Jesus has saved us from the forces of evil, and through the second advent of the Lord, the reconciliation of all things in God will be fully and finally accomplished. In Christ, we have been saved, we are being saved and we will be saved—the kingdom of God has come, it is coming and it will come. Past, present and future are organically united in the ongoing economy of redemption.

The Farewell Discourse contains several passages dealing with the ministry of the Holy Spirit. Jesus told his apostles that they were soon to receive the gift of the Holy Spirit, and that the Holy Spirit would dwell in them and enable them to comprehend the truth concerning salvation which Christ had shared with them during his earthly life (14:15-17, 25-26). But they were to receive the Holy Spirit only after the death, resurrection and ascension of Jesus (16:5-7). After his departure from the world, Jesus would send the third person of the Holy Trinity, "who proceeds from the Father," into the world to live in and to guide the apostles and, indeed, all members of Christ's Church (15: 26-27; see also Acts 2).

Jesus spoke of the Holy Spirit as "the Advocate" (Greek, *parakletos*) and as "the Spirit of Truth" (Jn 14:15-17, 26; 15:26-27; 16:7, 13). As Christ had been the advocate of his people (see 1 Jn 2:1), so the Holy Spirit would counsel, encourage, comfort and defend the Church before the onslaughts of the world, the flesh and the devil. Dwelling in the hearts of the apostles and in the life of the apostolic Church, the Spirit of Truth would teach the followers of Christ "all things," and would bring to their remembrance all that Jesus had taught during his days on earth (Jn 14:25-26). The Spirit would also reveal truths which had not been communicated by Christ because of the limited spiritual readiness of his disciples (16:12-13). As one commentator on these verses has written, "God's revelation is progressive. Christ revealed to the disciples only what they were ready to receive and understand. But he told them to expect further revelation after His ascension at the coming of the Holy Spirit, and to accept this revelation as the Word of God."[35]

The Farewell Discourse goes on to say that the Holy Spirit would empower the Church to witness effectively to the salvation which has come through Christ (Jn 15:26-27). Through the agency of the Holy Spirit, the Church will carry on Christ's work of salvation, and, indeed, will do even "greater works" than the Lord himself had done (14:12-14). This does not mean that the saving mission of the Church is superior to the work of Christ, but that through the mission of the Church, which is possible only in Christ, God's salvation will be made available on a world-wide scale.

Christ's teachings on the ministry of the Holy Spirit were presented to his disciples in the context of his preparing them—the Church—for the period of time after his departure from the world. The Church was not to be left desolate after Christ's departure from the world (Jn 14:18). Through the power and presence of the Holy Spirit, the Church was to receive the peace offered in Christ by the Father (14:27). Through the Holy Spirit, the followers of Christ would come to know that the Son is in the Father, that the Church is in the Son and that the Son is in the Church (14:19-20). The Holy Spirit would encourage and empower the Church to love and obey Christ (14:21); and in the Spirit, the Father and the Son would make their home in and with the Church (14:22-23). Thus, through the ministry of the Holy Spirit, Christ would be glorified in his Church, and the Church would live in union with the Holy Trinity (16:14-15).

The Gospel of John reports that the apostles did not comprehend the meaning of Christ's teachings at the last supper. They believed him to be the Messiah of Israel, and they were prepared to acknowledge his divine origin (16:29-30). But they were unable to understand him when he spoke of his departure from the world and of the advent of the Holy Spirit (see 14:5, 8-9, 22; and 16:17-18). It was this incomprehension which would lead the apostles to abandon Christ after his arrest (16:31-32). Even Peter, who professed to be willing to die for the Lord, was to deny him three times in a single night (13:36-38).

Knowing all this, Christ promised the apostles that they would become mighty witnesses to the good news of salvation. After the Lord's resurrection, and especially after Pentecost, the apostles would understand the true nature of Christ's saving mission. They would be rejected and even severely persecuted by the world (15:18-25 and 16:1-4). But through the Holy Spirit, they would be "made clean," they would learn how to live in Christ and how to love one another as Christ loved them, and they would carry the divine message of salvation to the very ends of the earth (see 15:1-17, 13:34-35, and 14:12-14). In and through the apostles, by the power of Christ and the Holy Spirit, the Church of the new covenant would be born, would "overcome the world" (16:33), and would grow eventually into the kingdom of God.

At the end of the Farewell Discourse, Jesus "lifted up his eyes to heaven" and prayed to his Father. This prayer is known as the "High Priestly Prayer," and it may be divided into three sections. First, Jesus prayed that his imminent "glorification" by way of his death and resurrection would bring his disciples to full knowledge of God and thus to eternal life; and looking beyond his death and resurrection, Christ also prayed to be reunited with his Father in the glory of heaven (17:1-5).

Second, Jesus prayed that the apostles would remain united in love, that they would have joy in spite of tribulation, that they would resist the designs of the devil, and that they would fulfil their evangelistic mission to the world:

> I have manifested thy name to the men whom thou gavest me out of the world. . . . Holy Father, keep them in thy name, which thou hast given me, that they may be one, even as we are one. . . . While I was with them, I kept them in thy name. . . . But now I am coming to thee; and these things I speak in the world, that they may have my joy fulfilled in themselves. I have given them thy word; and the world has hated them because they are not of the world, even as I am not of the world. I do not pray that thou shouldst take them out of the world, but that thou shouldst keep them from the evil one [the devil]. . . . Sanctify them in the truth; thy word is truth. As thou didst send me into the world, so I have sent them into the world. And for their sake I consecrate myself, that they also may be consecrated in truth (see 17:6-19).

Third, Jesus prayed for the entire Church, that she might live in love and unity throughout the ages to come: "I do not pray for . . . [the apostles] only, but also for those who believe in me through their word, that they may all be one. . . . The glory which thou hast given me I have given to them, that they may be one even as we are one, I in them and thou in me, that they may become perfectly one, so that the world may know thou hast sent me and hast loved them even as thou hast loved me. Father,

I desire that they also, whom thou hast given me, may be with me where I am, to behold my glory, which thou hast given me in thy love for me before the foundation of the world" (see 17:20-26).

The Trial and Death of Christ

After the last supper (which took place on Thursday evening of Holy Week), Jesus and the apostles went out to a garden "across the Kidron Valley" (Gethsemane—Jn 18:1). There, Jesus was arrested by the Temple police, who were sent by the Sanhedrin and led by the traitor, Judas Iscariot (18:2-11).

John does not describe the details of Christ's trial before the Sanhedrin. He does indicate that Jesus was convicted of the religious crime of blasphemy because he "made himself the Son of God" (19:7). While the Lord was being interrogated and tried by the Sanhedrin (18:12-14, 19-24), the apostle Peter was in the process of denying that he was a follower and friend of Jesus (18:15-18, 25-27). And most of the other disciples, as Christ had prophesied, also abandoned their Lord.

The Sanhedrin, following the law of Moses concerning the penalty for blasphemy, condemned Jesus to death. As already noted, the Jews were not permitted to execute criminals, but the sentence had to be confirmed by the Roman governor of Judea, Pontius Pilate. Upon his approval of the Sanhedrin's decision, the condemned man would be put to death by the Roman army. Thus, the high priest Caipahas ordered that Jesus be taken to the residence of the governor. Before Pilate, the leaders of the Sanhedrin accused Jesus of political intrigue as well as blasphemy (Jn 18:33-38 and 19:7).

Like the synoptics, John reports that "no crime" was found in the condemned man by the Roman authorities (18:38). Pilate sought by various means to release Jesus (18:38-40 and 19:1-11), but the Jewish leaders vehemently protested, crying out to the governor, "If you release this man, you are not Caesar's friend; every one who makes himself a king [in this case, "King of the Jews"] sets himself against Caesar" (19:12). When confronted with this choice—either Christ or Caesar—Pilate, needless to say, chose his emperor, Tiberias Caesar (r. 14-37 A.D.). The Jews, for their part, insisted that they had "no king but Caesar" (19:15). Pilate therefore confirmed the decision of the Sanhedrin and ordered that Jesus be crucified (19:13-16).

The Johannine account of the crucifixion of Christ is contained in John 19:17-37. According to John, Jesus was crucified with "two others"; and Pilate, against the objections of the Jewish authorities, had an inscription placed upon Christ's cross which read (in Hebrew, Latin and Greek), "Jesus of Nazareth, the King of the Jews" (19:17-22). Pilate's soldiers divided the Lord's garments among themselves, and cast lots for his tunic. This act, John points out, was a fulfilment of the messianic prophecy of Psalm 22:18: "They parted my garments among them, and for my clothing they cast lots" (see Jn 19:23-25).

Jesus' mother and some of his disciples were standing by his cross. One of these disciples was the "Beloved Disciple," who, tradition tells us, was the apostle John himself. "When Jesus saw his mother, and the disciple whom he loved standing near, he said to his mother, 'Woman, behold your son!' Then he said to the disciple, 'Behold, your mother!' " (Jn 19:25-27) The author of the fourth gospel then tells us that "from that hour the disciple took her to his own home" (19:27). Here, the Mother of God—the "Woman," the new Eve—becomes the mother of the beloved disciple, who represents the Church; and as a representative of the Church, the beloved disciple takes the holy mother into his own home.[36] As Mary was the intercessor on behalf of her friends at the marriage feast at Cana, so now she has become the intercessor on behalf of the entire people of God.

After his words to his mother and to the beloved disciple, "Jesus, knowing that all was now finished, said (to fulfil the scripture [Ps 69:21]), 'I thirst.' " The Roman guards gave him some vinegar to drink. "When Jesus had received the vinegar, he said, 'It is finished'; and he bowed his head and gave up his spirit" (Jn 19:28-30). John goes on to say that, because the crucifixion took place on the eve of the Sabbath, "the Jews asked Pilate that . . . [the legs of the crucified men] might be broken, and that they might be taken away [to die out of sight on the Sabbath?]" (19:31). The Roman soldiers therefore broke the legs of the two men who had been crucified with Christ, "but when they came to Jesus and saw that he was already dead, they did not break his legs" (19:32-33). But one of the soldiers pierced the Lord's side with a spear, "and at once there came out blood and water" (19:34). Thus, in fulfilment of Old Testament prophecies concerning the Messiah, not one of Christ's bones was broken (see Ex 12:46 and Ps 34:20), and he was "pierced" by a spear (Zc 12:10).

Joseph of Arimathea and Nicodemus, two members of the Sanhedrin who were "secret disciples" of the Lord, received permission from Pilate to take Christ's body away for burial. "They took the body of Jesus, and bound it in linen cloths with [embalming] spices as is the burial custom of the Jews." Joseph and Nicodemus (and perhaps some others) then laid the body in a nearby tomb, and they sealed the tomb with a large stone (Jn 19:38-42 and 20:1). It is likely that most of Christ's followers regarded his entombment as the final and definitive sign of his defeat by the forces of evil. Their hope for salvation through Christ was, no doubt, overwhelmed by their despair at his death.

The Resurrection of Christ

John's testimony concerning the resurrection of Christ is contained in chapters 20-21 of the fourth gospel. And again, John supplies us with material that supplements the resurrection narratives of the synoptic gospels. John tells us that Mary Magdalene went to the Lord's tomb early on the Sunday following his death. The evangelist does not mention the other myrrhbearing women, but that does not exclude the possibility that they were present. John 20:1-18 is written mainly from the point of view of Mary Magdalene, and it may well be that she was the source of most of the material contained in these verses. Discovering that the stone had been moved from the entrance to the tomb and that the tomb itself was empty, Mary ran and declared to Peter and the beloved disciple, "They have taken the Lord out of the tomb, and we [note the plural] do not know where they have laid him" (20:1-2). Peter and the beloved disciple ran to the tomb to see for themselves that it was empty. After witnessing the empty tomb, the two men "went back to their homes" (20:3-10).[37] Like Mary Magdalene, they probably assumed that the Lord's body had been removed by the Romans or the Jewish authorities (20:9).

Following his account of the discovery of the empty tomb, John records four post-resurrection appearances of Christ. First, he appeared to Mary Magdalene as she (and the other myrrh-bearers?) lingered at his tomb after Peter and the beloved disciple had gone home. Mary reported this appearance of Christ to the apostles, saying, "I have seen the Lord" (20:11-18).

The second appearance of the risen Lord which is reported by John took place on the evening of resurrection day. Jesus appeared to the apostles (in Jerusalem), showed them his pierced hands and side and then commissioned them to carry on his work (20:19-23).

> "Peace be with you. As the Father has sent me, even so I send you." And when he had said this, he breathed on them, and said to them, "Receive the Holy Spirit. If you forgive the sins of any, they are forgiven; if you retain the sins of any, they are retained." (20:21-23)

These words of Christ are among the scriptural foundations of the sacraments of holy orders and repentance. Through the consecration and empowerment of the apostles by the Lord, and through their ordination of others to continue their apostolic mission, Christ's own holy priesthood was communicated to the bishops and priests of the historical Church. It is also noteworthy that the communication of the Holy Spirit to the apostles on the occasion under discussion was distinct from the descent of the Spirit upon the Church at Pentecost (Ac 2).[38] There is a difference between the apostolic priesthood (into which only a few Christians are called) and the priesthood of all believers (which encompasses all Christians).

The apostle Thomas was not present when the Lord appeared to the other apostles on Easter evening. And when he heard of what had transpired, he refused to believe it (Jn 20:24-25). Eight days after the resurrection, the Lord appeared again to the apostles, including Thomas. Thus, St. Thomas—"doubting

Thomas"—had his doubts overthrown. And the deity of Christ, which had been recognized by a blind man (9:1-41), was now acknowledged by a skeptic (20:27-28). But Jesus chided Thomas for his insistence upon a physical vision, and praised those who were to believe in the resurrection without direct visible proof. It should be added, however, that, according to tradition, St. Thomas was consecrated to the apostolic priesthood by Christ and became a dedicated and effective minister of the gospel. Indeed, John implies that this third appearance of the risen Christ was especially intended to bring Thomas into the fulness of the apostolic brotherhood (20:26-29).

In John 21, a fourth post-resurrection appearance of Christ is recounted. Jesus appeared to seven of the apostles as they were fishing in Galilee (21:1-14). The highlight of this epiphany is a dialogue which took place between the Lord and the apostle Peter (see 21:15-19). Here, Peter does not boast that his love for the Lord is superior to that of the other apostles. And Peter's threefold denial of Christ on the night of the Lord's trial is reversed and forgiven in a threefold affirmation of Peter's love for his Master. Peter is charged to tend the Lord's flocks—a sign that Christ was confirming Peter's full membership in the apostolic college. And the concluding words of this passage (21:18-19) imply that Peter would thenceforth be a steadfast follower of Christ even though such faithful discipleship was to bring the apostle to his death.

With this final post-resurrection appearance of Christ, the Gospel of John comes to an end. In John 21:20-24, we are told that the beloved disciple was the primary source of the material contained in this gospel; and, as we have seen, it is likely that the author of the fourth gospel was St. John the Apostle. The author also tells us that his purpose in writing is that, through his testimony, we may come to believe "that Jesus is the Christ, the Son of God," and that in so believing we may "have life in his name" (20:30-31).

According to the Gospel of John, Jesus of Nazareth is the Messiah of Israel, the incarnate Son of God, "the Savior of the world" (Jn 4:42). In his incarnate life as Son of God and Son of Man, Jesus is the point of union between God and mankind.

Union with Christ, on the basis of faith and obedience, is union with God. In the words of St. Athanasius of Alexandria (d. 373 A.D.), "the Word of God Himself . . . assumed humanity that we might become [one with] God."[39] Christ is "the true vine" (Jn 15:1-17), and in him we are united to God, to the divine life of the Holy Trinity.

Through Christ the Enlightener, and by way of his ministry of signs and teachings, we receive the truth concerning God, man and the universe. Christ is "the light of the world" and "the light of life" (Jn 8:12), and he gives us the truth that makes us free from spiritual blindness, from sin and death, from eternal suffering (Jn 8:31-32 and 9:1-41). Christ's truth is a *saving* truth!

Christ is the good shepherd who leads us to pasture, to the kingdom of God (Jn 10:1-18). He is "the Door" to salvation, to union with God (10:7, 9). He is the Way, the Truth and the Life—the way to salvation, the truth of authentic enlightenment, and the life of God (14:6). No one can come to the Father who has not received Christ as the way, the truth and the life. Man is alienated from God as a result of sin; and Christ brings man to reconciliation and union with God through his own incarnate being, through his truth, and through his death, resurrection, ascension and exaltation. In dying, Christ identified himself with our sin and with our death, and he thereby freed us from the curse of sin and death. For when absolute righteousness becomes sin, sin is eradicated; and when the fulness of life dies, then death is vanquished—death is "trampled down" by death. In rising from the dead, Christ raised human nature from the grave and made "new life" in God a real possibility for all. And in his glorious ascension and exaltation to the right hand of God the Father, Christ opened "the door" to the deification of man. In and through Christ, we may "have life and have it abundantly" (10:10).

CHAPTER 7

The Theology of St. Paul

After the ascension of Christ, and the communication of the Holy Spirit to the Church on the day of Pentecost, the apostolic community began to grow significantly—both in numbers and in spiritual vitality (Ac 1-2). Through the illuminating power of the Holy Spirit, the apostles finally came to comprehend the full meaning of their Lord's ministry to the world, and they began to proclaim the gospel "with all boldness" to all who would listen. The center of the Church's life and activity was Jerusalem, and it was not long before the Jewish authorities became alarmed at the continued existence of the "Jesus movement" (Ac 3-4). Having failed to disperse the troublesome "heretics" by harassment and threats, the Sanhedrin decided upon a policy of outright persecution (Ac 4-5). During this persecution, St. Stephen, one of the first deacons of the Church, was arrested and brought before the Sanhedrin; and after making a strong and provocative defense of the Christian faith, he was stoned to death by an angry mob which the Jewish leaders made no real effort to control (Ac 6-7). Following Stephen's martyrdom, the Christian community was "scattered throughout the region of Judea and Samaria," although the apostles remained in Jerusalem (Ac 8:1). But this scattering through persecution only served to spread the gospel beyond the boundaries of the holy city.

One of the leading figures in the Jewish persecution of the Church was Saul of Tarsus (Ac 8:1, 3). Although he was born and raised outside of Palestine (Tarsus was a Greek city in Asia Minor), Saul was an Israelite "of the tribe of Benjamin, a Hebrew born of Hebrews . . . a Pharisee . . . [and] a persecutor of the church" (Ph 3:5-6). It is ironic, therefore, that, by the grace of God, this great enemy of Christianity was to become one of the greatest saints of the Church. While on his way to Damascus in Syria to arrest any Christians that he might find there, Saul had a direct and dramatic experience of the risen Christ (see Ac 9:1-19, 22:1-21 and 26:9-23). This experience revolutionized Saul's life. He was converted to the Christian faith, baptized and received into the church of Damascus—the very community he had set out to suppress (Ac 9:10-31). It was also revealed to him that he was Christ's "chosen instrument" to carry the gospel, not only to the Jews, but also to the Gentile world (Ac 9:15). Having grown up in a Greek city as a Roman citizen (see Ac 22:23-29), Saul was no doubt well prepared to communicate effectively in cosmopolitan terms. Thus, the persecutor of the Church had become one of Christ's apostles—the "apostle to the Gentiles." As a sign of his special mission to "the nations," the converted Pharisee ceased using his Hebrew name and used instead its Greek equivalent: Paul (Ac 13:9).

It was through the mission of St. Paul that Christianity, originally a small Jewish sect, became a world religion. After his conversion (c. 32 A.D.), Paul lived and preached in the region of Damascus for about three years (c. 32-35 A.D.—Ga 1:15-19 and Ac 9:20-25). He made a brief visit to Jerusalem in 35 A.D., and, following the counsel of the other apostles, he then returned to his native city of Tarsus (Ac 9:26-31). Paul remained in Tarsus for approximately nine years (c. 35-44 A.D.), no doubt preaching the gospel to both Jews and Gentiles. In the meantime, a Christian community including a "great number" of converted Greeks emerged in Syrian Antioch; and the church of Jerusalem sent the disciple Barnabas to minister to the new Antiochian fellowship. Barnabas, in turn, asked Paul to join him in the shepherding of the "large company" of Jewish and Gentile believers in Antioch. The ministry of Paul and Barnabas in Antioch lasted for a year or two (c. 45-46 A.D.—Ac 11:19-30). At the end of that time, they were commanded by the Holy Spirit to go out from Antioch and to preach the gospel of Christ throughout the Greco-Roman world (Ac 13:1-3). Paul's days as a pastor to local churches were over. Thenceforward, and in accordance with the will of God, the apostle to the Gentiles was to serve his Lord as an itinerant missionary to the world at large.

Paul made three major missionary tours. On the first of these tours (c. 47-49 A.D.) he carried the apostolic message of salvation to Cyprus and to a number of cities in Asia Minor (Ac 13-14). And on his second and third missionary journeys (c. 49-52 and c. 52-56 A.D.), Paul traveled extensively throughout Asia Minor, Macedonia and Greece (Ac 15:38-18:21 and 18:22-21:16). As a result of Paul's efforts, many Gentiles were converted to the faith and many local churches were established.

Paul's commitment to the Lord and his success in reaching out to the Gentile world were, of course, highly offensive to the Jews of his day. After his third missionary tour, and while he was visiting with the church in Jerusalem, Paul was attacked and almost killed by a Jewish mob. The apostle was rescued by a contingent of Roman soldiers and placed under arrest as a result of the public disturbance he had apparently caused (Ac 21-22). Through the legal and political maneuvers of the Sanhedrin and the Roman authorities, Paul was kept in prison—first in Jerusalem and then in Caesarea—for more than two years (c. 56-58 A.D.—Ac 23-24). Finally, having lost all hope of receiving a fair hearing from either the Jews or the Roman governor, Paul exercised his rights as a Roman citizen and appealed his case to the emperor in Rome (Ac 25:1-12). The Roman authorities in Judea thus sent Paul to Rome (Ac 27-28). After arriving in Rome, Paul was kept under a mild house arrest for another two years (c. 59-61 A.D.—Ac 28:17-30), until, at last, the charges against him were dropped and he was released. He continued to minister on behalf of Christ, preaching the gospel in Rome and, according to tradition, carrying the Christian message as far as Spain. Paul's freedom was, once again, taken from him in 64 A.D.—for in that year, the Emperor Nero (r. 54-68 A.D.) instituted the first great Roman persecution of the Church. Paul's second imprisonment in Rome lasted until 67 or 68 A.D., when he was (along with the apostle Peter and other leaders of the Church) executed by order of the emperor.[1]

THE WRITINGS OF ST. PAUL

Paul was primarily a preacher and teacher, not a writer. He wrote no systematic treatise expressing his theological perspective, nor did he live to set down in writing the gospel which he preached, although he was probably the major apostolic source of the Gospel according to St. Luke. Paul did, however, write a number of letters (or "epistles") during his thirty-five-year ministry; and thirteen of those letters have survived and are included in the canon of the New Testament. A fourteenth letter, Hebrews, has also been attributed to Paul, because it seems to be a development of his teaching about Christ; but since Hebrews was apparently composed after 70 A.D., it is almost certain that Paul (who died in 67 or 68 A.D.) was not its author. Scholars believe that the letter was composed by one of Paul's close associates, most often suggesting Barnabas, Luke or Apollos.

Some of Paul's letters were written to specific Christian communities (Romans, 1 and 2 Corinthians, Galatians, Philippians, Colossians, 1 and 2 Thessalonians); others were addressed to individuals (1 and 2 Timothy, Titus, Philemon); and one was intended for the Church at large (Ephesians, which scholars believe to have been originally a circular letter). Hebrews, which is more in the form of a sermon or treatise than a letter, was apparently intended for a community of Jewish Christians located either in Rome, Jerusalem or Ephesus.

Although these writings are not systematic theological treatises, they do contain lucid and profound expositions of the metaphysical and ethical doctrines of the Christian Church. Paul's major purpose in writing his letters was to encourage the newly emerging churches of the Greco-Roman world to remain both theologically and morally steadfast in their discipleship to Christ. Paul was especially concerned with the problem of heresy in the early Church, for many enthusiastic but untutored Christians were following unsound doctrines which were inconsistent with the apostolic tradition. The two major heresies that had infected the first-century Church were propagated by the Judaizers and the gnostics. The Judaizers insisted that Christianity was a form of Judaism and that all Gentile converts to the faith must follow all of the stipulations of the Mosaic law (circumcision, dietary laws, Sabbath observances, and so on). The gnostics taught a kind of spiritualism in which the goodness of the material world was denied; they rejected the biblical view that God had created the physical universe; they denied the bodily incarnation and resurrection of Jesus; they considered Christ to be only one of a multitude of semi-divine, angelic saviors; and they held that God's truth was available only to a small number of "illuminati."[2] Much of Paul's letter-writing was intended to counteract the subversive influence of the Judaizers and the gnostics. Throughout his writings, the apostle insists that the Christian, whether Jew or Gentile, is free of the Jewish ritual law. He also insists that God is the Creator of the world, that our salvation has been embodied in Christ and his Church and that the apostolic message of salvation through Jesus Christ is available to all mankind.

Paul's New Testament epistles are commonly grouped into four categories, reflecting the chronological order in which the documents were written. Paul's "early letters," 1 and 2 Thessalonians, were written from Corinth (in Greece) c. 50 A.D., during his second missionary tour. Paul was one of the founders of the church in Thessalonica (in Macedonia), and in his letters to the Thessalonian Christians the apostle encourages them to remain both theologically and morally pure. In both letters, Paul speaks of the second coming of Christ and the last judgment, and he cautions the Thessalonians to await the day of the Lord with vigilance and with patience (1 Th 4-5 and 2 Th 2). Like many enthusiastic Christians, the Thessalonians were so excited about the return of the Lord that they were neglecting the day-to-day and down-to-earth requirements of the Christian life. Paul therefore exhorts them not to allow their "eschatological expectations" to distract them from the daily moral and spiritual practice of their faith.

The "great letters" were composed during Paul's third missionary journey (c. 52-56 A.D.). Paul wrote his letter to the Galatians (probably from Ephesus) in 52 or 53 A.D. Galatia was a large Roman province in Asia Minor, and Galatians was most likely intended for all of the churches in that region. The letter contains a defense of Paul's apostolic authority and a strong critique of the Judaizers, who had apparently made inroads into the Christian communities in Galatia. First and Second Corinthians were written from Ephesus (on the west coast of Asia Minor) in 55 A.D. Corinth was a cosmopolitan city in Greece, notorious for its corruption and immorality. Paul was apparently the founder of the church in Corinth, and he was disturbed by the news he received of the moral and spiritual disorder that had grown up there. First Corinthians (as well as two other letters that have been lost) was intended to correct the irregularities that were undermining the Christian life in Corinth. After a difficult struggle (which went on for several months), Paul finally convinced the Corinthians of the errors of their ways, and in 2 Corinthians expresses his thanks to God for the cleansing of the church in Corinth. After writing 2 Corinthians, Paul traveled to Corinth and stayed with his repentant flock for about three months. During that time, in 56 A.D., he wrote his letter to the Romans (that is, to the Christian community in Rome). Paul hoped to visit the church in Rome, and in his letter to them he discusses the nature of salvation through Christ (chapters 1-8), the relationship between Jews and Gentiles in God's plan of salvation (9-11) and the life of practical holiness which all Christians should strive to live (12-15). Romans is one of Paul's most extended and systematic statements of his overall theological understanding of the gospel of Christ.

During his first imprisonment in Rome (c. 59-61 A.D.), Paul wrote the "prison letters." Philemon, Colossians and Ephesians were all written in 59 A.D., and Philippians was produced in 60 A.D. Philemon was a well-to-do Christian of Colossae in Asia Minor whose slave, Onesimus, had run away to Rome. Onesimus visited Paul, who was a friend of Philemon, and was converted to Christianity. In his letter to Philemon, Paul appeals to his friend to receive Onesimus back as a Christian brother; the apostle also promises to pay back whatever money or property the runaway slave had stolen from his master. The letter to the Colossians was written in opposition to the gnosticism that had sprung up in the church at Colossae. Accordingly, Paul stresses that Jesus Christ is the only Savior of the world, that through Christ God created the world and that in Christ "the whole fulness of deity dwells bodily" (Col 2:9). The document known as the "Letter to the Ephesians" was probably a circular letter sent by Paul to all of the churches of the Ephesian region (eastern Asia Minor). The central theme of Ephesians is the relationship between Christ and his Church; the Church is depicted as the mystical body of Christ which, in the power of the Holy Spirit, is God's sacrament of salvation offered to the world. The church in Philippi (a Roman colony in Macedonia) was another of the Christian communities founded by Paul. Knowing of Paul's imprisonment in Rome, the Philippians sent him a gift in order to comfort him; and the letter to the Philippians is a highly personal and spontaneous response by Paul to the generosity and concern of his flock. He expresses joy at their continuing faith in Christ, warns them against the heretical teachings of the Judaizers, exhorts them to persist in their efforts to live the full Christian life and thanks them for the gift that they had sent him.

The "pastoral letters" were written after Paul's first Roman imprisonment. Titus and 1 Timothy were composed between 61 and 64 A.D., while 2 Timothy is a product of the period of Paul's second imprisonment in Rome (c. 64-67/8 A.D.). In these letters, Paul speaks of the nature and functions of the Christian ministry; and he appeals to Titus and Timothy, ministers of the gospel who were ordained by Paul himself, to work diligently for the maintenance of sound doctrine and good order in the churches of Christ.

The document known as the "Letter to the Hebrews" is in fact an anonymous treatise or sermon presenting a lengthy and sustained argument concerning the superiority of Christianity over Judaism. The intended readers of the letter seem to have been Jewish Christians who, as a result of persecution, were at the point of renouncing their faith and lapsing back into Judaism. In an effort to save his readers from apostasy (Heb 6:1-12) and to win them back to a firm commitment to Christianity, the author of Hebrews develops three major themes: (1) the superiority of Christ over the prophets of Judaism (1:1-3), over the angels (1:4-2:18) and over Moses and Joshua (3:1-4:13); (2) the superiority of Christ's high priesthood over the Levitical priesthood (4:14-7:28); and (3) the superiority of the new covenant in Christ over the old covenant of ancient Israel (8:1-10:18). Hebrews also contains a profound meditation on the life of faith (10:19-12:29) and a concluding exhortation in which Christians are warned not to be "led away by diverse and strange teachings" (13:1-15). The overall message of Hebrews is that the old covenant of ancient Israel has been fulfilled and transcended in the new covenant of Jesus Christ, and that, in Christ, God's work of salvation has been made both perfect and final.

Because of their complexity and profundity, it would require a book-length study to do justice to the specific content of each of Paul's letters.[3] In the remainder of this chapter, therefore, we will concentrate not upon a detailed exegesis of the Pauline corpus but rather upon the overall theological message of Paul's New Testament writings.

THE OVERALL MESSAGE OF ST. PAUL

The Divine Plan of Salvation

The gospel of Christ, according to St. Paul, is, in the first place, a revelation of the human condition and of the human need for salvation (see Rm 1:18-3:20); and, in the second place, it is a revelation of God the Father's plan for the salvation of mankind and the world (see Eph 1:3-14, 3:4-12; and Col 1:24-29). Paul's analysis of the human condition will be presented in the next section. Here, we must summarize briefly the apostle's overall conception of God's economy of redemption.

Sin has separated the human race from the full presence and life of God; but God's love for mankind is an enduring love, and God has graciously decided to redeem mankind from the clutches of sin and death, from bondage to the devil. God's will and purpose is to reconcile not only mankind but "all things" to himself through his Son, Jesus Christ, and through the power of the Holy Spirit. In Paul's view, the general pattern of "salvation history" may be defined in terms of the following stages: (1) the creation of the world and of the human race; (2) the fall of mankind from the grace of God; and (3) God's redemption of humanity and of the cosmos through the old covenant with ancient Israel and through the new covenant of Christ and the

Holy Spirit. God's new covenant with the human race is realized in Christ's earthly ministry; in the life of the Church, which is inspired by the Holy Spirit; and in the second coming of Christ, which will usher in the kingdom of God (see Rm 8; 1 Co 1-2, 15; 2 Co 3-5; Eph 1-6; 1 Th 4-5; 2 Th 1-2).

Paul speaks of the divine economy of salvation as a "mystery hidden for ages and generations but now made manifest to . . . [God's] saints" (Col 1:26). God the Father "has blessed us in Christ with every spiritual blessing in the heavenly places" and has chosen us in Christ "before the foundation of the world." We are "destined . . . in love" to be the sons of God "through Jesus Christ," through the saving grace which the Father has freely bestowed upon us in his beloved Son (Eph 1:3-6). From the beginning, it has been "the purpose of . . . [God's] will" to effect the redemption of the world from evil through the person and work of Jesus Christ. And those who have acknowledged Christ as Savior and Lord have been destined for glorification as children of God (Rm 8:14-17). The gospel is a revelation of "a secret and hidden wisdom of God, which God decreed before the ages for our glorification" (1 Co 2:7). "For those whom he foreknew he also predestined to be conformed to the image of his Son . . . And those whom he predestined he also called; and those whom he called he also justified; and those whom he justified he also glorified" (Rm 8:29-30).

God's predestinating will for Christians does not cancel out their spiritual freedom. From an Orthodox point of view, we are led to Christ by the Holy Spirit; but we remain free to accept or to reject the salvation offered to us by God in Christ. God has known from all eternity who would accept and who would reject the gospel, and he has ordained that the former shall enter into the divine sonship of Christ and that the latter shall be forever separated from the divine presence. God does not foreordain our spiritual choices, but rather the spiritual destiny which is contingent upon those choices. Throughout our lives in this world, we remain free to cooperate with or to resist the leading of the Holy Spirit.

Salvation, then, is the work of the Holy Trinity. But in Paul's "Christocentric" doctrine of redemption (soteriology),[4] the pivotal figure in the divine drama of salvation is Jesus Christ. We have redemption through the blood of Christ, and in Christ the meaning and goal of all creation are revealed. Christ is the consummation of "all things"; in him both heaven and earth have been united and reconciled with God (Eph 1:7-10). Christ, who is both true God and true man, is the one and only mediator between God and man (1 Tm 2:5-6), and through faith in him we may be liberated from "the law of sin and death" (Rm 8:2). This is the "mystery" of which Paul speaks, "the mystery of Christ, which was not made known to the sons of men in other generations as it has now been revealed to his holy apostles and prophets by the [Holy] Spirit" (Eph 3:4-5). In one of his letters to Timothy, Paul writes, "It is a great mystery we worship: Revelation made in human nature, justification won in the realm of the Spirit; a vision seen by angels, a mystery preached to the Gentiles; Christ in this world, accepted by faith; Christ, on high, taken up to Glory" (1 Tm 3:16).[5] Through the person and work of Christ, the eternal redemptive purpose of the Father has been realized, and the ministry of the Holy Spirit in and through the Church has been made possible.

The Human Condition

The Bible teaches that man was originally intended to live in communion with God (Gn 1-2). It was God's eternal and original purpose to associate mankind and the cosmos to himself in perfect harmony; and in that harmony, man was to receive and enjoy the fulness of the divine life. But instead of responding in love and obedience to his gracious Creator, man turned from God to himself; he yielded to the temptations of the devil and was thus enslaved to the forces of evil.[6] The Bible proclaims the *fact* of man's alienation from God as a result of sin, but gives no systematic explanation of the fall of man. We are told of the angelic rebellion against God which occurred prior to the creation of man (Rv 12:1-17; Is 14:5-15; Ezk 28:11-19), and of the satanic temptation of Adam and Eve (Gn 3). But Holy Scripture does not tell us precisely *why* angels and men, whose relationship with God was direct and uncorrupted by sin, should have chosen to set themselves in opposition to their Creator.

Like other biblical writers, Paul makes no attempt to explain the mystery of man's original rebellion against God. Instead, he presupposes the fall of man and concentrates his attention upon the postlapsarian condition of alienation into which the human race has fallen. Between the fall and the advent of Christ, man lived without access to the presence and life of God and was subjected to the powers of sin and death. According to Paul, "sin came into the world through . . . [Adam] and death through sin, and so death spread to all men because all men sinned" (Rm 5:12), for "the wages of sin are death" (Rm 6:23). These words of the apostle do not mean that all men have sinned *in* Adam, that we are all "born guilty" of Adam's sin. The Orthodox Church teaches that we have inherited the consequences of Adam's sin—a world pervaded by evil—but we have not inherited Adam's guilt. Living in a fallen world, we are continually tempted to sin; and we all succumb to that temptation and thus incur guilt in the sight of God. But that guilt is our own and not Adam's.

Many Orthodox theologians, building upon St. Paul's analysis of the relationship between sin and death, have argued that human mortality is itself a major cause of human sinfulness in the postlapsarian era.[7] Through the sin of Adam, the human race was excluded from "the tree of life," from immortality in God, and death became a universal and permanent structure of human existence. As a result of his inherited mortality—the curse of death—post-Adamic man has been enslaved by his passions and thus tends toward sin. Afflicted with anxiety concerning death and its accompanying effects—for example, bodily weakness, old age, disease—man tends to become self-centered and self-indulgent, to despair of God's goodness and wisdom and to place his ultimate concern in his own pleasure, safety and security rather than in God. Post-Adamic man is born into bondage— bondage to sin and bondage to death. And his subjection to the tyranny of death deepens his subjection to the tyranny of sin.[8]

Paul sometimes describes man's subjection to sin and death as a subjection to the "flesh" (Greek, *sarx*—Rm 8:3-11; Ga 5:16-24). The "flesh" is not simply identical with the body (Greek, *soma*). The human body, like the rest of the material creation, is essentially good (Gn 1:31). The "flesh," for Paul, represents those human inclinations that seek fulfilment in that which is contrary to the will and being of God. The "desires of the flesh" run counter to the "desires of the Spirit" (Ga 5:17). To "walk by the Spirit" is to lead a life of "love, joy, peace, patience, kindness, goodness, faithfulness, gentleness, self-control" (Ga 5:22-23). But to follow the way of the flesh is to immerse oneself in "fornication, impurity, licentiousness, idolatry, sorcery, enmity, strife, jealousy, anger, selfishness, dissension, party spirit, envy, drunkenness, carousing, and the like" (Ga 5:19-21). As a result of the fall, man was enslaved to his passions, appetites and lusts; his mind and will were set upon "the things of the flesh" rather than upon "the things of the Spirit" (Rm 8:5-6). "For the mind that is set on the flesh is hostile to God; it does not submit to God's law, indeed it cannot; and those who are in the flesh cannot please God" (Rm 8:7-8). To live "according to the flesh" rather than "according to the Spirit" is to be estranged from the "life and peace" of the Lord (Rm 8:6).

Another effect of the fall, Paul argues, is spiritual blindness, a corruption of the mind that deprives man of the knowledge of God. In his sinful failure to honor God as God, man "became futile" in his thinking, and his "senseless mind . . . [was] darkened" (Rm 1:21). Seeking wisdom outside of God (see Gn 3), and "claiming to be wise," man became a fool (Rm 1:22; see also 1 Co 1:18-2:16). "Let no one deceive himself. If any one among you thinks that he is wise in this age, let him become a fool that he may become wise. For the wisdom of this world is folly with God" (1 Co 3:18-19).

Spiritual ignorance, like mortality, is both a consequence and a cause of human sin. Without knowledge of God and his will, the human understanding is "darkened," and man is given over to "licentiousness" and to the practice of "every kind of uncleanness" (Eph 4:17-19). Having lost contact with "the glory of the immortal God" (Rm 1:23), the human mind is turned from light to darkness (Eph 5:8-14; Col 1:9-14). In Paul's view, much of the spiritual and moral impurity which pervades the world follows from the darkness and ignorance of the fallen human mind (Rm 1:24-32; Eph 4:17-19; Col 3:5-10; 1 Th 4:3-6; Tt 3:3). It is not that everyone commits every sin but that everyone fails in countless ways to live for God and to walk perfectly in the "paths of righteousness" (Ps 23:3). Insofar as our hearts are primarily oriented not toward God but toward that which is not God, we are guilty of the grave offense of idolatry and we become infected with the general sinfulness of the world.

The ancient Jews, and especially the Pharisees, were proud of the fact that God had chosen them to be the custodians of his divine law. They believed that they were saved through the law, for the law was a revelation of the will of God, a deliverance from the curse of spiritual blindness. Knowledge of God and his will, which had been lost as a result of the fall, was made once more available to mankind. In giving his law to Israel through Moses, the Lord made manifest his own holiness and the moral and religious standards by which man must live. But to be saved under the old covenant, man had to obey the divine law. And many Jews apparently believed that they were capable of living according to the requirements of the Mosaic code (Rm 2:17-20). In the writings of St. Paul, however, the idea that man can be saved through "works of the law" is repeatedly rejected (see Rm 2:17-8:2; Ga 3-5; Ph 3).

For Paul, the revelation of the divine law was an illumination of the human condition, of the human need for salvation. The law did not, in itself, bring salvation to the human race; on the contrary, it was a revelation of the vast distance that separates sinful man from the absolute moral and spiritual perfection of God. Anyone who contemplates seriously the rigorous standards of God's law will realize that he is incapable of living up to those standards (see Rm 2:21-23, 7:7-25). Man may even be provoked to sin by the law, for his sinful soul naturally rebels against the commandments and prohibitions issued by God (Rm 7:5, 8, 11). The law is therefore "a curse" for those who believe that the way of salvation is conformity to its requirements. For as Paul points out, the Mosaic code itself stipulates (in Dt 27:26) that everyone who does not abide by the law *in its entirety* is "cursed" (Ga 3:10). And on this basis, the apostle concludes "that no man is justified before God by the law" (Ga 3:11). The law demonstrated the extremely desperate situation into which man had fallen, yet it did not supply man with the moral and spiritual power needed to extricate himself from his plight. But the law was also a great blessing. It was, as the Jews believed, a revelation of the divine nature, a remedy for the spiritual ignor-

ance of post-Adamic man. And in showing the full reality of
man's moral and spiritual desolation—in revealing the human
need for salvation—the Mosaic law served to prepare the world
for the redemptive work of Jesus Christ (Ga 3:21-22).

To the Jews of his day, then, St. Paul proclaimed that although
the law was a source of enlightenment, it was not the key to
salvation (Rm 3:20). What the law reveals is that man, in his
fallen state, cannot live according to the will of God. All men—
Jews as well as Gentiles—are "under the power of sin" (Rm
3:10). Quoting Psalm 14:1-3, Paul declares, "None is righteous,
no, not one; no one understands, no one seeks for God. All have
turned aside, together they have gone wrong; no one does good,
not even one" (Rm 3:10-12). Both Jews and Gentiles are in
desperate need of the salvation offered in Christ, for "all have
sinned and [thus] fall short of the glory of God" (Rm 3:23).
Only through faith in Jesus Christ, and not through "works of
the law," can man be justified in the sight of God (Rm 3:21-30).
Through the perfect obedience of Christ—the Son of God incarnate—the requirements of the law have been met. Christians,
therefore, are not bound by the ritual and ceremonial laws of
Judaism, for purification now comes through Christ and through
the sacraments of his Church; and while the moral law revealed
in the Old Testament remains valid, it is only through faith in
Christ and through the power of the Holy Spirit that the struggle
to live righteously can contribute to our final deliverance from
evil.

Yet another dimension of man's fallenness is his subjection
to the tyranny of the devil and other demonic forces. Presupposing
the ancient Jewish tradition concerning Satan's original role as
the angelic guardian of the earth,[9] Paul speaks of the devil as
"the god of this world" (2 Co 4:4). After the primeval angelic
rebellion against the divine order, and as part of the mystery and
drama of God's plan of redemption, Satan was permitted to
continue his association with our world. Adam and Eve, making
bad use of the gift of freedom, responded to the enticements of
the devil and sought fulfilment in that which had been forbidden
by God (Gn 3:1-6), and thus brought the human race under "the
dominion of darkness" (Col 1:13), the jurisdiction of Satan.
Alienated from God, fallen man must follow "the course ['aeon,'

or angel] of this world, . . . the prince of the power of the air, the spirit that is now at work in the sons of disobedience [fallen angels as well as men]" (Eph 2:1-2). Because of "the wiles of the devil," the human race has been subjected to "the principalities and powers" and "the elemental spirits of the universe" which do the bidding of the Prince of Darkness (see Eph 6:11-12; Col 2:15, 20; Ga 4:1-3, 8-9). Having lost his relationship with God, man was brought into bondage "to beings that by nature are no gods" (Ga 4:8), to "all the forces in the universe opposed to God and man."[10] And, indeed, the other powers that govern the existence of postlapsarian man—sin, death, the "flesh," spiritual blindness—are the instruments through which the satanic tyranny over mankind is exercised (see Eph 2:1-3, 5:3-14).

In consequence of the fall, then, man lost his full spiritual freedom under God, was alienated from the presence and life of God and was enslaved by the devil. Under the tyranny of Satan, man is condemned to death, dominated by sin, driven by "the desires of the flesh" and bereft of moral and spiritual wisdom. So desperate is the human condition after the fall that the divine law itself, revealed by God to Israel, is experienced as a curse of conviction and condemnation—since no one can fulfil the requirements of the law. Estranged from the divine presence and from his own spiritual liberty, man lives in a condition of desolation, unable to actualize his original potentiality for participation in the life of God. Thus, man's deepest need is for liberation from his fallen state, for deliverance from his demonic captivity, for redemption.

The Person and Work of Jesus Christ

As indicated earlier, Paul's theory of redemption, or soteriology, is "Christocentric"—centered upon the person and work of Jesus Christ. Speaking out of the apostolic tradition of the early Church and in accord with the other authors of the New Testament, Paul proclaimed Jesus of Nazareth to be both the Messiah of Israel and the divine Son of God. Jesus was "the Christ," the anointed descendant and successor of King David, promised by God to Israel through the prophets of the Old Testament (Rm

1:1-3). He was also the incarnation of God the Son, the manifestation of the power, wisdom and glory of God in human form
(see Ph 2:6-11; Col 1:15-20, 2:9; 1 Co 1:24, 2:8). Thus, Paul
speaks repeatedly of Jesus as "Lord" (Greek, *kyrios*—see Ph
2:11; Rm 5:1, 10:9; 1 Co 12:3, 15:57; 2 Co 8:9), a title which
the Jews reserved exclusively for God. According to Paul, the
eternally preexistent Son of God became man in Jesus of Nazareth; he "emptied himself" (or "divested himself") of his divine
prerogatives and took "the form of a servant" (Ph 2:6-7). Paul
also speaks of God the Son as the source and sustenance of the
created order: ". . . In him all things were created, in heaven
and on earth, visible and invisible. . . . All things were created
through him and for him. He is before all things, and in him all
things hold together" (Col 1:16-17). This same divine Son was
"born of woman" (Ga 4:4), and his divine nature was made one
with human nature in the person of Jesus Christ. Christ is true
God—"for in him all the fulness of deity dwells bodily" (Col
2:9, 1:19); and he is also true man, the perfect image and likeness of the invisible God (Col 1:15; 2 Co 4:4). In and through
the saving work of Christ—and especially through his death and
resurrection—mankind and the cosmos have been saved from the
forces of evil.

Paul recognized that the apostolic proclamation of Jesus as
the divine-human Christ who has suffered and died for the sins
of the world was difficult for many to accept: "We preach Christ
crucified, a stumbling block to Jews and folly to Gentiles" (1
Co 1:23). From at least as early as the second century B.C.,
Judaism depicted the Messiah as a great man—a king anointed by
God—who would lead the nation of Israel to victory over her
enemies and prepare the world for the advent of the kingdom of
God. Thus, most Jews regarded the idea of a divine and yet
crucified Messiah as a scandal—indeed, blasphemy.[11] And the
Gentiles of Paul's time—especially the "sophisticated" Greeks and
Romans—regarded Christianity as nothing more than a particularly
superstitious and fanatical sect of Judaism, just another religious
cult propagating its own peculiar brand of "foolishness."[12] Believing that the "scandal" and "foolishness" of the Christian
faith was, in fact, the very wisdom of God (1 Co 1:18-2:5), Paul
saw it as his divinely ordained duty to bring the apostolic message

of salvation through Christ to both Jews and Gentiles (see Ac 9:15, 26:12-23; Rm 1:1-3:20, 9:1-11:36; Ga 2:7-8; Eph 3:7-8).

The New Testament teaches that the divine plan of salvation has been carried into effect by the Holy Trinity. The Father has purposed the redemption of the world from all eternity, and, in the fulness of time, he has sent the Son and the Holy Spirit into the world to make possible and to proclaim the good news of salvation from evil. While not ignoring the "economy of the Father" or the "economy of the Spirit," the New Testament concentrates its attention upon the "economy of the Son."[13] The mission of Jesus Christ, the Son of God incarnate, is presented as the key element in the redemptive plan of God. Even the ministry of the Holy Spirit in and through the Church is a product of the "economy of the Son," for the Church was able to receive the indwelling power and life of the Spirit only after Christ had ascended to the Father (see Jn 15:26-27, 16:5-11).

In proclaiming the apostolic message of salvation through Christ, theologians of the ancient Church emphasized some aspects of Christ's ministry more than others. The elements of the Lord's work most often selected for special consideration were his incarnation, his passion and death and his resurrection. When speaking of the resurrection, most ancient Christian writers—including St. John the Apostle and St. Paul—were also thinking of Christ's ascension and exaltation: they were three phases of a single divine act.[14] Through the incarnation of God the Son in Jesus Christ, human nature was united with the divine and thus transfigured and deified; through the passion and death of the perfectly righteous Christ, mankind can be absolved of sin and thus delivered from the dominion of death; and through the resurrection-ascension-exaltation of the Lord, the liberation of the human race from the curse of mortality was made manifest to all the world.[15]

St. Paul's account of the redemptive ministry of Christ is centered upon the saving effects of the passion, death and resurrection of the Lord. Paul presupposes the incarnation as the basis of Christ's saving work, for only he who is both true God and true man can save the world by dying and rising again. Through his passion, death and resurrection, Christ has effected the *expiation* (or remission) of man's sins, the *justification* of man in the

sight of God, the *redemption* of man from the forces of evil and
the *reconciliation* of God and man. To share in these effects of
Christ's work, of course, man must acknowledge Jesus as Savior
and Lord (Col 1:23). Fallen man needs reconciliation, or at-one-
ment, with God; and Paul's testimony is that Christ has made
such reconciliation possible. Through faith in Christ, the believer's
sins are washed away, his life is rededicated to the service of
God, he is constituted as righteous before God, he is liberated
from the demonic powers of sin and death and he is adopted as
a son of God (Ga 4:5).

To be reconciled with God, fallen man must *repent,* he must
give up his self-centeredness in favor of a God-centered life. But
in his bondage to the world, the flesh and the devil, man is incapable of true repentance, for repentance is the death of self-
centeredness, a complete surrender, submission and devotion to
God; and sinful man, having no direct experience of God's reality and life, is unwilling to undergo this self-abasement. To
repent in the true and full sense, man needs God's help (just as
he needs God's help in order to reason or to love). To help man
repent, God had to become man. In Christ (the God-man), man
surrenders, suffers, submits and dies *perfectly.* Christ pays the
"debt" which man, by himself, could never pay—the debt of
perfect love and obedience owed to God (Col 2:14). By identifying ourselves in faith with Christ in his passion and death, it is
possible for us to repent and, on that basis, to enter into union
with God through the resurrection, ascension and exaltation of
Christ.[16] "Redeemed, justified, reconciled, man is elevated from
the status of slave to that of son, and becomes 'an heir through
God' [Ga 4:7] of the promised salvation."[17]

The Ministry of the Holy Spirit and the Life of the Church

Paul's doctrine of the Holy Spirit (*pneumatology*) and his
doctrine of the Church (*ecclesiology*) are developed in conjunc-
tion with one another. For there is a close relationship between
"the economy of the Holy Spirit" and the ministry of the Church.
Paul's analysis of that relationship contains the following the-
matic elements: the Church and the work of salvation; the unity

of the Church; the mission of the Church; the Church and the process of sanctification; and the Church and the glorification of man.

The Church and the Work of Salvation. The salvation offered by God in Christ is made fully available to the human race through the ministry of the Church; and the ministry of the Church is possible only on the basis of the indwelling power of the Holy Spirit, who descended upon the apostolic community on the day of Pentecost. For Paul, the Church is the mystical body of Christ, filled with the Holy Spirit—God's sacrament of salvation to the world. To be delivered from the bondage of evil and to be raised into the presence and life of the triune God, we must be "made one" with Christ, we must be incorporated into Christ through the devotional, sacramental and moral life of the Church. Salvation must be appropriated by the individual through faith in and obedience to Christ as Savior and Lord. But Paul does not teach a "doctrine of solitary salvation." On the contrary, "to be 'in Christ' is, for St. Paul, to participate in the solidarity of all Christians with one another and with their Lord: it is to be a member of the Church which is the Body of Christ (1 Cor. 12:12), Christ Himself being the Head."[18]

The individual is led to faith in Christ by the Holy Spirit and, on the basis of his faith, he receives the Holy Spirit as an indwelling presence in his life (regeneration). He who hears and believes "the word of truth, the gospel of . . . salvation," is "sealed with the promised Holy Spirit" and enters into the life of Christ in his Church (Eph 1:13-14). Through the power of the Holy Spirit, the individual is to become a "new creation"—built into Christ through the life of the Church (edification), made holy through the performance of "good works" (sanctification) and, finally, united with the eternal and divine life of the Holy Trinity (glorification). Through the redemptive and reconciling work of Christ, and through the regenerating, edifying, sanctifying and glorifying ministry of the Holy Spirit, "all men can share in the glory of God and become participants in God's own holiness."[19]

The work of the Holy Spirit, then, is carried out within the body of Christ, the Church. The Church is God's holy temple, a dwelling-place for the Holy Spirit (Eph 2:19-22). Through the ministry of the Holy Spirit in the Church, "we receive adoption as sons of God," and we become co-heirs of Christ's inheritance as the Son of God. Thus, full participation, on the basis of faith, in the life of the Church is the path to salvation. Faith, in other words, must be an active response to the Lord, an "existential" engagement of one's total self in the life of Christ and in the power of the Holy Spirit. And this existential faith must therefore involve a full incorporation of the individual into the life of the Church. In Christ and his Church, man receives his full inheritance as a child of God; he is "raised up" with Christ and exalted into the very power and presence of God the Father (Eph 2:4-7).

The Unity of the Church. Paul proclaims the unity of all believers in the undivided body of Christ—in the one, holy, catholic and apostolic Church. And he exhorts the Christians of his day "to maintain the unity of the Spirit in the bond of peace" (Eph 4:3). "There is one body and one Spirit, just as you were called to the one hope that belongs to your call, one Lord, one faith, one baptism, one God and Father of us all, who is above all and through all and in all" (Eph 4:4-6). Before the creation of the Church on Pentecost, the entire Gentile world was "uncircumcised . . . alienated from the commonwealth of Israel . . . [estranged from] the covenants of God's promise" (Eph 2:11-12). But through Christ and his Church, both Jews and Gentiles have been incorporated into the Israel of God. All those who have faith in Christ have been constituted as "one new man," having access "in one Spirit to the Father" (Eph 2:13-18). Speaking to the Gentile Christians of the mid-first century, Paul declares, "So then you are no longer strangers and sojourners, but you are fellow citizens with the saints and members of the household of God" (Eph 2:19). In Christ and in his Church, all believers are united as sons of God through faith. "For as many of you as were baptized into Christ have put on Christ. There is neither Jew nor Greek, there is neither slave nor free, there is neither male nor female; for you are all one in Christ Jesus. And if you are Christ's, then you are Abraham's offspring, heirs according to promise" (Ga 3:26-29).

To give practical expression to the unity of the Church, to experience "the unity given by the Spirit," Christians must live "in the bond of peace." They must practice humility, gentleness, patience, forbearance and love. The unity of the Church cannot be experienced when Christians fail to "lead a life worthy of their calling." And such a life is possible only insofar as we are guided and led—edified and sanctified—by the Holy Spirit (see Eph 4:1-3).

In discussing the practical expression of the unity of the Church, Paul elaborates upon the work of the Holy Spirit in and through the body of Christ. The Spirit, as Christ's "gift" to the Church, is also the source of the Church's "gifts" (or *charisms*, special powers). Paul refers to a *general* dispensation of the Holy Spirit whereby all members of the Church are constituted as a holy priesthood ("the priesthood of all believers") as well as a *special* dispensation of the Holy Spirit which raises up an ordained spiritual leadership (Eph 4:7-12).[20] Through the general dispensation of the Holy Spirit (at Pentecost; see Ac 2), the Church as a whole has received "Christ's gift." Each member of the Church has received his own measure (or share) of grace by which he is enabled (or empowered) to live the Christian life. It is through this general ministry of the Holy Spirit, filling all members of the Church with "sanctifying grace," that Christ "fills all things with his presence" (Eph 4:10).[21] The spiritual leadership raised up through the special dispensation of the Holy Spirit (apostles, prophets, bishops, presbyters, deacons, teachers, evangelists) is "gifted," "called" and "ordained" by Christ and the Holy Spirit in order to equip the Church for the proper performance of her ministry to the world (Eph 4:11-12; see also Jn 20:21-23).

In his letters to Timothy and to Titus, Paul speaks at length of the role of ordained leaders in the life and mission of the Church. He states some of the personal and moral qualifications required of those who are called to be bishops, presbyters (or priests) and deacons (see 1 Tm 3:1-13; and Tt 1:5-9); and he emphasizes that those who are ordained through "the laying on of hands" receive "a spirit of power and love and self-control" which will enable them to carry out their ministries in the Church (2 Tm 1:6-14). The Christian minister will need both moral and doctrinal fortitude, grounded in God's promises, if he is to complete his mission on behalf of God in Christ (2 Tm 2:1-13).

The central task of the Christian leader is to practice and defend the faith of the Church. To practice the faith is to live according to godliness, placing one's hope in God alone (1 Tm 4:7-10). On the basis of a "sincere faith," the Christian leader must live righteously. He must have a "pure heart" and a "good conscience" (1 Tm 1:5). His conduct must be guided by the virtues of love, patience, gentleness and steadfastness (see 1 Tm 6:11; and 2 Tm 4:10). The Christian leader must also defend and hold on to the deposit of faith—the "sound doctrine"—which has been passed on to him from the apostles (see 1 Tm 1:10, 4:6, 6:14). The defense of the faith requires the faithful preservation of the apostolic tradition and the steadfast adherence to the teachings of Holy Scripture (2 Tm 3:14-17). The apostolic faith—"the word of truth"—must be "rightly handled" and "faithfully interpreted and dispensed" (2 Tm 2:15). The Christian leader (especially the bishop and the priest) is to dispense the rule of faith through the liturgical reading of scripture (1 Tm 4:13), and he must also preach the gospel in a convincing manner, rebuking and exhorting those who are not fully in accord with the true faith. This he must do with patience and yet also with a sense of urgency, both "in season and out of season," whether this activity is considered "appropriate" or not (2 Tm 4:2). In this way, the pastoral ministry will contribute to the sustenance of the spiritual and moral unity of the body of Christ.

The Mission of the Church. The task of the Church is to proclaim the mystery of God's plan of salvation through Christ to the world, and to make participation in the body of Christ available to all who sincerely seek it (see Eph 3:1-21; Col 1:24-29). The Church is God's sacrament of salvation, the visible means by which the saving grace of the Holy Trinity is made available to the human race. Through her preaching and teaching, through her works of mercy and charity and through her liturgical and sacramental ministry, the Church is to "make the word of God fully known" throughout the world (Col 1:25). God has commanded the Church to "warn every man and teach every man in wisdom," and to bring all believers to maturity in Christ (Col 1:28).

In addition to his definition of the general mission of the Church, Paul also speaks of the sacramental life of the body of Christ. Baptism, he argues, is an immersion in the death of Christ and a participation in the resurrection of Christ from the dead. "We were buried therefore with him by baptism into death, so that as Christ was raised from the dead by the glory of the Father, we too might walk in newness of life. For if we have been united with him in a death like his, we shall certainly be united with him in a resurrection like his" (Rm 6:3-11; see also Col 2:11-15). Through baptism, which is a "washing of regeneration and renewal in the Holy Spirit" (Tt 3:5),[22] we may "put off" our "old nature," which was dominated by the forces of evil, and "be renewed in the spirit of . . . [our] minds," putting on "the new nature, created after the likeness of God in true righteousness and holiness" (Eph 4:22-24).

Paul's teachings on the holy eucharist are contained in 1 Corinthians 10:16 and 11:17-34. The apostle recounts the institution of the eucharist by Christ at the last supper (11:23-25). He also states that to partake of the bread and wine of holy communion is to participate in the body and blood of the Lord (10:16). And he warns the Corinthian church that to partake of the consecrated bread and wine in an unrepentant spirit is to eat and drink condemnation upon oneself (11:27-29).

Paul's writings contain references to two other sacraments of the Church: matrimony and holy orders. In Eph 5:21-33, the marriage relationship between husband and wife is depicted as an iconic representation of the relationship between Christ (the bridegroom) and his Church (the bride of Christ) (see also Rv 19:1-10, 21:2, 9; and 2 Co 11:2). And in 1 Timothy 3:1-13, 2 Timothy 1:6-7 and Titus 1:5-9, Paul comments on the significance of the "gift of God" received through the rite of ordination. To be an ordained leader in the Church is to participate in the high priesthood of Christ himself (2 Tm 2:1; see also Heb 4:14-7:28).

The point of Paul's "sacramental theology" is that through responding to "the word of truth" propagated by the Church, and through participating in the sacramental acts of the Church, the individual can be incorporated into Christ himself and thus into the life of the Holy Trinity. The mission of the Church is accomplished through the preaching of the gospel to all nations and through the sacramental incorporation of all believers into the divine sonship of Christ.

The Church and the Process of Sanctification. To enter into the fulness of salvation made available in Christ, the individual must place his faith in Christ and struggle to live according to the will of God. By cooperating with the Holy Spirit, the Christian is enabled to do those "good works" which are "pleasing to God" (Eph 2:10, 5:10). The Christian, in other words, must *practice* his faith: he must participate in the devotional, liturgical and sacramental life of the Church (Rm 12:3-8; 1 Co 11-14; Eph 1:3-4:16; 1 Tm 2:1-7); and he must strive to live a morally upright life, after the example of Christ himself (Rm 12:1-15:3; 1 Co 6:9-20; Ga 5:13-6:10; Eph 4:17-6:9; Col 3:5-4:6). It is through the practical expression of his faith—through good works —that the Christian is "sanctified" (or "made holy") through the grace of the Holy Spirit. And through the process of sanctification, the Christian is prepared for his final "glorification," when he will enter into the divine sonship of Christ and become a participant in the eternal life of God (1 Th 4:3; 2 Th 2:13-14; Rm 15:16; 1 Co 6:11). Thus, sanctification is a progressive and life-long process of moral and spiritual growth "by which the believer dies more and more to self and sin and lives more and more to Christ and righteousness."[23]

Paul's teaching on the relationship between "faith and works" in the process of sanctification is complex and has thus often been misinterpreted. On the one hand, Paul holds "that a man is not justified by works of the law but through faith in Jesus Christ" (Ga 2:16; see also Rm 3:20-4:25). But on the other hand, Paul repeatedly exhorts his Christian readers to "work out your own salvation with fear and trembling" (Ph 2:12), to struggle toward holiness and righteousness under the lordship of Christ and through the power and guidance of the Holy Spirit (see Rm 12:9-21; 1 Co 6:9-11; Ga 6:7-10; Eph 4:17-6:9; Col 3:5-17).

There is no contradiction between these two dimensions of the Pauline doctrine of sanctification. In arguing that we are justified by faith and not by "works of the law," the apostle was seeking to repudiate the Judaizers, who, as we have seen, maintained that the Christian must live according to the Mosaic law as interpreted by the Scribes and Pharisees. According to Paul, the law was fulfilled and transcended in Christ (Rm 10:10), and through the perfect righteousness of the Lord Christians have been freed from the bondage of Jewish legalism (Rm 7:1-6; Ga 2-5; Col 2:20-23). But in his controversies with the Judaizers, Paul never intended to deny that the Christian must struggle to live a life of "true righteousness and holiness" before God (Eph 4:24). The Christian is not "without law toward God" (1 Co 9:21). Although he has been liberated from the minute rules and regulations of the Jewish law, the Christian has come under a new law—"the law of the Spirit of life in Christ Jesus" (Rm 8:2; see also 1 Co 9:21)—revealed in the teachings of Christ and in the life of his Spirit-filled Church. The Christian is called not merely to *believe in* Christ but to *live in* Christ; his faith, to be authentic, must be expressed in those good works which are willed by God (Eph 2:8-10). No one can achieve holiness and righteousness entirely through his own efforts. It is only by the grace of God and through faith in Christ that man can receive the gift of the Holy Spirit and so begin the difficult process of sanctification, a process in which "faith and works" are indivisibly conjoined. The Christian life is a life of "faith working through love" (Ga 5:6).

Paul's teachings on the process of sanctification have played a significant role in the development of Orthodox theology, especially with reference to the doctrine of the deification of man.[24] Man responds to the gospel as preached by the Church through the prompting and guidance of the Holy Spirit. But prior to full conversion, the operation of the Holy Spirit upon the individual is external and not yet "infused." Only on the basis of an explicit faith which leads to active membership in the Church of Christ does the believer receive the Holy Spirit as an indwelling presence in his life. It is in this sense that "the Word took flesh that we might receive the Holy Spirit."[25] Through the economy of the Holy Spirit, our desire to conform to God's will becomes an *inward* power—the divine will "is no longer external to ourselves" but is present "within our very person" through the ministry of the Holy Spirit. This indwelling (or "infused") presence of the Holy Spirit is the foundation of the process of sanctification.[26]

Through the process of sanctification, the "corruptible and depraved nature" of man is transformed and adapted to eternal life.[27] This transformation of the believer is not automatic, not coerced: he must cooperate willingly with the Spirit in order to be "made holy." There is no contradiction between God's grace and man's liberty. In Christ, the incarnation of God the Son, the will of God and the will of man are united and thus collaborative. Thus, grace and free will are, in the life of one who is in Christ, synergically coordinated; the divine will and the human will cooperate, God's sovereignty and human liberty are united. This "synergy," this free cooperation with God, is the metaphysical foundation and presupposition of the performance of good works. Thus, the very distinction between faith and works, based upon the false dichotomy of grace and liberty, is meaningless.[28]

Through the "infused grace" of the Holy Spirit, the Christian is empowered to live the life of faith, hope and love (1 Co 13). In order to be sanctified, the Christian must cooperate with the Holy Spirit. Such cooperation (or synergy) is possible, as we have seen, only insofar as the believer is built *into* Christ by faith and by membership in the Church; for through his incorporation into Christ, the believer is able to share in Christ's human nature, a human nature which cooperated freely and perfectly with the will of God the Father. By this means, the Christian is himself enabled to cooperate freely and perfectly with the will of God as present in the indwelling grace of the Holy Spirit. Insofar as he *does* cooperate with the grace of the Holy Spirit, the Christian is sanctified, that is, he "grows in grace" through good works based upon his faith in Christ. And by this process of moral and spiritual growth, the Christian enters into an ever-deepening communion with God. In sacramental terms, we might say that, through the works of sanctification, the Christian *actualizes* a relationship with God which is *potential* in the mysteries of baptism and chrismation (the works of *regeneration*). Through the works of sanctification, the fact of the believer's union with God in Christ is *realized* and experienced. Thus, God became one with man in the incarnation of Christ; and man can become one with

God through the sanctifying work of the Holy Spirit. This process of sanctification enables the Christian to partake of Christ's transfiguration, resurrection, ascension and exaltation.[29]

When one systematically rejects the guidance of the Holy Spirit, one cannot meaningfully claim to be, or be characterized as, a believer in Christ. Insofar as one truly believes in Christ, one *cannot* fail in the process of sanctification, in the sense that one who believes in Christ *must* and *will* struggle toward holiness and righteousness. To engage in such a struggle against the devil, against the world, and even against oneself, *is* to cooperate with the Holy Spirit in the work of sanctification; and such cooperation, showing itself in good works, is an expression and "outworking" of one's faith in Christ. To accept and to cooperate with the grace of the Holy Spirit is, in fact, an integral and therefore necessary dimension of the Christian faith. "Faith without works" is a meaningless notion; and thus, St. James tells us that "faith without works is dead" (Jm 2:26), not just figuratively but literally dead! Where there are no good works, there is simply no faith!

Contrary to Martin Luther and his followers, then, mankind is not justified in the sight of God "by faith alone."[30] We are saved by a faith which issues in good works. Good works and virtues are the "symptoms, the outer manifestations of the Christian life."[31]

Following the teaching of St. Paul, the Orthodox Church proclaims that we must cooperate with the Holy Spirit by struggling toward holiness. On the basis of our free and willing response to his guidance, the Holy Spirit will bring us to victory over sin and death through the process of sanctification and will elevate us into the life of the Holy Trinity. Thus, while we do not "merit" our salvation through good works, we must, nonetheless, *earn* it by responding with our whole heart, soul and mind to the "second chance" which God has given us in the "economy of the Son" and the "economy of the Holy Spirit."

The Church and the Glorification of Man. The ultimate goal of the Holy Spirit's edification and sanctification of the Church is the realization, by all members of the body of Christ, of "the unity inherent in our faith and our knowledge of the Son of

God." Paul defines this unity of the faith as the unity of "mature manhood, measured by nothing less than the full stature of Christ" (Eph 4:13).[32] In and through the ministry of the Holy Spirit, believers in Christ are to realize their "common unity through faith in the Son of God."[33] Our task, according to Paul, is to cease being unsteady, confused and impressionable children —immature in our faith, tossed about by the storms of life, misled by heretical "winds of doctrine"—and to "grow up," through the profession and maintenance of the truth and through the practice of love, into the "perfect manhood" of Christ himself (Eph 4:13-15).[34] We are called to acquire "the full measure of perfection found in Christ,"[35] and we are empowered to do so by Christ's gift of the Holy Spirit (Eph 4:7-10). We are to "grow up into Christ" in and through the Church—the body of Christ—which depends upon Christ as "the source which supplies it," and which grows toward Christ, who is its head (Eph 4:15-16).[36] Thus, Christ is both the source and the goal of the Church's spiritual growth.

The end of the process of sanctification, then, is the glorification (or deification) of man in Christ. Through our faith, "we have peace with God through our Lord Jesus Christ . . . [for in him] we have obtained access to this grace in which we stand, and we rejoice in our hope of sharing the glory of God" (Rm 5:1-2). Through the process of sanctification, "we all, with unveiled face, beholding the glory of the Lord, are being changed into his likeness from one degree of glory to another; for this comes from the Lord who is the Spirit" (2 Co 3:17-18; see also 2 Co 4:6). In the power of the Holy Spirit, we may be "raised with Christ" to the "right hand of God." For the true Christian is dead to the world, the flesh and the devil; and his life is "hid with Christ in God." "When Christ who is our life appears [at his second coming], then . . . [we] also will appear with him in glory" (Col 3:1-4).

Through the Church, believers are one in faith and one with Christ. Christ, through the Holy Spirit, has created special ministries within the Church in order to train all believers for the works of service that make for the edification (or building up) of the body of Christ. The aim of this process of training and edification is the achievement, by the Church as a whole (that is, as a *body*), of a unified faith based upon a unified "knowledge of the Son of God." When this unity of faith has been attained, then every member of the Church will have "grown up" to the "complete manhood" of Christ, each "attaining the full measure of perfection found in Christ." It follows, therefore, that attainment of full growth in Christ cannot take place outside of the Church. It also follows that the unity of believers in and through the Church is subordinate to and instrumental in the attainment of a still higher unity—the unity of the Church with Christ himself, with the "perfect manhood" found in Christ. We must be built into the Church in order to be built into Christ. And being built into Christ, we enter into full union with the eternal and divine life of the Holy Trinity, into communion with God. Through the life of the Holy Spirit in the Church, the deification of the believer, which began with the incarnation of the divine Word, is carried through to completion.[37]

The Second Coming of Christ and the General Resurrection of the Dead

The apostolic message of salvation through Christ is fundamentally "eschatological," pointing toward the "last things" which will bring the redemptive plan of God to completion. The center of biblical eschatology is the coming of the kingdom of God. The prophets of the Old Testament foretold that, "in the last days," God would send his Messiah to prepare Israel and the world for the great day of judgment which would usher in the heavenly kingdom.[38] The authors of the New Testament depict Jesus of Nazareth as the fulfilment of Israel's messianic hopes. Through the first advent of Christ—through his life, death, resurrection and ascension—the kingdom of God has been inaugurated; and during the "last days" of world history—the Church age— the Spirit of God has been "poured out" upon the followers of Christ (see Jl 2:28-32; Ezk 36:24-28; and Ac 2) in order to make them ready for the consummation of the divine economy. With his second advent, Christ will bring "all things" to fruition. The second coming of the Lord will be followed by the general resurrection of the dead, the last judgment and the final establishment of the kingdom of God.

Like the other writings of the New Testament, the letters of St. Paul are pervaded with the eschatological spirit of the early apostolic community. Paul characterizes the era between the ascension and the second coming of Christ as a time of tension and conflict for the Church, a time during which the people of God are locked in spiritual combat with the devil and his servants (see Rm 12:12; 2 Co 4:4, 11:14, 12:7; Ga 1:4; Eph 2:2-3, 6:11-12). Although the Church has been liberated from the domination of evil, her spiritual warfare with the powers of darkness (Eph 6:10-20) must continue until "the day of our Lord Jesus Christ" (1 Co 1:8).

Toward the end of the Church age, Satan will mount an all-out attack against the disciples of Christ. A "man of sin [or lawlessness]" will emerge and will be empowered by the devil to perform "signs and wonders" (2 Th 2:3, 9). This "antichrist" (see 1 Jn 2:18, 22) will become the ruler of the world and proclaim himself to be God (2 Th 2:4, 9). Through the "wicked deceptions" of this satanic world leader—this "son of perdition" —many (both within and without the Church) will be deluded, believing what is false and taking "pleasure in unrighteousness" (2 Th 2:10-11). Those who are so deceived, refusing "to love the truth and so be saved," will be separated from God and condemned (2 Th 2:10-11). Paul also implies that those who remain faithful to Christ during that time will suffer intense persecution and tribulation (see Rm 8:35; and Mt 24:15-28).

The second advent of Christ will bring the reign of evil on earth to an end. Paul speaks of "the day of the Lord" as a sudden "arrival" (Greek, *parousia*), an "unveiling," "disclosure" or "revelation" (Greek, *apokalypsis*) and an "epiphany" or "appearance" (Greek, *epiphaneia*—see 1 Th 3:13; 2 Th 1:7; 1 Tm 6:14). "The day of the Lord will come like a thief in the night," suddenly and unexpectedly, and the antichrist and all who follow him will be utterly destroyed (1 Th 5:2; 2 Th 2:8; see also 2 Th 1:7-10). Because of the suddenness and unpredictability of "that day," Paul exhorts his Christian readers to keep the faith and to be vigilant at all times in order that they might be ready when the Lord returns (see 1 Th 5:1-11).

The second coming of Christ will also bring with it the general resurrection of the dead. "For the Lord himself will descend from heaven with a cry of command, with the archangel's call, and with the sound of the trumpet of God. And the dead in Christ will rise first; then we who are alive, who are left, shall be caught up together with him in the clouds to meet the Lord in the air; and so we shall always be with the Lord" (1 Th 4:16-17). Although he does not say so explicitly, Paul clearly assumes that all the dead, and not only "the dead in Christ," will rise at Christ's second advent; for he refers frequently to the last judgment (see Rm 2:1-16, 14:10-12; 1 Co 4:5; 2 Co 5:10; Ga 6:7-10; 2 Th 1:9; 2 Tm 4:8). At the last judgment, those who have been faithful to Christ will enter into glory (Col 3:1-3); and those who have been faithless (either through apostasy or outright rejection of the gospel) will suffer eternal separation from the presence and glory of God (Rm 2:8; 2 Th 1:8-9).[39]

Paul's most extended discussion of the resurrection of the dead appears in 1 Corinthians 15.[40] In this passage, the apostle does not speak of the resurrection of unbelievers, but instead concentrates his attention upon the resurrection of the redeemed. The foundation of the Christian belief in the general resurrection is the resurrection of Christ himself. The testimony of the apostolic Church is "that Christ died for our sins in accordance with the scriptures, that he was buried, [and] that he was raised on the third day in accordance with the scriptures" (1 Co 15:3-4). In quoting this early credal formula, Paul also refers to several post-resurrection appearances of the Lord to his apostles and disciples, including Paul's own encounter with the risen Christ on the road to Damascus (1 Co 15:5-11).

Through the resurrection of Christ, mankind as a whole has been liberated from the grave. Paul argues that "if Christ has not been raised then our preaching is in vain and your faith is in vain" (1 Co 15:14). For without Christ's victory over the powers of sin and death, a victory certified by his resurrection, the human race would remain alienated from the love and life of God, it would remain under the bondage of sin and death (1 Co 15:17-19). If our only hope in Christ is for peace and prosperity in our natural lives, then "we are of all men most to be pitied"; for the good things of this life are always subverted by

evil, and our natural lives are continually haunted by the prospect
of death and its accompanying symptoms (bodily weakness, disease, old age, etc.—see 1 Co 15:18-19). For Paul, the resurrection
of the Lord is the center of the Christian faith and the necessary
foundation of our hope for ultimate deliverance from evil. If
that faith and hope are without substance, then we ought to
devote our lives to the pleasures of the moment, "for tomorrow
we die" (1 Co 15:32).

Paul goes on to discuss the relationship between the resurrection of Christ, the general resurrection of the dead and the coming of the kingdom of God. Through the sin of Adam, mortality
became a permanent condition of human existence; but in Christ,
the human race has been delivered from the curse of mortality.
"For as in Adam all die, so also in Christ shall all be made alive"
(1 Co 15:20-22; see also Rm 5:12-21). For those who have
believed in Christ and who have been incorporated into his
Church, the general resurrection will bring the glory of eternal
life in the kingdom of God. At the second coming of the Lord,
"those who belong to Christ" will be raised with him into the
power and presence of God the Father (1 Co 15:23-28). Following the last judgment, the kingdom of God will be established as
an eternal dwelling place for God's people. God and his creation
will be finally and totally reunited (1 Co 15:24-28).

Paul also discusses the nature of the resurrected body. At the
general resurrection, the bodies of the dead in Christ will be
transformed. The natural body is to the resurrected body as the
seed is to the plant: "There is continuity between the seed and
the plant, but no resemblance."[41] "What is sown is perishable,
what is raised is imperishable." The natural body is "sown in
dishonor," as a sign of man's alienation from God, but it is
"raised in glory"; "it is sown in weakness, [but] it is raised in
power"; "it is sown a physical body, [but] it is raised a spiritual
body" (1 Co 15:36-37, 42-44). In Christ, we are delivered from
the mortality which we inherited from Adam; we are raised into
the presence of God, to live on a plane of existence that is
radically different from our present state. "Just as we have borne
the image of . . . [Adam], we shall also bear the image of . . .
[Christ]" (1 Co 15:45-49). In Christ, our humanity has been

transfigured and deified, and our bodies have been reconstituted
and infused with the Spirit of God.

At the second coming of Christ, then, the dead will be raised,
and the believers will be translated to a new level of being.

> Lo! I tell you a mystery. We shall not all sleep, but we
> shall all be changed, in a moment, in the twinkling of an
> eye, at the last trumpet. For the trumpet will sound, and
> the dead will be raised imperishable, and we shall be
> changed. For this perishable nature must put on the
> imperishable, and this mortal nature must put on immortal-
> ity. When the perishable puts on the imperishable, and
> the mortal puts on immortality, then shall come to pass
> the saying that is written: "Death is swallowed up in vic-
> tory." "O death, where is thy victory? O death, where is
> thy sting?" (1 Co 15:51-55)

Through the victory of Christ, all believers have been liberated
from the condemnation of sin and death (1 Co 15:56-58). And
thus, in his letter to the Romans, Paul writes: "I consider that the
sufferings of this present time are not worth comparing with the
glory that is to be revealed to us" (Rm 8:18). When the Church
is raised into the divine sonship of Christ at the second coming,
the entire creation, which "has been groaning in travail," will be
liberated from its subjection to "futility" and its "bondage to
decay." The cosmos itself will be transfigured on "the day of
Jesus Christ" (Rm 8:19-25). From that day forward, the faithful
in Christ will live forever in God, and "neither death, nor life,
nor angels, nor principalities, nor things present, nor things to
come, nor powers, nor height, nor depth, nor anything else in
all creation, will be able to separate us from the love of God in
Christ Jesus our Lord" (Rm 8:38-39).

In this chapter, we have surveyed the major themes in the
New Testament letters of St. Paul. Paul tells us of the divine
plan for the salvation of mankind and the world, a plan put into
effect by the three persons of the Holy Trinity. Man is in radical need
of salvation, for in his fallen state, he is in bondage to the powers of sin and death, to the darkness of spiritual ignorance and to

the demonic tyranny of the devil. Through the incarnation of God the Son in Jesus Christ, and through the ministry of Christ, man is offered redemption from the forces of evil, forgiveness of sins and reconciliation with God. And through the work of the Holy Spirit in and through the Church—the body of Christ—man may receive the gifts of edification, sanctification and glorification. By living a life in Christ, in the Church and in the power of the Holy Spirit, man may rise from the dead on the last day and be transformed into the perfect image and likeness of God.

CHAPTER 8

The Testimony of the "Catholic Epistles"

Seven of the twenty-one letters contained in the New Testament are known as the "catholic epistles": the letter of St. James; the first and second letters of St. Peter; the first, second and third letters of St. John; and the letter of St. Jude. These epistles were originally grouped together (probably during the second century A.D.) primarily because of their non-Pauline authorship.[1] They became known as the "catholic epistles" during the third and fourth centuries. The term "catholic" (Greek, *katholikos*, "universal") was apparently used to designate the "universal" (or general) nature of these letters, that is, the fact that they were intended for the Church at large and not for particular churches or individuals. The appellation, however, does not fit the second and third letters of St. John: 2 John was directed to an unnamed local church (probably in Asia Minor), and 3 John is a personal letter from the author to "Gaius." These two epistles were no doubt included in the "catholic" collection because of their Johannine origin. The catholic epistles were written during the last three or four decades of the first century A.D.

The catholic epistles are centrally concerned with the problems stemming from the dispersion of the Church throughout the world during the period between the ascension and the second coming of Christ. The relationship between the Church and "the world" has always been a source of difficulty for the followers of Christ, for it is not easy to be *in* and yet not *of* the world. There is, in fact, a certain ambivalence in the Christian attitude toward the world.

On the one hand, the world is God's world, created by
God and loved by God, currently alienated from God, it
is true, but destined to be redeemed and reconciled to God.
On the other hand, the world is dominated by a spirit
[the devil] totally opposed to God, organized in such a
way as to exclude God, drawn towards unworthy goals of
material status and self-interest, quite different from the
goals towards which the Christian way leads. . . . The
Christian is sent into the godless world to reclaim it for
its rightful Lord, but while it remains the "godless world"
it is an uncongenial environment for the Christian: he cannot feel at home there . . . [because his] true homeland
[is] elsewhere.[2]

In this sense, the Church is a "stranger and exile on the earth"
(Heb 11:13), and Christians, while they are in the world, must
live as "aliens and exiles" (1 Pt 2:11).

Like other human beings, the Christian is tempted by the
"passions of the flesh" (1 Pt 2:11), and may well be attracted to
the ways of the fallen world. The devil is continually seeking to
entice us into worldliness, into sin, into a life of self-centered
gratification. And if we refuse to follow the path of worldliness,
the devil works to turn the world against us, and the Church
must then face persecution. The catholic epistles warn their
readers of the spiritual dangers of "worldly temptation" *and* of
the likelihood of persecution when worldliness is effectively
resisted. Christians are to work in the world for the salvation of
mankind, but they must beware of the infection of worldly corruption, and they must be always ready and willing to suffer on
behalf of the gospel of Christ. They must not allow the world—
either through temptation or through persecution—to subvert and
defeat the divinely ordained purposes of the Church.

One aspect of the problem of worldliness that was particularly
disturbing to the authors of the New Testament was the rise of
heresy within the Christian community itself. Heresy—the enter-
taining, acceptance and propagation of doctrines that are inconsistent with the apostolic tradition—is a sign of the "worldly
invasion" of the Church. During the first century, there were
three heretical movements within the Church of grave concern

to the apostles and their disciples. First, there was a Jewish Christian legalism (taught by the "Judaizers") which claimed that salvation depended upon adherence to every jot of the Mosaic code, that salvation came through "works of the law." Much of the preaching and writing of St. Paul was directed against the heresy of the Judaizers.[3] Second, there was a heresy according to which salvation was a product of true belief alone; there was no need to worry about "good works." From the standpoint of this Jewish Christian "intellectualism," orthodoxy of belief was all that mattered, and the practical conduct of life was of no salvific importance.[4] The letter of St. James was written mainly in order to counteract this intellectualist heresy. The third and perhaps most dangerous heresy of the first century was Christian gnosticism. Like apostolic Christianity, gnosticism was opposed to worldliness. But unlike apostolic Christianity, gnosticism was based upon the belief that the created order was originally and inherently evil, created by the devil rather than by God and utterly contrary to the life of the spirit. The gnostics, as we have seen above,[5] taught a radical spirit-matter dualism in which matter was the principle of evil, and they accordingly denied that Christ had "become flesh" and that God intended to redeem the entire material universe. An interesting aspect of gnostic teaching was the view that because matter has nothing to do with spirit, sexual licentiousness and other forms of physical sin, if engaged in with the proper "mental attitude," could actually contribute to man's liberation from the material world! The letters of St. Peter, St. John and St. Jude were all aimed at refuting the doctrinal and moral errors of gnosticism.

In seeking to uphold the apostolic tradition of Christian theory and practice, the catholic epistles insist upon the need for "godliness" and upon the necessity of avoiding "worldliness"; and they define godliness in terms of both knowledge of the truth (faith) *and* moral righteousness (good works).

The Letter of James

The first of the catholic epistles was written by "James, a servant of God and of the Lord Jesus Christ," to Jewish Christian

communities "in the Dispersion" (that is, throughout the world—
1:1). Tradition tells us that the author of this letter was St.
James of Jerusalem, "James the Just," a "brother" (that is, relative) of the Lord and first bishop of the church in Jerusalem.
His letter is a "parenesis," an "exhortation and teaching of wisdom in a popular style."[6] This parenesis, which was written c. 60
A.D., contains the author's views concerning true religion, true
wisdom and true Christian living; and it was directed primarily
against the heretical teachings of the Jewish Christian intellectualists mentioned above.

For James, Christianity is the one true faith. But in opposition
to those who would deny the importance of good works to the
Christian faith, James argues that an authentic faith in Christ
will express itself in an active and practical moral life. "Be doers
of the word, and not hearers only" (1:22), for "faith by itself,
if it has no works, is dead" (2:17). An authentic Christian faith
must be active and must "complete itself" in righteous moral
works (2:22). Just as "the body apart from the spirit is dead, so
faith apart from works is dead" (2:26).

In line with his view of the nature of true religion—of the
relationship between faith and works—James gives a number of
examples to illustrate how moral works can express and complete
the Christian's faith. "Religion that is pure and undefiled before
God and the Father is this: to visit orphans and widows in their
affliction, and to keep oneself unstained from the world" (1:27).
The Christian, that is, is to avoid worldliness and to concern himself actively with the affliction of others. According to "the royal
law" of love, the Church is to "show no partiality" to the rich
at the expense of the poor. If anything, the poor are to be pre-
ferred over the rich, for, in James' view, the rich are most often
oppressors and exploiters! (2:1-13, 5:1-6) Also, the Christian
must struggle to attain self-control. But this is not easy; for man
has a tendency to be "lured and enticed by his own desire," and
human desire (or lust) "gives birth to sin, and sin . . . brings
forth death" (1:14-15). This tendency toward lust, sin and
death must be (and therefore *can* be) resisted, no matter how
difficult such resistance may be. James illustrates the difficulties
of attaining self-control by commenting on the problem of con-
trolling the tongue (see 3:1-12). He issues a series of warnings

concerning the evil of slander (4:11-12), the dangers of false confidence with reference to one's status in this world and the next (4:13-17) and the temptations of wealth (5:1-6). He also exhorts his readers to be patient concerning the second advent of the Lord (5:7-11) and to avoid the making of sworn oaths (5:12).

James also discusses the nature of true wisdom. He contrasts the wisdom of the world with the wisdom of God.

> Who is wise and understanding among you? By his good life let him show his works in the meekness of wisdom. But if you have bitter jealousy and selfish ambition in your hearts, do not boast and be false to the truth. This wisdom is not such as comes down from above, but is earthly, unspiritual, devilish. . . . But the wisdom from above is first pure, then peaceable, gentle, open to reason, full of mercy and good fruits, without uncertainty or insincerity. (3:13-18)

Like much of the wisdom literature of the Old Testament, the letter of James depicts wisdom as a practical understanding of the will of God, an understanding which enables a man to live at peace with the Lord and with his fellow man.

The predominantly ethical character of James' conception of wisdom is manifest in his view of the relationship between faith and works. To be wise is to seek friendship with God (on the basis of faith and obedience) rather than "friendship with the world." Worldliness, especially in the form of immoral conduct ("bad works"), leads one into demonic bondage (the bondage of sin and death) and makes one "an enemy of God" (4:1-10). "Submit yourselves therefore to God. Resist the Devil and he will flee from you. Draw near to God and he will draw near to you. Cleanse your hands, you sinners, and purify your hearts, you men of double mind" (4:7-8). A life guided by "the wisdom from above" is a life in Christ, a life in which one's faith in the Lord is enacted in those works that make for righteousness.[7]

The First Letter of Peter

First Peter was written from Rome c. 60-68 A.D. to certain
Christian communities in Asia Minor composed mainly of converts from paganism (1:1-2). Many scholars believe that the
letter was dictated by the apostle Peter to his amanuensis, Silvanus
(or Silas).[8] Peter exhorts those who have been "chosen and
destined by God the Father and sanctified by the Spirit for obedience to Jesus Christ and for sprinkling with his blood" (1:2) to
maintain their hope in Christ, to practice holiness within the life
of the Church and to live lives of moral probity. His two major
themes in this letter are the meaning of Christian baptism and
the problem of persecution.

The Meaning of Baptism. First Peter 1:3-4:11 is a baptismal
address to newly converted and baptized Christians concerning
the meaning of their conversion from paganism to Christianity.
To these "newborn babes," Peter declares that to be baptized
is to be "born anew to a living hope through the resurrection of
Jesus Christ from the dead, and to an inheritance which is imperishable, undefiled, and unfading, kept in heaven for you, who
by God's power are guarded through faith for a salvation ready
to be revealed in the last time" (1:3-5). Although the genuine-
ness of one's faith must be "tested by fire"—that is, through trials
and suffering—those who prevail in the struggle against the powers of darkness will obtain salvation of their souls (1:6-9).

True spiritual rebirth, Peter continues, must express itself in
holiness. An authentic faith must issue in good works.

> As obedient children, do not be conformed to the passions
> of your former ignorance, but as he who called you is holy,
> be holy yourselves in all your conduct. . . . And if you
> invoke as Father him who judges each one impartially
> according to his deeds, conduct yourselves with fear
> throughout the time of your exile [in the fallen world].
> You know that you were ransomed from the futile ways
> inherited from your fathers, not with perishable things
> such as silver and gold, but with the precious blood of

> Christ, like that of a lamb without blemish or spot. . . .
> Having purified your souls by your obedience to the truth
> for a sincere love of the brethren, love one another earn-
> estly from the heart. . . . So put away all malice and all
> guile and insincerity and envy and all slander. (1:13-2:3)

We are "born anew" in Christ in order that we might live according to the will of God.

Through baptism and spiritual rebirth, the believer becomes
a part of Christ and his Church, a "living stone" in God's "spiritual house." Peter describes the Church as "a chosen race, a royal
priesthood, a holy nation, God's own people"—the new Israel—
whose task it is to "declare the wonderful deeds of him who
called you out of darkness into his marvelous light" (2:4-10).

Since the new Christian must learn to grow in holiness in and
through the Church, Peter issues a number of moral admonitions
on the nature of righteous living. He exhorts his readers to "maintain good conduct among the Gentiles" (2:11-12) and to submit
to established secular powers and institutions (2:13-20). He
comments on the proper relations between husbands and wives
(3:1-7). And, finally, he calls all Christians to a life of moral
seriousness: "Finally, all of you, have unity of spirit, sympathy,
love of the brethren, a tender heart and a humble mind. Do not
return evil for evil or reviling for reviling; but on the contrary
bless, for to this you have been called, that you may obtain a
blessing. . . . For the eyes of the Lord are upon the righteous,
and his ears are open to their prayer. But the face of the Lord
is against those that do evil" (3:8-9, 12).

The Meaning of Persecution. The conclusion to Peter's baptismal address (see 3:13-4:11) touches upon the second major
theme of his letter: the problem of persecution and of suffering
in general. Baptism, he argues, is a participation in the suffering,
death, burial and resurrection of Jesus Christ (3:13-22; see also
2:21-25). It is also a preparation for the second coming of Christ,
an opportunity to "make oneself ready" for "the end of all things"
which is "at hand" (see 4:1-11). The suffering of the Church as
a result of persecution by the world is a sign of God's coming
judgment upon the powers of evil. Thus, Peter exhorts his read-

ers to steadfastness in the faith, describing how to live and how not to live under persecution and in "the last days" (see 4:12-5:11). "Be sober, be watchful. Your adversary the devil prowls around like a roaring lion, seeking some one to devour." But he also assures his readers that "after you have suffered a little while, the God of all grace, who has called you to his eternal glory in Christ, will himself restore, establish, and strengthen you" (5:6-11). To be baptized into Christ is to be baptized into his passion and death; but it is also to be raised with him in his resurrection and exaltation.

Thus, Peter places the problem of suffering in an eschatological context, looking toward the second coming of Christ for the meaning of the Church's tribulation. And with St. Paul, St. Peter would no doubt agree: "I consider that the sufferings of this present time are not worth comparing with the glory that is to be revealed to us" (Rm 8:18).

The Second Letter of Peter

The authorship and date of composition of 2 Peter is a matter of dispute among biblical scholars. Tradition and most conservative commentators attribute the letter to St. Peter and assume that it was written c. 60-68 A.D. Many contemporary and less conservative scholars believe that the letter was written no earlier than 90 A.D. (long after Peter's death, c. 67 A.D.) by a Christian who saw himself as continuing Peter's apostolic witness.[9] The present analysis, however, will follow tradition and view the letter as the work of St. Peter the Apostle. From that point of view, 2 Peter was written (probably from Rome) to the Christian churches of Asia Minor. It is a statement of Peter's views on the process of salvation, the problem of heresy in the Church and the second coming of Christ.

The Relationship between Faith, Works and Salvation. In the first chapter of 2 Peter, the author urges Christians to put their faith into practice in the form of good works. To live the Christian life, one must have "righteousness" as well as "knowledge." Having "knowledge of God" through Jesus Christ, we must also strive to live according to "the righteousness of our God and Savior Jesus Christ" (1:1-2). On the basis of our faith in Christ, God "has granted to us all things that pertain to life and godliness"; and through Christ, we have been called into the very glory and excellence of God (1:3). The ultimate goal of our life in Christ is to "escape from the corruption that is in the world because of passion [that is, the lust of the 'flesh'], and become partakers of the divine nature" (1:4). But to actualize the salvation which has been offered in Christ, we must "make every effort to supplement . . . [our] faith with virtue," living lives that give practical expression to our "knowledge" of God. We must strive for self-control, steadfastness, godliness, brotherly affection and love—a life that is not "ineffective or unfruitful in the knowledge of our Lord Jesus Christ" (1:5-8). We must confirm our faith and our "call and election" through holy and righteous conduct in the world. For it is by way of a living faith that one may find "an entrance into the eternal kingdom of our Lord and Savior Jesus Christ" (1:9-11).

The Problem of Heresy. The heresies of intellectualism and gnosticism differed from one another in many ways. The intellectualists within the first-century Church accepted the apostolic faith in almost all respects, but going to the opposite extreme from the Judaizers, they argued that salvation was a product of "faith alone," that good works were not a necessary part of the process of redemption. The gnostics went much further. As we have seen, gnosticism denied the inherent goodness of the material creation and that God was the Creator of the world, and thought of Jesus as an angel who had taken on the appearance (but not the reality) of a man in order to bring the special "knowledge" (*gnosis*) required for deliverance from the "evil" of materiality. The key to salvation, then, was the separation of "spirit" from "matter." Man's basic need, from the gnostic point of view, is to be liberated from the material realm and ushered into the realm of "pure spirit."

Gnosticism, then, was much more unorthodox than intellectualism. But in spite of their differences, gnosticism and intellectualism did have one thing in common: they both taught moral antinomianism. In Greek, *anti* means "against," and *nomos* means "law." An "antinomian" is one who denies the authority of the moral law. The intellectualists were antinomians because of their belief that one can be saved through faith and without good works. Many of them, therefore, lived in opposition to the moral teachings of the Church, especially those teachings relating to sexual behavior. The gnostics, too, rejected the moral teachings of the apostolic community; they were particularly notorious for their reputed sexual libertinism. Gnosticism, however, was not indifferent to the spiritual value of good works, as was intellectualism. Physical sin, from the gnostic point of view, might actually be considered a form of "good" behavior. If it is true that spirit alone is good and that matter is absolutely evil, then to engage in physical debauchery may be construed as a sign of one's contempt for the body, of one's denial of the moral and spiritual value of the material world. Gluttony, drunkenness, promiscuity and other physical "sins," therefore, may well lead us into the life of the spirit!

Peter's insistence upon the necessity of both orthodox belief and good conduct in the process of salvation is directed against the intellectualists and gnostics. These "false prophets" and "false teachers," following "cleverly devised myths," have insidiously introduced "destructive heresies" into the Christian community (1:16, 2:1). These heresies are contrary to Christ and will lead many people into "licentiousness" (2:1-2); many unsteady Christians will be swept away by "the lust of defiling passion" and will come to despise the authority of the moral law (2:10). Some who are enticed "with licentious passions of the flesh," and thus entangled in and overpowered by "the defilements of the world," may actually apostasize (that is, renounce their faith) and so lose their salvation in Christ (2:18-22; see also Heb 6:4-8).

Peter warns his readers that those who reject or abandon the apostolic faith, and those who teach and practice moral antinomianism, will face condemnation and eternal punishment on the day of judgment, along with the devil and his fallen angels. Those who keep the faith and live righteously, however, will be ultimately delivered from all evil and live forever in the kingdom of God (see 2:4-10).

The Second Coming of Christ. Second Peter was written at least thirty years after the crucifixion, resurrection and ascension of Christ. During his earthly ministry, the Lord had promised his disciples that he would "come again" some day to lead the people of God into the heavenly kingdom (see Mt 24:29-31; Mk 13:24-27; Lk 21:25-28; Jn 14:1-4). Many of the first Christians were convinced that the second advent of Christ would occur during their own lifetime. But with the passage of time, it became clear that the Lord's return could not be predicted and that it might not take place according to human expectations. By the time Peter wrote his second epistle (c. 60-68 A.D.), the "delay" of the second coming had become something of a problem for the Church. Those who were seeking to discredit the apostolic witness seized upon this "problem" and scoffed at the faith of the Church. Peter quotes these scoffers as saying, "Where is the promise of his coming? For ever since the fathers [the Old Testament patriarchs] fell asleep, all things have continued as they were from the beginning of creation" (3:3-4). Chapter 3 of 2 Peter was penned in response to this criticism.

Peter warns that "the heavens and earth that now exist have been stored up for fire, being kept until the day of judgment and [the] destruction of ungodly men" (3:7). He goes on to explain that the Lord's "delay" in returning to the world is based upon his forbearance toward sinners: "The Lord is not slow about his promise as some count slowness, but is forbearing toward you, not wishing that any should perish, but that all should reach repentance" (3:9). But the time allotted to sinners to see the errors of their ways and to repent is not infinite in duration. And Peter exhorts his readers to make themselves ready without hesitation for the second advent of Christ and for the divine judgment which is coming upon the world (see 3:14-18).

Peter proclaims that "the day of the Lord will come like a thief [that is, suddenly and unexpectedly], and then the heavens will pass away with a loud noise, and the elements will be dissolved with fire, and the earth and the works that are upon it will be burned up" (3:10). Looking toward and hoping for "the coming of the day of the Lord," Christians must strive to live according to holiness and godliness (3:11-12). Until that day, we must struggle to "grow in the grace and knowledge of our

Lord Jesus Christ" (3:18), that we may enter into the "new heavens and . . . new earth" that will follow the great and dreadful day of the Lord (3:13).

The Letters of John

The three letters of John were written from Ephesus c. 90 A.D. The fathers of the Church attributed these letters to the apostle John, who, as bishop of the churches in Asia Minor, lived in Ephesus during the later years of the first century.[10] As indicated earlier, only 1 John is a "catholic" letter in the strict sense; 2 John was intended for one of the local congregations in Asia Minor, and 3 John is addressed to "Gaius," apparently a personal friend of the author.

The letters of St. John (and especially 1 and 2 John) were written in order to counteract the spread of gnosticism in the early Church. We have already noted that the central doctrine of the gnostics was a spirit-matter dualism in which the goodness and spiritual significance of the material creation were denied. The gnostics also taught a doctrine of "salvation through illumination," according to which man's deliverance from material bondage was to be effected by the acquisition of a special kind of "knowledge." Only those who were initiated into the gnostic fellowship could receive this "knowledge," for God had revealed his "truth" to the gnostics alone. Thus, the gnostics distinguished between three different kinds of people: the "men of spirit" (or *pneumatikoi*), who had been fully introduced into the gnostic mysteries; the "men of soul" (or *psychikoi*), who were seekers after the wisdom of gnosticism; and the "men of flesh" (or *sarkikoi*), who were not interested in gnosticism and therefore hopelessly lost in an evil world. There were only a few "men of soul" and still fewer "men of spirit"; the vast majority of the human race were "men of flesh." Gnosticism, therefore, was a kind of spiritual elitism that depicted most human beings as beneath contempt.

Those Christians who were led astray by gnosticism, who regarded the gnostic worldview as the true but esoteric version of Christianity, saw themselves as a spiritual elite within the Church.

They considered the apostolic faith, which was proclaimed to all rather than whispered to a few, to be both false and vulgar. The apostolic teaching that the material universe had been created by God and was thus essentially good, and that the divine Word had "become flesh" in the person of Jesus of Nazareth, was incompatible with the radical antimaterialism of gnosticism. Those who adhered to the "materialistic" witness of the apostles, therefore, were "men of flesh," or, at best, "men of soul," to be recruited into the "true faith" of gnostic spiritualism. Thus, in those Christian communities where gnosticism gained a foothold, there sprang up divisions and factions which threatened the unity of the body of Christ. For the gnostics "were religious snobs, claiming to have a special revelation of their own. They were the 'spiritual' ones, the enlightened aristocracy, the religious *elite*."[11]

In his letters, John repudiates the spiritual elitism of the gnostics as well as their moral antinomianism and their rejection of the Christian doctrine of the incarnation. In response to the false doctrine, immorality and religious snobbery of the gnostics, John stresses the need for right belief concerning the person and work of Jesus Christ, the seriousness of sin and the need for obedience to God's moral law, and the need for all Christians to love one another as brothers and sisters in Christ.

The form of gnosticism criticized in the Johannine letters is known as "Cerinthianism." Cerinthus was the leader of a gnostic sect in Ephesus, and he claimed to possess the secret key to the "real truth" of Christianity. Like all gnostics, Cerinthus denied the full divinity and the real humanity of Christ. He made a distinction between the Father and the Son, according to which the Son (or "the Christ") was an angelic emanation from the Father and thus not "true God." Cerinthus also maintained that "the Son and Christ" only *seemed* to take on human flesh in Jesus of Nazareth. Because the Greek for the verb "to seem" is *dokeo,* the gnostic view of the incarnation is sometimes called "docetism." In Cerinthus' version of docetism, Jesus of Nazareth was an ordinary man until he was baptized by John the Baptist. "At that point the heavenly Christ descended upon him, and remained until the completion of the revelation that he had come to communicate. Thereupon the supernatural [but not divine] Christ left Jesus, who became a man again and as such was crucified. His death, however, signified nothing, since Christ had by that time left him."[12]

The apostle John denounces Cerinthus as an "antichrist." Insisting upon the unity of the Father and the Son, John declares that "no one who denies [the deity of] the Son has the Father," and that "he who confesses the Son [as divine] has the Father also" (1 Jn 2:22-23). John also insists upon the incarnation of the divine Son of God in the person of Jesus of Nazareth:

> *That which was from the beginning,* which we have *heard,* which we have *seen* with our eyes, which we have *looked upon* [with our eyes] and *touched* with our hands, concerning *the word of life*—the life was *made manifest,* and we saw it, and testify to it, and proclaim to you the eternal life which *was with the Father* [*from all eternity*] and was *made manifest* to us. (1 Jn 1:1-2)

He who denies that the Word of life was "made manifest" in Jesus of Nazareth, that Jesus is the Christ or that "Jesus Christ has come in the flesh" is a liar and false prophet (see 1 Jn 2:22, 4:2; and 2 Jn 7-11).

John goes on to argue, against Cerinthus, that the divine identity of Jesus was made manifest both in his baptism and in his crucifixion: "Jesus is the [divine] Son of God. This is he who came by water [his baptism] and blood [his crucifixion], not with the water only but with the water and the blood. And the [Holy] Spirit [who lives in and inspires the apostolic Church] is the witness [to the divinity of Jesus], because the Spirit is the truth. There are three witnesses, the Spirit, the water, and the blood; and these three agree" (1 Jn 5:5-13).

In John's view, the maintenance of right belief concerning the incarnation of God the Son in Jesus Christ is necessary to salvation. Through faith in Jesus as the "hypostatic (or personal) union" of God and man, the believer may enter into the eternal life of heaven. "Every one who believes that Jesus is the Christ is a child of God. . . . [and] whatever is born of God overcomes the world; and this is the victory that overcomes the world, *our faith.* Who is it that overcomes the world but he who believes that Jesus is the Son of God?" (1 Jn 5:1, 4-5) "Any one who goes ahead and does not abide in the *doctrine* of Christ [as preached by the apostles] does not have God; he who abides in the *doctrine* has both the Father and the Son" (2 Jn 9).

In addition to his emphasis upon the need for right belief, John also exhorts his Christian readers to practice right conduct. "God is light and in him there is no darkness at all" (1 Jn 1:5). If we are to have fellowship with God, therefore, we must not walk in the darkness of sin but rather in the light of Christ, who has delivered us from the power of sin (1 Jn 1:6-2:2). We must make every effort to keep the moral commandments of God and to conform ourselves to the image and likeness of God in Christ; and "he who says he abides in . . . [Christ] ought to walk in the same way in which he walked [that is, in perfect obedience to God]" (1 Jn 2: 3-6). Christians, of course, do not measure up to the perfection of Christ. The followers of Christ sin frequently, and sometimes grievously (1 Jn 1:8, 10). But he who is "born of God," according to John, can never live a life of moral indifference or outright immorality, he will never make sin the standard practice of his life. The true Christian has "God's nature" abiding in him in the person of the Holy Spirit, and he will seek to cooperate with the Holy Spirit in the process of sanctification (see 1 Jn 3:4-10, 4:13-15). And when a Christian fails to live up to the moral and spiritual standards of God, he will confess his sins to the Lord and seek forgiveness and renewal in and through Christ and his Church (1 Jn 1:9-2:2). Contrary to the antinomian teaching of the gnostics, if we are to enter into the divine sonship of Christ and the eternal life of the Holy Trinity, we must live righteous lives according to the moral law of God (see 1 Jn 3:1-3; 2 Jn 4-6). For "he who does good is of God; [and] he who does evil has not seen God" (3 Jn 11).

John also attacks the spiritual elitism of the gnostics. He who has received true enlightenment through Christ, John argues, will love his brothers and sisters in the Church. "He who loves his brother abides in the light. . . . But he who hates his brother is in the darkness and walks in the darkness, and does not know where he is going, because the darkness has blinded his eyes" (1 Jn 2:9-11). A true Christian will not, unlike the gnostics, despise his fellow Christians because of their ignorance. He will love them in Christ and pray for their edification in the truth of the faith.

A life of Christian love is essential to a life in God, for God is himself the source and foundation of love.

> Beloved, let us love one another; for love is of God, and he who loves is born of God and knows God. He who does not love does not know God; for God is love. In this the love of God was made manifest among us, that God sent his only Son into the world, so that we might live through him. In this is love, not that we loved God but that he loved us and sent his Son to be the expiation for our sins. Beloved, if God has so loved us, we also ought to love one another. . . . God is love, and he who abides in love abides in God, and God abides in him. If any one says, "I love God," and hates his brother, he is a liar; for he who does not love his brother whom he has seen, cannot love God whom he has not seen. And this commandment we have from him, that he who loves God should love his brother also. (1 Jn 4:7-12, 16-17, 19-21)

We are to live, then, not only in the truth of God, but also in his love (2 Jn 1-6). He who holds to the truth of the apostolic faith and seeks to live in the unity of love with all members of the Church of Christ, will live in the "grace, mercy, and peace" of God the Father.

Life in God, then, requires right belief, right conduct and right love. Our life in the world must be grounded in our love of God and of our brethren in the Church. We must, in the name of the gospel of Christ, be in the world; but we must not be of the world. John admonishes us not to "love the world or the things in the world." To live according to "the lust of the flesh and the lust of the eyes and the pride of life" is to live in violation of the will of God. We must always remember that "the world passes away, and the lust of it; but he who does the will of God abides for ever" (1 Jn 3:15-17). If we will accept Christ as Savior and Lord and struggle to live according to the will of God, then we will receive the fulness of the Holy Spirit, our glorification (1 Jn 3:21-24, 4:13). Speaking for the apostolic community,

John proclaims, "we have seen and testify that the Father has sent his Son as the Savior of the world. Whoever confesses that Jesus is the Son of God, God abides in him, and he in God" (1 Jn 4:14-15). If we live in God through right belief, then we will practice right conduct under the authority of God's moral law and we will love our fellow Christians in the love which has been shown to us in Jesus Christ.

The Letter of Jude

The last of the catholic epistles was written by "Jude, a servant of Jesus Christ and brother of James." It is not known who this Jude was. Some believe him to have been one of the early disciples of Christ, perhaps even an apostle, while others hold that he was a church leader of the late first century.[13] There is also controversy concerning the date of composition of Jude's epistle. "Some date this letter in the sixties of the first century, others around A.D. 150."[14] The canonicity of the letter of St. Jude was disputed by a number of ecclesiastical authorities in the early Church, but it was ultimately accepted as part of the New Testament canon during the fourth century A.D.

The letter is addressed to all Christians, and, like the other catholic epistles, it expresses grave concern with reference to the rise of heresy in the Church. Jude's intention is to defend "the faith which was once delivered to the saints," that is, the apostolic witness to Christ (v. 3). He points out that the Church had been infiltrated by false teachers, "ungodly persons who pervert the grace of our God into licentiousness and deny our only Master and Lord, Jesus Christ" (v. 4). It would appear, therefore, that the heresy Jude had in mind was gnosticism; for as we have seen, the gnostics denied the deity of Jesus Christ and encouraged their followers to practice moral antinomianism.

Jude warns his readers that doctrinal and moral heresy will be punished by God (vv. 15-16), and he calls upon them to live according to the teachings of the apostles (vv. 2, 20-21). All heretics will have to face the judgment of God on the last day; "but you, beloved, build yourselves up on your most holy faith; pray in the Holy Spirit; keep yourselves in the love of God; wait for the mercy of our Lord Jesus Christ unto eternal life" (vv. 20-21). Christians must also work to save weak souls from the abomination of heresy: "convince some, who doubt; save some, by snatching them out of the fire; on some have mercy with fear, hating even the garment spotted by flesh" (v. 22).

The letter of Jude ends with a beautiful benediction: "Now to him who is able to keep you from falling and to present you without blemish before the presence of his glory with rejoicing, to the only God, our Savior through Jesus Christ our Lord, be glory, majesty, dominion, and authority, before all time and now and for ever. Amen" (vv. 24-25).

The catholic epistles are especially concerned with the problem of heresy in the Church, with the corruption of the Church by the temptations of the world and with the practical as well as the theoretical meaning of the Christian faith. James, Peter, John and Jude insist that the Christian faith requires both true belief and good works. We are not saved by "faith alone," nor are we saved by "works alone." According to the apostolic tradition, we enter into fellowship with God—we become "partakers of the divine nature"—through faith in Christ and through a life of moral and spiritual struggle and growth in the power of the Holy Spirit. Our life in the Church is a life of growth toward union with God, through faith in the person and work of Jesus Christ and in the sanctifying grace of the Holy Spirit. Such is the perspective of the catholic epistles.

CHAPTER 9

Revelation: St. John's Vision of the Kingdom of God

The last book in the Holy Bible is the book of Revelation, also known as the Revelation to John or the Apocalypse. The term "apocalypse" (Greek, *apokalypsis*) means an unveiling of things not normally accessible to human knowledge, a prophecy based upon ecstatic visions. In ancient Jewish and Christian thought, apocalyptic prophecies and revelations had to do with the final events in God's plan for the universe. Thus, apocalyptic thought is essentially eschatological, having to do with the "last things" of cosmic history. We must recall, however, that the eschatology of the New Testament is not exclusively "futuristic." To be sure, the authors of the New Testament were deeply concerned with the *coming* of the kingdom of God; but they were also convinced that the kingdom *had come* in and through the person and work of Jesus Christ. As indicated in chapter 6, the New Testament contains an eschatological vision in which the coming of the kingdom of God is both a future event and a realized fact. The kingdom *has come* in Christ, it *is coming* through the ministry of the Holy Spirit in the Church and it *will come* with the second advent of Christ. The eschatology of the New Testament is neither a "futurist" nor a "realized" eschatology, but rather an "inaugurated" eschatology.

Revelation, then, must not be read as a "coded" description of what had already taken place by the time the book was written. Nor must it be read as "nothing but" a predictive prophecy of events that have not yet taken place. This highly symbolic and

difficult to understand book is a prophecy that points to the supernatural realities of world history. It is oriented simultaneously
toward the past, the present and the future. The message of
Revelation was intended for the Christians of the late first century
A.D. as well as for believers of all subsequent ages. It *is* an eschatological prophecy which speaks dramatically of the second coming
of Christ, the last judgment and the final establishment of the
kingdom of God. But it also depicts the heavenly kingdom as
an ever-present reality which has been made manifest in Christ
and in his Church.

Tradition tells us that the author of Revelation was St. John
the Apostle. St. John was bishop of Asia Minor during the later
years of the first century. In 93 A.D., the Emperor Domitian (r.
81-96 A.D.) instituted an empire-wide persecution against the
Church because of her opposition to the Roman cult of emperor
worship. "Calling himself 'August,' 'Savior,' 'Lord,' and even
'God,' the Emperor had statues [of himself] built throughout
the empire, and required citizens to offer sacrifices, as evidence
of their allegiance to him. Christians, for whom there was only
one God, and one Lord, . . . refused to participate in this idolatry,
and consequently suffered persecution in the form of arrest, loss
of possessions, economic boycott, and in many cases, death."[1]
During this persecution, which lasted until Domitian's death in
96 A.D., the apostle John was sent into exile on the island of
Patmos, off the west coast of Asia Minor.

While in exile on Patmos, John had a vision of Christ in his
heavenly glory (see Rv 1:9-18). The Lord granted John a revelation of the ultimate destiny of the world, and commanded him
to record that revelation in a book in order that all Christians
might know "what is and what is to take place hereafter" (see
1:11, 19). In the book of Revelation, John shares his vision of
Christ's enduring love for his Church, God's judgment upon and
eventual victory over the forces of evil and the final entry of
God's people into the fulness of the heavenly kingdom. The
churches of John's day were threatened both by the enticements of
heresy and by the evil of persecution. And these threats have
continued to pose problems for Christians of later times as well.
The "revelation of Jesus Christ" was given to the Church through
John as an encouragement to Christians of all ages who are

afflicted by spiritual confusion and suffering. "Here is a call for the endurance of the saints, those who keep the commandments of God and the faith of Jesus" (14:12). According to Revelation, the trials and tribulations of the Church are experiential manifestations of the spiritual warfare which is going on between the kingdom of heaven and the legions of Satan. Christians are urged to patient endurance and faithful confession in the light of Christ's certain victory over the kingdom of darkness. We will all "overcome" the world, the flesh and the devil in the triumph of Christ and the kingdom of heaven.

John's apocalypse was written c. 95 A.D. In order to communicate to his readers the mystical and astonishing character of his ecstatic visions, John adopted the style of ancient Jewish apocalyptic literature.[2] Thus, his book is full of symbols, metaphors, figures of speech, pseudonyms, mysterious numbers, depictions of supernatural events and unearthly creatures, and so on. "Perhaps not even the original readers of the book understood the precise meaning of all these strange symbols and metaphors; among modern commentators there is no agreement as to what they all mean."[3] It was largely because of "the great difficulty of interpreting the apocalyptic symbols of the book" that the early Church hesitated to include Revelation in the canon of the New Testament.[4] And throughout the centuries since John's time, "the book of *Revelation* has been more mishandled by religious cranks than any other book in the Bible."[5] But in spite of its obscurity and its misuse by heretics, the Apocalypse, primarily because of its Johannine authorship and the divine origin of its testimony, was finally accepted by the historic Church as the last installment of the written Word of God.[6] The fact that it "is never read liturgically in the Orthodox Church" is a reminder of the early Church's reservations concerning this powerful but difficult book.[7]

The visions recounted in Revelation must not be understood as depicting an exact chronology of God's salvific work. Through his encounter with the glorified Christ, John witnessed the divine plan of salvation from several different although complementary perspectives. His book does point toward the "end-time" events that will accompany the second advent of Christ; but the succession of chapters in the book does not represent the exact sequence of historical events and epochs leading up to the final reconstitution of all things. As Stott puts it, John had "successive visions of Christ [and the kingdom]"; but these were not strictly chronological "visions of successive events."[8] One major dimension of the message of Revelation is that Christ is continually present to his Church, that the kingdom of God is forever coming upon us so long as we live in the current historical age, and that one day the kingdom will be finally and fully established. We can never know when that day—the day of the Lord—will come; we must therefore struggle to maintain our faith and to live according to the will of God, making ourselves always ready for the sudden advent of the kingdom.

Christ's Concern for His Church

John's apocalypse was written as a long letter "to the seven churches that are in Asia," that is, to the churches of Asia Minor in Ephesus, Smyrna, Pergamum, Thyatira, Sardis, Philadelphia and Laodicea (Rv 1:4, 11). For John, the number "seven," derived from the creation story in Genesis 1, symbolizes completeness and perfection. The "seven churches that are in Asia," therefore, represent the entire or universal Church of Christ. The message of Revelation is intended for all true Christians at all times.

John begins his address to the Church with a description of his vision on Patmos of the risen and glorified Christ:

I was in the Spirit on the Lord's day, and I heard behind me a loud voice like a trumpet saying, "Write what you see in a book and send it to the seven churches. . . ." [Then] I saw seven golden lampstands, . . . and in the midst of the lampstands one like a son of man, clothed with a long robe and with a golden girdle round his breast; . . . and in his right hand he held seven stars, . . . from his mouth issued a sharp two-edged sword, and his face was like the sun shining in full strength. When I saw him, I fell at his feet as though dead. But he laid his right hand upon me, saying, "Fear not, I am the first and the last, and the living one; I died, and behold I am alive

for evermore, and I have the keys of Death and Hades."
(1:9-18)

In this spectacular epiphany, Christ commanded John to send
messages to each of the seven churches in Asia. These seven
messages constitute a prophetic statement concerning the trials,
tribulations and characteristics of the true Church of Christ. In
the first message (2:1-7), the Lord praises the church in Ephesus
for her doctrinal orthodoxy and her patient endurance during
times of trouble. He chastises her, however, for her loss of her
"first love," that is, her enthusiastic desire to bring the gospel of
Christ to those outside the Church. The second message, to the
church in Smyrna, warns of the tribulation and suffering, insti-
gated by Satan, which Christians must be always ready to face
and to bear (2:8-11). The third message takes note of the steadfast faith of most members of the church in Pergamum, even
during periods of intense persecution; but Christ also denounces
the Pergamum Christians for their tolerance toward the heretics
in their midst (probably gnostics), and he urges them to institute
a strict moral and doctrinal discipline in their church community
(2:12-17). The content of the fourth message, addressed to the
church in Thyatira, is essentially identical with that of the message to the church in Pergamum. The majority of the Christians
in Thyatira are credited for their personal orthodoxy, but they
are severely admonished for their toleration of those members
of their community who adhere to false doctrines and who
"practice immorality" (2:18-29).

In his fifth message (3:1-6), Christ accuses the church in
Sardis of being spiritually dead—filled with people who are
nominally Christian but actually not very different from the pagans
around them. The Lord calls upon the Christians in Sardis to
repent, and he reminds them of his unpredictable second advent:
"I will come like a thief, and you will not know at what hour
I will come upon you" (3:3). The sixth message depicts the
church in Philadelphia as a model Christian community, rich in
both faith and works. The Lord promises the Philadelphians that
they will one day enter into the full enjoyment of the kingdom
of God (3:7-13). The seventh and final message of Christ to the
churches of Asia is addressed to the Christian community in

Laodicea (3:14-22). The church in Laodicea was apparently filled with people who were economically affluent and socially prominent, who felt at peace with the world. For in the message to the Laodiceans, Christ charges them with being outwardly prosperous but inwardly "wretched, pitiable, poor, blind, and naked" (3:17). The Lord expresses particular displeasure with the "lukewarm" faith of the Christians in Laodicea, and he calls upon them to change their ways before it is too late.

These seven messages to "the churches of Asia" represent a challenge from Christ to the Christian Church at all times and in all places. Are we like the ancient Ephesian Christians, basically orthodox and steadfast in our faith, but lacking in the evangelistic zeal which should lead us to "make disciples of all nations, baptizing them in the name of the Father and of the Son and of the Holy Spirit" (Mt 28:19-20)? Are we willing and ready to suffer and even die in defense of our faith? Do we, like those in the ancient churches of Pergamum and Thyatira, tolerate the breakdown of moral and doctrinal discipline in the Church? Do we close our eyes to the worldly immorality into which so many Christians have fallen? Have we, following the pattern of the church in ancient Sardis, become spiritually dead and virtually indistinguishable from those who do not follow Christ? Or have we achieved the exemplary orthodoxy of the ancient Philadelphian Christians, adhering steadfastly to the apostolic faith and expressing that faith in a life of good works? Have we managed, like the Philadelphians, to avoid the spiritual lukewarmness and emptiness of the church in ancient Laodicea? Honest answers to these questions will demonstrate whether or not we are living up to the standards Christ has set for his Church.

In his messages to the seven churches of Asia, the Lord has graciously revealed his will for his people throughout the ages until his coming again. Those who respond to those messages and who struggle to live according to the standards disclosed therein will be incorporated into the victorious life of Christ himself (see Rv 2:7, 10-11, 26-29) and be exalted with Christ to the throne of the Father (3:21-22).

The Heavenly Assembly

During his encounter with Christ on the island of Patmos, St.
John had several visions of heaven. Three of these visions are
recorded in Revelation 4, 5 and 7. In chapter 4, John describes
his vision of God enthroned and worshiped in heaven:

> At once I was in the Spirit, and lo, a throne stood in
> heaven, with one seated on the throne! And he who sat
> there appeared like jasper and carnelian . . . Round the
> throne were twenty-four thrones, and seated on the thrones
> were twenty-four elders, clad in white garments, with
> golden crowns upon their heads. . . . And round the throne,
> on each side of the throne, are four living creatures, full
> of eyes in front and behind: the first living creature like
> a lion, the second living creature like an ox, the third living
> creature with the face of a man, and the fourth living
> creature like a flying eagle. And the four living creatures,
> each of them with six wings, are full of eyes all round
> and within, and day and night they never cease to sing,
> "Holy, Holy, Holy, is the Lord God Almighty, who was
> and is and is to come!" And whenever the living creatures
> give glory and honor and thanks to him who is seated on
> the throne, . . . the twenty-four elders cast their crowns
> before the throne [thereby showing their subservience to
> the Supreme King], singing, "Worthy art thou, our Lord
> and God, to receive glory and honor and power, for thou
> didst create all things, and by thy will they existed and
> were created." (4:2-11)

In this vision, God appears as the absolute Lord of heaven
and earth, enthroned above all things and powers. In Revelation,
the number "twelve" and multiples thereof symbolize the people
of God, the true Israel, the Church. The twenty-four crowned and
enthroned elders, therefore, are representative of the Church which
will be glorified in heaven. Twelve of the elders represent the
patriarchs of the twelve tribes of ancient Israel as well as the
entire body of Old Testament saints; and the other twelve elders

stand for the people of the new covenant, nurtured on the faith of the twelve apostles.

Like the prophet Ezekiel (see Ezk 1:10-14), John speaks of the "four living creatures" who surround the heavenly throne. These are the angelic beings referred to in the Divine Liturgy as "the Cherubim and the Seraphim, six-winged, many-eyed, who soar aloft, borne on their pinions [or wings]."[9] We must remember, of course, that angels are "strictly spiritual beings" with no physical bodies, and that John's descriptions of these heavenly powers are symbolic rather than literal.[10] For John, the number "four" is symbolic of the created universe and of the absolute dependence of the creation upon its Creator. Thus, the Cherubim and Seraphim in heaven do what all creation ought to do: worship God without ceasing. The "eyes" and "wings" of the four living creatures symbolize God's omnipresence in the created order. The four living creatures also represent what is best in the realm of created life: the nobility of the lion, the strength of the ox, the wisdom of man and the swift and soaring flight of the eagle. Through the Cherubim and Seraphim, then, "the whole of creation is . . . represented before the throne of God, worshiping his divine Majesty and fulfilling his will."[11]

Another of John's visions of heaven is recounted in Revelation 5. This is a vision of Christ, venerated by the heavenly host as "the Lamb of God":

> And between the throne and the four living creatures and among the elders, I saw a Lamb standing, as though it had been slain, with seven horns and with seven eyes, which are the seven spirits of God [the angels of the Church] sent out into all the earth. . . . [The] four living creatures and the twenty-four elders fell down before the Lamb, each holding a harp, and with golden bowls full of incense, which are the prayers of the saints; and they sang a new song, saying, "Worthy art thou to take the scroll and to open its seals, for thou wast slain and by thy blood didst ransom men for God from every tribe and tongue and people and nation, and hast made them a kingdom of priests to our God, and they shall reign on earth." (5:6-10)

During the period between the completion of the Old Testament and the writing of the New Testament, the apocalyptic literature of the Jews frequently portrayed the Messiah as a horned lamb who would do battle on behalf of his people and conquer the forces of evil. The Jews, of course, never expected this warrior-lamb to suffer and to die for the sins of the world. The death of Jesus, therefore, was proof for most Jews that he was not the Christ. But for Christians, Jesus is both "the lamb who was slain" (our Passover lamb) *and* the lamb "with seven horns" who has conquered the powers of darkness. Indeed, as we have seen in earlier chapters, the death of Christ was a crucial element in his victory over evil. John's vision of the heavenly adoration of the lamb does full justice to the dialectical nature of Christ's work of salvation: the lamb of God is he who was slain and yet was victorious. Christ's conquest of evil is symbolized by the image of the "seven horns." In the Old Testament, the horn of an animal (especially the ram) is a sign of royal dignity and power; and, as indicated above, John employs the number "seven" as a symbol of completeness and perfection. Thus, Christ possesses the full power and glory of his heavenly Father and is worthy of the worship offered him by the entire redeemed universe.

John's description of the position of the heavenly lamb is also significant. An alternative translation of Revelation 5:6 is: "And I saw, and behold, *in the midst of the throne and of the four living creatures, and in the midst of the elders,* a Lamb standing. . . ." Christ is depicted as standing "in the midst" of God's throne and in the midst of the elders (that is, the Church). John's vision portrays the exaltation of Christ to the throne of his Father and his continuing presence "in the midst" of his people. He is, as we have seen throughout this book, the point of union between God and man. By living in Christ, we live in God.

The vision recorded in Revelation 7 is a twofold revelation concerning the destiny of the Church. In the first place, we see the Church of history, preserved for glorification in spite of her trials and tribulations during her sojourn in the world; and in the second place, we are shown a picture of the final redemption and exaltation of the people of God. John describes the Church of history as those in the world who have been sealed for salvation by God. He speaks of them as "a hundred and forty-four

thousand sealed, [twelve thousand] out of every tribe of Israel"
(see 7:4-8). "Israel," of course, is the biblical name for God's
chosen people, those chosen under the old covenant as well as
those chosen under the new. And, as usual, John's use of numbers
must be understood symbolically rather than literally. We have
seen that the number "twelve" and multiples thereof are representative of the people of God. We must add here that the number "ten" and multiples thereof are used by John to indicate
indefiniteness and magnitude. John's reference to the hundred and
forty-four thousand members of the Church should be understood
as follows: 144,000 = 12 x 12 x 1,000. The Church of history
contains an indefinitely large number of Old Testament saints
as well as countless Christians who have lived since the time of
Christ. Literally considered, there will be far more than 144,000
redeemed saints in heaven.

In Revelation 7:9-17, John describes his vision of the Church
in heaven and beyond tribulation:

> After this I looked, and behold, a great multitude *which
> no man could number,* from every nation, from all tribes
> and peoples and tongues, standing before the throne and
> before the Lamb, clothed in white robes, with palm
> branches in their hands, and crying out with a loud voice,
> "Salvation belongs to our God who sits upon the throne,
> and to the Lamb!" . . . Then one of the elders . . . said
> to me, "These are they who have come out of the great
> tribulation; they have washed their robes and made them
> white in the blood of the Lamb. Therefore are they at the
> throne of God, and serve him day and night within his
> temple; and he who sits upon the throne will shelter them
> with his presence. They shall hunger no more, neither
> thirst any more; the sun shall not strike them, nor any
> scorching heat. For the Lamb in the midst of the throne
> will be their shepherd, and he will guide them to springs
> of living water [see Jn 4:7-15, 7:37-39]; and God will
> wipe away every tear from their eyes."

Christ taught that, just prior to his second coming, the devil
would mount a final and almost overwhelming attack on the

Church (see Mt 24:15-28). For a period of time, known as "the great tribulation," the people of God would face "unprecedented trial and affliction."[12] John's vision of the Church in heaven depicts the people of God as they will be following the great tribulation: finally redeemed, made absolutely pure through the blood of the lamb, exalted to the throne of God and participating in the ceaseless celebration of the "celestial liturgy."[13] In intimate union with God the Father, through God the Son and in God the Holy Spirit,[14] the Church will dwell forever in the house of God.

Although Revelation is never read in the liturgies of the Orthodox Church, the book has had a major impact upon Orthodox liturgical life. "The worship of the Church," writes Father Thomas Hopko, "has traditionally, quite consciously, been patterned after the divine and eternal realities revealed in [Revelation]. The prayer of the Church and its mystical celebration are one with the prayer and celebration of the kingdom of heaven. Thus, in Church, with the angels and saints, through Christ the Word and the Lamb, inspired by the Holy Spirit, the faithful believers of the assembly of the saved offer perpetual adoration to God the Father Almighty."[15] While waiting for the final reconciliation of all things at the second coming of Christ, the Church of history lives in mystical anticipation of and in real union with the heavenly assembly.

God's Judgment upon a Sinful World

The biblical witness speaks frequently of the "day of the Lord" and the last judgment. On that day, and before "the dread judgment seat of Christ" (2 Co 5:10),[16] the forces of evil will be finally and decisively blasted by God and banished from the heavens and the earth. But the Bible also makes it quite clear that, between the fall of man and the last judgment, the wrath of God is continuously directed toward the sins of the world.

God's continuing and historical judgment of the fallen world is depicted vividly in Revelation. John describes two visions of God's wrathful condemnation of sin: the vision of the seven seals (chapter 6), and the vision of the seven trumpets (chapters 8-11). In the vision of the seven seals, the divine scroll of judgment

—"a scroll written within and on the back, sealed with seven seals"—is given to the lamb of God ("the Lion of the tribe of Judah, the Root of David"—that is, the Christ). As the lamb breaks the seals on the scroll, great calamities are visited upon the earth. With the breaking of the first four seals, the "four horsemen of the Apocalypse" go forth to bring war, famine and pestilence to the world of men (see 6:1-8). As the fifth and sixth seals are broken, God's holy martyrs—"those who had been slain for the word of God and for the witness they had borne"—cry out for the final destruction of the powers of darkness which will take place on the day of the Lord (see 6:9-17). The opening of the seventh seal brings "silence in heaven," for the scroll of judgment is now completely open, signifying the fulness (the number "seven" again) of the judgment which is yet to come (see 8:1).

In his vision of the seven trumpets, "the seven angels who stand before God" announce, with trumpet blast, the incredible catastrophes that are to occur just prior to the end of days. The imagery of this vision is very difficult to decipher in detail. As the seven trumpets are sounded by the angels, the earth is devastated by a series of afflictions: hailstorms of fire and blood; vast and extremely destructive fires; the pollution of the rivers and the seas; worldwide warfare; the contamination of the atmosphere by great clouds of smoke and sulphur; the darkening of the sun, moon and stars; the death of millions of human beings; and so on (see 8:7-11:14). Even the Church of Christ will suffer tremendously during the last days; but because of her faithfulness, she will be finally delivered and exalted into the kingdom of God (see 11:1-19).

The breaking of the seven seals and the blasting of the seven trumpets signify the utter ungodliness of sin and the disasters which sin has brought upon the world. John's visions of God's judgment upon the sinful world constitute, on the one hand, a kind of explanation of the great suffering that takes place in the present world order, and, on the other hand, a call to repentance. The most devastating judgment of all still lies before us— beyond the world, beyond death, beyond time. To enter into the ultimate glory of the kingdom of heaven, we must make ourselves ready for the last judgment. By living faithfully and obediently in Christ and in his Church, we will one day hear the Lord say to us, "Come, O blessed of my Father, inherit the kingdom prepared for you from the foundation of the world" (Mt 25:34).

The Coming of the Kingdom of God

The series of visions recounted in Revelation 12-22 tells of the original satanic rebellion against God, the spiritual warfare between Christ and the devil which forms the supernatural background of world history, the ultimate victory of Christ over the powers of darkness and the final establishment of the kingdom of God.

The Satanic Rebellion against God. According to ancient Jewish and Christian traditions, the devil was originally one of the angels of God. But seeking to exalt himself to the heavenly throne, this celestial creature led an angelic rebellion against God. Revelation tells us that one-third of the angelic host was implicated in Satan's revolt (see 12:3-4). Depicting the devil as "a great red dragon," John writes:

> Now war arose in heaven, Michael [the archangel] and his angels fighting against the dragon; and the dragon and his angels fought, but they were defeated and there was no longer any place for them in heaven. And the great dragon was thrown down, that ancient serpent [see Gn 3], who is called the Devil and Satan, the deceiver of the whole world—he was thrown down to the earth, and his angels were thrown down with him. (12:7-9)

According to tradition, the devil was thrown down to earth because he was originally ordained to be the guardian spirit of that planet, and during the epoch of world history he has been permitted to continue his association with our world (see Ezk 28:11-19). It was through his position as "the god of this world" (2 Co 4:4) that Satan was able to entice Adam and Eve into the realm of evil.

The Spiritual Warfare between the Lamb and the Dragon.
Revelation takes the fall of man for granted and concentrates
upon the devil's attempts to subvert God's plan for the salvation
of the fallen world. John portrays ancient Israel as "a woman
clothed with the sun, with the moon under her feet, and on her
head a crown of twelve stars." The woman was "with child and
she cried out in her pangs of birth, in anguish for delivery"
(12:1-2). The "child," of course, is the Messiah promised by
God to the people of the old covenant, he "who is to rule all the
nations with a rod of iron" (12:5). The devil—the "great red
dragon"—sought to destroy the Messiah of Israel, but the Holy
One "was caught up to God and to his throne" (12:3-5). As
we know, Satan did see the Messiah suffer and die on the cross,
but through the Lord's resurrection, ascension and exaltation
Satan has himself been defeated, as will be made finally clear at
the second coming.

Realizing his defeat and final destiny, the devil, out of sheer
malice, has devoted his remaining time to the devastation of the
earth and to the oppression of the human race. The Bible tells
us that he is especially concerned with the persecution of the
Church and of individual Christians. Seeing that he could no
longer hope to defeat God, Satan

> pursued the woman who had borne the male child [the
> woman now represents the people of the new covenant,
> the Church]. But the woman was given the two wings of
> the great eagle that she might fly from the serpent into
> the wilderness, to the place where she is to be nourished
> for a time, and times, and half the time. . . . Then the
> dragon was angry with the woman, and went off to make
> war on the rest of her offspring, on those who keep the
> commandments of God and bear testimony to Jesus.
> (12:13-17)

The Church, as the body of Christ, will never be destroyed.
Individual Christians, John tells us, are very much at the mercy
of demonic temptation and oppression, but they can conquer the
devil and his agents by believing in the saving power of "the
blood of the Lamb" and by maintaining their faith ("the word

of their testimony") during times of tribulation (12:11).

In his tyranny over the earth, Satan employs two major instruments of oppression and temptation: worldly power and worldly ideology. Revelation describes these forces of evil as animate in nature. Worldly power is represented as "a beast rising out of the sea, with ten horns and seven heads, with ten diadems upon its horns and a blasphemous name upon its heads" (13:1). This beast from the sea is given authority by Satan to rule "every tribe and people and tongue and nation, and all who dwell on earth will worship it [that is, worldly power], every one . . . [except those who belong to] the Lamb that was slain" (13:10). The Christian must not allow himself to be swept away in admiration for the power of state and empire, for the glory of race and nation. He must keep his heart and mind free from "the political illusion," the illusion that the salvation of the human race can be effected through social, economic, political or military means.[17]

John's symbol for worldly ideology is "another beast which rose out of the earth" (13:11). Of this beast, John writes:

> It exercises all the authority of the first beast in its presence, and makes the earth and its inhabitants worship the first beast. . . . It works great signs, even making fire come down from heaven [the sky] to earth in the sight of men; and by the signs which it is allowed to work in the presence of the [first] beast, it deceives those who dwell on earth, bidding them . . . [to worship the first beast], and . . . [causing] those who would not worship the image of the [first] beast to be slain. (13:12-15)

For John, this imagery was no doubt symbolic of the Roman empire (the first beast) and its cult of emperor worship (the second beast). The famous "number of the beast"—666—is a Hebraic cryptogram symbolizing the Roman emperor, Domitian (see 13:18).[18] But the beast from the earth stands for any ideology or belief system that would lead us to devote our ultimate concern to worldly power. Christians of all ages can find meaning in the vision of the two beasts.

In John's day, as has been indicated, the center of worldly power and worldly ideology was Rome. In Revelation Rome is presented in symbolic guise as "Babylon, the great harlot." John, carried away in the Spirit by an angel of the Lord, is shown

> the great harlot who is seated upon many waters, with whom the kings of the earth have committed fornication, and with the wine of whose fornication the dwellers on earth have become drunk. . . . [He saw] a woman sitting on a scarlet beast which was full of blasphemous names, and it had seven heads and ten horns. The woman was arrayed in purple and scarlet, and bedecked with gold and jewels and pearls, holding in her hand a golden cup full of abominations and the impurities of her fornication; and on her head was written the name of a mystery: "Babylon the great, mother of harlots and of earth's abominations." And I saw the woman, drunk with the blood of the saints and the blood of the martyrs of Jesus. (17:1-6)

The "mystery" of the great harlot's identity is cleared up in Revelation 17:7-18. John tells us that she is "the great city which has dominion over the kings of the earth" (17:18). But, again, the symbolism of the Apocalypse has universal significance. The image of the great harlot, based upon the Old Testament symbol of Babylon, represents "every society which fights against God, every body of persons united in wickedness and fleshliness." The great harlot of Revelation is the biblical type of "all who are corrupted by their passions and lusts, unfaithful to God Who has made them and loves them."[19]

These, then, are the forces against which the Church of Christ must contend throughout the duration of world history: demonic oppression and temptation, the enticements and threats of worldly power, the delusions of false religion and philosophy, a worldly morality based upon the renunciation of God, and so on. During the Christian era, the Lamb of God does battle with the devil in and through the Church. For those of us who follow Christ, the spiritual warfare of our Savior has become our warfare. And we must always remember, with St. Paul, that "we are not contending [merely] against flesh and blood, but against the principalities, against the powers, against the world rulers of this present darkness, against the spiritual hosts of wickedness [which are in league with the devil]" (Eph 6:11-12).

The Victory of Christ and his Church over the Powers of Darkness. According to the "inaugurated eschatology" of New Testament thought, our salvation through Christ is simultaneously past, present and future: we have been saved, we are being saved, we will be saved; the kingdom of God has come, it is coming and it will come. This "collapsed time" of the redemptive process is evident in John's prophetic vision of the victory of Christ and his Church over the powers of darkness. The work of Christ at his first advent, his ongoing work through the Holy Spirit and in his Church and the work he will perform at his second coming are depicted in Revelation 14-20 as phases of a single process.

In the last days, John tells us once again, the earth will be afflicted by the wrath of God. In chapters 15-16, we are presented with a vision of "the seven bowls of the wrath of God" which are poured out by angels upon the world. All those who had followed the satanic beasts of worldly power and worldly ideology are covered with "foul and evil sores"; the sea becomes like blood, and all sea-life dies; all the rivers and fountains of the earth, too, become like blood; the land is covered with complete darkness; the earth is wracked by a devastating earthquake, and so on (see Rv 16). While the seven bowls of wrath are being poured out, the legions of God are secretly gathered and made ready for the final battle with evil, which will take place at the second advent of Christ (see Rv 14 and 19:1-10).

In Revelation 17-19, John presents his vision of Christ's final victory over the great harlot and the two beasts—the powers of worldliness through which the devil had ruled the world since the fall of man. And in chapter 20, the final defeat of the devil and his demonic legions is described. John tells us that, through the power of Christ, the devil will be bound up in chains by an angel and cast into "the bottomless pit." The devil is to remain in the bottomless pit for "a thousand years," and, after that, "he must be loosed for a little while" (20:1-3). During that thousand-year period, Christ and his saints will reign over the world (20:4-6). "And when the thousand years are ended, Satan will be loosed from his prison" and will come forth to do battle for the last time against God. At the battle of Armageddon (see 16:13-16), the devil and his legions will be utterly routed. They will be "thrown into the lake of fire and sulphur where the . . . [two beasts] were, and they will be tormented day and night for ever and ever" (20:7-10).

The thousand-year period mentioned in Revelation 20 is often referred to as "the millennium" (the Latin term for "thousand-year period"). Christians have held several different views of the millennial reign of Christ. One of these views is known as pre-millennialism. The pre-millennialists hold that all of the events described in Revelation 20 will follow the second coming of Christ, and that the Lord will literally rule the earth for a thousand years prior to the final institution of the kingdom of God. Another view, that of the post-millennialists, is that, through the missionary work of the Church, the world will experience a long golden age (the millennium) which will be *followed* by the second coming. A third perspective is that of a-millennialism, which denies "that there will ever be a literal earth-rule of a thousand years, either before or after Christ's return."[20] The Orthodox Church (as well as the majority of Christians through the centuries) subscribes to the a-millennialist point of view. We must recall that, for John, the number "ten" and multiples thereof signify an indefinite magnitude. The Orthodox Church regards the thousand-year period of Revelation 20 as symbolic of Christ's reign in and with his Church during the indefinitely long period between his first and second advents. At the Lord's first coming, the power of the devil was placed in chains (although not utterly and finally obliterated); and when Christ returns, at the end of "the millennium," the devil will be "loosed" and finally reduced to a hellish impotence.

Following the second coming and the battle of Armageddon, the general resurrection of the dead will take place. At the last judgment, the saved will be separated from the damned, and the latter will be eternally separated from the presence of God (see Rv 20:11-15; see also Mt 25:31-46). With the "great divorce" of God's people from those who belong to darkness, the victory of Christ and his Church over the forces of evil will be complete.[21]

The Final Establishment of the Kingdom of God. After the

last judgment, the glorious kingdom of God will be fully and
finally established. The final vision recorded in the Apocalypse
portrays that ultimate eschatological event.

> Then I saw a new heaven and a new earth; for the first
> heaven and the first earth had passed away. . . . And I
> saw the holy city, new Jerusalem, coming down out of
> heaven from God, prepared as a bride adorned for her
> husband; and I heard a loud voice from the throne saying,
> "Behold, the dwelling of God is with men. He will dwell
> with them, and they shall be his people, and God himself
> will be with them; he will wipe away every tear from
> their eyes, and death shall be no more, neither shall there
> be mourning nor crying nor pain any more, for the former
> things have passed away." And he who sat upon the throne
> said, "Behold, I make all things new . . . It is done! I am
> the Alpha and the Omega, the beginning and the end.
> To the thirsty I will give from the fountain of the water
> of life without payment. He who conquers shall have this
> heritage, and I will be his God and he shall be my son."
> (21:1-7)

John goes on to describe the glory of the new Jerusalem, the
fully deified bride of Christ, the Church (21:9-27). The union
of God and his Church is presented as complete: the glorified
Church lives in God, and God lives in his Church. In the glorified
union of God and the Church, "there shall no more be anything
accursed . . . [and the saints] shall see . . . [the] face [of God],
and his name shall be on their foreheads. And night shall be no
more; they need no light or lamp or sun, for the Lord God will
be their light, and they shall reign [with him] for ever and
ever" (22:3-5).

John brings Revelation to a close with a series of exhortations
and warnings (22:6-21). We are all called into the glorious
kingdom of God; but to enter that kingdom, we must first
respond to the invitation of Christ and his Church with diligence,
constancy and obedience. And we are reminded, again and again,
to make ourselves ready for the sudden and unpredictable second
coming of Christ. The Lord has told us, "Surely I am coming

soon." May we all say, with John, "Amen. Come, Lord Jesus!"

From the standpoint of the Orthodox Church, the book of Revelation is an enduring message of encouragement and consolation to a sinful, doubtful and fearful world. John calls us to turn sincerely to Christ in order that we might overcome our sin, our doubt and our fear. For only in Christ can we receive forgiveness of sins as well as the strength to avoid the temptations of sin; only through the knowledge of Christ which comes from prayer and participation in the sacraments of the Church can we be delivered from the demon of doubt; and only in the salvation which is available in and through Christ can our fears be removed. We have been invited by the Holy Spirit and the Church to enter into the life of Christ: "And the Spirit and the Bride say, 'Come!' And let him who heareth say, 'Come!' And let him that is athirst come. And whosoever will, let him take the water of life freely!" (22:17; King James Version). And in response to this invitation, we must ourselves invite Christ into our lives: "Behold [said Christ], I stand at the door [of your life] and knock; if any one hears my voice and opens the door, I will come in to him and eat with him, and he with me" (3:20).

The Message of the Bible

Having gone through a detailed examination of all the books of the Bible, let us now close with a brief summary of the contents and message of Holy Scripture.

According to the holy tradition of the Church, the Bible is the book of salvation. Through the books of the law, the historical writings of ancient Israel, the wisdom literature, the writings of the prophets, through the New Testament revelation of the "good news" of salvation in Jesus Christ, the records of the earliest Christian communities, and ending with St. John's revelation of the last days, we have manifested to us the entire history of salvation—God's plan for the redemption of mankind and the world from the forces of evil and for the ultimate glorification of man and the world in the kingdom of heaven.

In the first chapters of Genesis, we see God's original plan for mankind. The Bible tells us that men and women are created in the image and after the likeness of God, and that God has granted them dominion over the earth and all that is within it. The divine image is man's potentiality for perfect communion with God, and the divine likeness is the actualization of that potentiality. Thus, man was created in order that he might grow into union with God (deification, *theosis*), and, standing at the head of all creation, that he might bring with himself the entire cosmos to its Creator.

The first chapters of Genesis also relate to us, however, that instead of freely accepting God's gracious offer of union with himself, man chose to follow his own will, to rebel against and to reject the love and will of God. This is the "fall" of mankind,

269

symbolized by Adam and Eve's partaking of the forbidden fruit, as depicted in the third chapter of Genesis. Thus, man failed to actualize his potentiality as the likeness of God; because of his alienation from the lifegiving presence of God, man's need to participate in the divine nature has been frustrated. And as a result of this fall, man has come under the domination of evil, the fruits of which are spiritual blindness, mortality and sin.

The entire history of the people of Israel given in the Old Testament scriptures is a striking illustration of this fallen condition of mankind. The slavery of the house of Israel in Egypt, told of in the later chapters of Genesis; the wanderings in the wilderness as described in Exodus; the struggles to capture the promised land during the days of Joshua; the continual struggle for national survival led by the judges; the tribulations of the two kingdoms, together with their downfall and exile and captivity, recorded in the books of Samuel, Kings and Chronicles—all reveal the desperate situation and fragile condition of man in a world ruled by sin and evil. As human beings, the people of ancient Israel—like ourselves, like all peoples everywhere—owed their love and obedience to God alone. But we have all submitted our wills to the temptations of the world, the flesh and the devil; we have devoted ourselves to self-love rather than to God-love. The human race has thus been separated from the presence and life of God, and in forsaking his gracious love and will, mankind has become completely subject to the tyranny of evil, death and sin.

Even after the fall, however, God did not leave his creation entirely without his grace and without the promise of ultimate deliverance. In Genesis, even as man is cast out of the garden of paradise, God shows his loving care by himself making the garments with which Adam and Eve are clothed. Genesis also records two covenants that God makes with man: the Noahic covenant, under which God promises not to remove life from the world, no matter how widespread evil becomes; and the covenant with Abraham, under which God makes for himself a chosen people, who would eventually bear the Messiah of the human race. In renewing this covenant with Moses, God reveals his law to his people, showing them the way in which they must live in order to restore themselves to God's loving fellowship. Furthermore, God inspires holy writers of the old covenant to reveal his wisdom unto his people, to teach them how to praise his name (e.g., the Psalms), to give them practical precepts for fulfilling his law (e.g., Proverbs) and to guide them into understanding the injustice and miseries of this fallen world (e.g., Job, Ecclesiastes). Finally, God sends his prophets to speak the light of truth in the darkness of the fallen world, and to reveal the great promise of future deliverance from the powers of this world.

All of these signs of God's providential care for his people are manifestations of God's holiness. In response to them, God requires from us our own holiness—i.e., perfect love of God and absolute obedience to his law. This holiness is the prerequisite for man's entering into the fulness of the divine presence. But the testimony of the scriptures is that man can do nothing through his own efforts to restore himself to God's love and fellowship. No matter how many times God delivers his chosen people from their enemies, no matter how often he reveals his truth, love and holiness to them, no matter how many prophets and wise men he inspires to lead them back to the truth they have forsaken, mankind continues to fall prey to the temptations of the devil, to turn away from God and honor false idols—whether made of wood or clay, or of self-love, pride and self-interest. The message is clear: man, existing under the conditions created by the fall, is utterly lost and is thus in radical need of salvation. Fallen man needs a Savior—he needs to be saved by God himself.

All the above manifestations of God's holiness are fulfilled in Jesus of Nazareth. He is the only man to completely follow the precepts of the law; he is himself the eternal Wisdom of God; he is the inspirer of the words of the prophets and the realization of their prophecy; he is the promised Messiah of the chosen people of Israel, and the light to all nations. The New Testament—the book of the "new covenant" between God and man—begins with the four gospels. The word "gospel," as we have already seen, means "good news," and this good news is that God the Son—the divine Logos—"became man" in order to draw mankind back into communion with the Holy Trinity. The gospels testify how God himself, in the incarnation of the Son, took upon himself all our suffering and travail, how in his perfect love for his fallen creatures, even though he himself was without sin, he paid the price for all of our sins, voluntarily accepting death on the cross to atone for our sins, and then destroying sin and its consequences through his glorious resurrection on the third day. And now, through the incarnation, life, death, resurrection, ascension, exaltation and second coming of the Son of God, man can be liberated from the powers of darkness, from evil and emptiness, from "the law of sin and death," from spiritual ignorance, mortality and sin.

In his Farewell Discourse in the Gospel of St. John, Christ promises to send his disciples the Holy Spirit, the "Comforter," who will guide them into all truth. And in the first chapters of the Acts of the Apostles, we see this promise fulfilled, as the Spirit descends on the early Christian community on the day of Pentecost in "tongues as of fire." Through this gift of the Holy Spirit, which comes to all who are "in Christ," we can be *sanctified* and so resume the original human project of growing morally and spiritually into the likeness of God. Through the "economy of the Son" and the "economy of the Holy Spirit," man can be reconciled with God and, on the basis of this reconciliation, he can receive his ultimate *glorification* as a son of God, a participant in the fulness of the divine life. Only through faith in Christ, and through the ministry of the Holy Spirit, can men and women be reconciled to God and so escape everlasting condemnation when Jesus returns to the world at the end of days to judge both the living and the dead.

God the Father has offered us salvation through the mission of his Son and through the ministry of the Holy Spirit. However, this offer is made to us as free human beings, and we must accept it freely into our lives in order to realize its redemptive and glorifying effect. The testimony of the apostles to the early church communities in Acts and in the New Testament epistles is that we must "work out" the salvation offered and made possible by the Holy Trinity "in fear and trembling"; we must appropriate this salvation; we must explicitly and freely respond to the mercy and love of God shown in his redemptive purpose. To be saved, we must first of all admit our sinful alienation from God and recognize our inability to make ourselves right with God through our own efforts. Because of his fallenness, all of man's attempts at "self-salvation" are pathetic and futile. Man must, therefore, accept through faith what God has done for us in Christ; he must, with the help of the Holy Spirit, submit to Christ as the Lord and Master of his life. Only on this basis can we become right with God and be restored to a condition of divine sonship.

God's salvation comes to those who, on the basis of a personal, decisive and freely chosen faith, acknowledge Jesus as Savior, and who through continual repentance and obedience to God's will, submit to Jesus as Lord. But to be obedient to Christ and to submit to God's will means to become wholly a part of his body. The door to the kingdom of heaven has been opened by Jesus Christ, through his incarnate life and through his redemptive and reconciling ministry. But to pass through that door, fallen man must accept Christ's gift of the Holy Spirit, which was first bestowed not on Christians as individuals, but on the entire body of the Christian community—the Church—and which is now given in and through the life of the Church. Through the sacramental, devotional and moral ministry of the mystical body of Christ, Christians are regenerated, edified and, ultimately, glorified in the power and indwelling presence of the Holy Spirit. With a few exceptions (e.g., Timothy and Titus, who themselves stood at the head of church communities), all the epistles of the New Testament were addressed not to individuals but to either specific church communities or to the Church at large. The book of Revelation is also addressed primarily to seven local communities which are named in the text; and modern scholarship shows that the gospels themselves were all composed in the context of specific major church communities. God's salvation comes to us through the mediation of Christ's body, the Church. Thus, the Church is God's sacrament of salvation to the world, the visible means of grace by which man may be elevated to the divine energies and life of the Holy Trinity.

The continuity of the life of the Church throughout all ages is assured by her holy tradition. It is this tradition which first carefully preserved the memory of Christ's words and deeds in oral form, which guaranteed the harmony of the content of all the written records of Christ's revelation, and which then passed down from generation to generation the New Testament scriptures for the edification and sanctification of all believers of all times. Thus, there can be no opposition between scripture and tradition. For, first of all, the New Testament is itself a primary and normative articulation of the Church's tradition. Secondly, but equally, all who wish to know and to be faithful to that tradition will turn first of all to the Bible, and will continually read and study it, treasuring its words in their hearts, and reciting and singing these holy words out loud together, with their brothers and sisters in the Church, in her liturgy and throughout her life.

In sum, our salvation is a result of man's identification with Christ through faith. Through faith, man enters into the life of Christ, which is the life of God, lived through the grace of the Holy Spirit in the fulness of the body of the Church. Through the grace of the Holy Spirit, man receives power to grow morally and spiritually into the perfect image of Christ. Through freely and personally responding to God's offer of salvation, each one of us can be delivered from the bondage of evil, sin and death. And through the life of the Church, we may therefore enter into communion with God the Father, through God the Son, and in God the Holy Spirit. Through the divine economy of salvation, revealed in the Holy Scriptures of the Church and passed on to all generations in her holy tradition, each one of us may become a partaker of the divine nature, a participant in the glorious energies and life of the Holy Trinity, a living icon of God!

APPENDIX

Major English-Language Versions of the Bible

English-speaking persons who wish to study Holy Scripture must first find a readable and accurate version of the Bible. And there are many—some would say *too* many—English-language versions of the Bible available today. Which of these many versions is most appropriate for the purposes of the fledgling Bible student?

The classic English-language version of the Bible is the *King James Version* (KJV), which was published in England in 1611 under the sponsorship of King James I (r. 1603-1625). This is a wonderfully poetic and beautiful translation of Holy Scripture, often called "the noblest monument of English prose." Many contemporary readers, however, find the seventeenth-century English of the KJV to be rather obscure and quite difficult to understand. Furthermore, many ancient Hebrew, Greek, Latin and Syriac manuscripts and manuscript fragments of the Bible have been unearthed by scholars since the seventeenth century; and many of these materials are thought to be older and more accurate than were the manuscripts upon which the KJV is based.

On the basis of these manuscript discoveries, the KJV was revised twice during the late nineteenth century. The *English Revised Version* (RV) of 1885 and the *American Standard Version* (ASV) of 1901 have eliminated many of the inaccuracies contained in the KJV of 1611. But these revisions have preserved the difficult English diction of the KJV and are thus not wholly suitable for most beginning Bible students.

One of the best and most widely used contemporary versions of the Bible is the *Revised Standard Version* (RSV), which was published in 1952. The RSV is an updated revision of the American Standard Version of 1901 and thus stands in the tradition of the King James Version. Its language is dignified, grand and beautiful, but, at the same time, contemporary and readable. And scholars consider the RSV a highly accurate rendering of the biblical text. All in all, the RSV well deserves its current popularity.

The *New English Bible* (NEB), published in 1970, is a direct translation of Holy Scripture from ancient Hebrew and Greek manuscripts. The language of the NEB is readable, but not very poetic. And many scholars have questioned the accuracy of this rather free and interpretive translation of the biblical text.

Two contemporary Roman Catholic translations of the Bible are the *Jerusalem Bible* (JB) of 1966 and the *New American Bible* (NAB) of 1970. Like the New English Bible, these translations are readable but less than accurate.

The *New American Standard Bible* (NASB) of 1971 and the *New International Version* (NIV) of 1978 are recent translations of Holy Scripture which are popular among conservative Protestants. These translations are both accurate and readable, although the language of the NIV flows a bit more smoothly than that of the NASB.

Two other versions of the Bible currently in general use are the *Living Bible* (LB) of 1971 and *Today's English Version* (TEV) of 1976. The latter is also known as the "Good News Bible." The LB is not a new translation, but a contemporary paraphrase of the King James Version. And the TEV is a highly colloquial and, in my opinion, excessively interpretive translation from Hebrew and Greek texts of the Bible. Both the LB and the TEV are written in ordinary, current English. They are thus quite readable, but their language is utterly pedestrian and lacking in poetic grandeur. The textual accuracy of these versions is also open to serious question.

All things considered, I should prefer the Revised Standard Version (RSV) over any of the other versions of the Bible described in the preceding paragraphs. The King James Version is both less readable and less accurate than the RSV. The English

Revised Version and the American Standard Version, although quite accurate, are written in a form of English that is much less contemporary than the prose of the RSV. The New American Standard Bible and the New International Version, in spite of their very considerable strengths, are somewhat less readable and therefore less useful for the purposes of Bible study than is the RSV. The RSV is also preferable to the New English Bible, the Jerusalem Bible and the New American Bible, which are readable but not entirely reliable translations of Holy Scripture. And the Living Bible and Today's English Version, while quite easy to read, are inferior to the RSV in both literary beauty and textual accuracy.

In addition to the question of the readability and accuracy of current English-language versions of the Bible, the Orthodox Christian will also seek an edition of Holy Scripture containing the "deuterocanonical" books of the Old Testament. These books (with the exception of 1 Esdras, 3 Maccabees, Psalm 151 and the Prayer of Manasseh) are contained in the Old Testament portions of such Roman Catholic editions of the Bible as the Jerusalem Bible and the New American Bible. And there are editions of the King James Version, the English Revised Version, the Revised Standard Version and the New English Bible that follow the Protestant practice of placing the deuterocanonical books in special sections of "Apocrypha" either between the Old and New Testaments or at the end of the New Testament. Most of these editions, however, like Roman Catholic versions of the Bible, do not include 1 Esdras, 3 Maccabees, Psalm 151 and the Prayer of Manasseh. The only English-language edition of the Bible containing all of the Old Testament deuterocanonical books accepted by the Orthodox Church is the expanded edition of *The New Oxford Annotated Bible with the Apocrypha,* published in 1977. This is a study Bible which provides the reader with verse-by-verse annotations and commentaries on each book of Holy Scripture, special articles by distinguished scholars dealing with the use and general understanding of the Bible, detailed maps of Bible lands, and so on. And since this edition also contains the most recent form of the Revised Standard Version, it is perhaps the English-language version of the Bible that will prove most useful to the Orthodox Christian reader of Holy Scripture.

Notes

CHAPTER 1

[1]Timothy (Fr. Kallistos) Ware, *The Orthodox Church* (Penguin Books, 1972) 209.

[2]Ibid., 204.

[3]Ibid.

[4]Georges Florovsky, *Bible, Church, Tradition: An Eastern Orthodox View* (Nordland Publishing Co., 1972) 9-16.

[5]Georges A. Barrois, *The Face of Christ in the Old Testament* (SVS Press, 1974), 19.

[6]Ware, *The Orthodox Church*, 208.

[7]Ibid., 209.

[8]Ibid., 207.

[9]Thomas Hopko, *The Orthodox Faith*, vol. 4: *Bible and Church History* (Orthodox Church in America, Department of Religious Education, 1973) 5-6.

[10]Ibid., 5.

[11]Ibid.

[12]Raymond E. Brown, et al., eds., *The Jerome Biblical Commentary*, vol. 2: "The New Testament" (Prentice-Hall, 1968) 512.

[13]Hopko, *The Orthodox Faith*, vol. 1: *Doctrine*, 2d ed. (Orthodox Church in America, Department of Religious Education, 1976) 12.

[14]Ibid.

[15]Ware, *The Orthodox Church*, 205.

[16]Hopko, *Bible and Church History*, 9.

CHAPTER 2

[1]Barrois, *The Face of Christ in the Old Testament*, 63.

[2]*The New Oxford Annotated Bible with the Apocrypha*, "Introduction to the Old Testament" (Oxford University Press, 1977) xxviii.

[3]Adam W. Miller, *Introduction to the Old Testament* (Pillar Books, 1976) 31.

[4]Fr. Kallistos Ware, *The Orthodox Way* (SVS Press, 1979) 56.

[5]Ibid., 58.

[6]Barrois, *The Face of Christ in the Old Testament*, 56.

[7]Ware, *The Orthodox Way*, 66.

[8]Ibid.

[9]Ibid.

[10]Vladimir Lossky, *The Mystical Theology of the Eastern Church* (SVS Press, 1976) 112-3.

[11]Ware, *The Orthodox Way*, 67.

[12]Thomas Hopko, "On the Male Character of Christian Priesthood," St. *Vladimir's Theological Quarterly* 19:3 (1975) 149. It must be emphasized, however, that in partaking of the divine nature, man does not become identical with God. To understand the Orthodox doctrine of deification, it is most helpful to refer to the writings of St. Gregory Palamas (1296-1359), who makes a distinction between the essence (*ousia*) and the energies (*energeia*—actions, operations) of God. The divine energies are those "forces proper to and inseparable from God's essence, in which He goes forth from Himself, manifests, communicates, and gives Himself," for example, his wisdom, life, truth, love, glory, light, and so on (Lossky, *The Mystical Theology of the Eastern Church*, 70). God is *really present* to us in his energies, and by the grace of God we are able to participate in his energies and thus in his nature; but there is no sense in which we can enter into or partake of the essence of God, which is always transcendent. As Lossky has written, deification "is union with God in His energies, or union by grace making us participate in the divine nature, without our essence becoming thereby the essence of God. In deification, we are by grace (that is to say, in the divine energies), all that God is by nature, save only identity of nature" (ibid., 87). In this process of theosis, then, we remain creatures, distinct but not separate from God; in communion with, but not absorbed into, the divine nature.

[13]Barrois, *The Face of Christ in the Old Testament*, 66.

[14]It is true that after Adam and Eve had disobeyed God and had partaken of the forbidden fruit, God cast them out of the garden of Eden, saying, "Behold, the man has become like one of us, knowing good and evil" (Gn 3:22). This does *not*, however, mean that God or his angels are immersed in evil as well as good. The point is that the serpent of Genesis 3 had beguiled the man and the woman into disobeying God by promising them that if they did so they would become like angels, "knowing good and evil." God's statement in Genesis 3:22, therefore, is ironic or even sarcastic, for as a result of their violation of divine law, Adam and Eve had become radically alienated from the life of heaven, contrary to the serpent's promise!

[15]*The New Oxford Annotated Bible with the Apocrypha*, "The Old Testament," footnote on p. 4.

[16]For biblical reflections of these ancient traditions concerning the fallen angels, see Isaiah 14:5-15, Ezekiel 28:11-19 and Revelation 12:1-17.

[17]Jean Danielou, *The Angels and their Mission* (Christian Classics, 1976) 41-2.

[18]Ibid., 45-7.

[19]Ware, *The Orthodox Way*, 74.

[20]Ibid., 75.

[21]Barrois, *The Face of Christ in the Old Testament*, 60.

[22]William Neil, *Harper's Bible Commentary* (Harper & Row, 1975) 20.

[23]*The New Oxford Annotated Bible with the Apocrypha*, "The Old Testament," footnote on p. 5.

[24]Ware, *The Orthodox Church*, 228.

[25]Ware, *The Orthodox Way*, 80. Fr. Kallistos points out that, indeed, "any

action, performed by any member of the human race, inevitably affects all the other members" (ibid., 81).

[26]*The Harper Study Bible* (Zondervan Publishing House, 1965) footnote on p. 9.

[27]*Jerome Biblical Commentary*, vol. 1: "The Old Testament," 13.

[28]The serpent of Genesis 3 is not an "incarnation" of the devil, but merely a symbol of his evil presence in the life of the human race.

[29]*The Harper Study Bible*, footnote on p. 14.

[30]Neil, 31.

[31]*Jerome Biblical Commentary*, vol. 1: "The Old Testament," 15.

[32]Paul Lazor, *Baptism* (Orthodox Church in America, Department of Religious Education, 1972) 10.

[33]*Jerome Biblical Commentary*, vol. 1: "The Old Testament," 16. Some interpreters have argued that there are two additional covenants contained implicitly in the early chapters of Genesis. The first is the *Edenic covenant* (Gn 1-2), which describes the original, prelapsarian relationship between God and man; and the second is the *Adamic covenant* (Gn 3:14-19), which reveals the consequences of man's fall from grace. The Edenic covenant is formed between God and Adam, and requires perfect obedience from the latter, and its sign is the tree of life. The Adamic covenant, which extends through Adam to the whole human race, requires no moral or spiritual response from man but sets down the conditions of existence for fallen man—conditions that must prevail until the coming of the kingdom of God. The unavoidability of man's death may be regarded as the sign of this covenant. This so-called Adamic covenant also contains, as we have seen, God's first promise of a Redeemer in the form of "the seed of the woman" (Gn 3:15), typified by the "garments of skins" given to Adam and Eve by God (3:21). We have, in essence, already surveyed the ground covered by the Edenic and Adamic covenants (see above, 35-46), and we shall consider the covenants with Abraham and Israel in chapter 3 (below, 57-8).

[34]Ibid.

[35]According to modern biblical scholars, Genesis 9:20-27 contains a combination of two curses: one against Ham and one against Canaan. Ham is representative of the land of Egypt, where Israel was enslaved during the pre-Mosaic era. Canaan was the father of the pagan peoples of ancient Palestine, against whom Israel was destined to struggle for centuries during the post-Mosaic era. Japheth was the ancestor of the Philistines, also subsequent enemies of Israel but never so threatening to or despised by the Hebrews as were the Canaanites. The author of the text in question retrojected the sin of Canaan into the times of Ham and combined the two curses into one.

[36]Miller, 38.

CHAPTER 3

[1]*The Harper Study Bible*, 190.

[2]Ibid., footnote on p. 110.

[3]The choice of Saul, a Benjaminite, as king presents a problem, for the Lord, through a prophecy of Jacob, had designated Judah as the kingly tribe in Israel (see Gn 49:10). Perhaps the choice of Saul, and his acceptance by the people,

is intended to illustrate just how far Israel had departed from the path of God's plan for them. And the kingship of Saul ends in catastrophe.

[4]Miller, 76.

[5]Georges Barrois, "Survey of the Geography, History, and Archaeology of the Bible Lands," in The New Oxford Annotated Bible with the Apocrypha, 1542.

[6]Ibid., 1543.

[7]See above, in chapter 2, 31-5.

[8]From the Nicene Creed.

[9]From the Anaphora of the Liturgy of St. John Chrysostom.

[10]See above in chapter 2, 34-5.

[11]The Harper Study Bible, footnote on p. 1835.

[12]In the Epistle to the Hebrews, Christ is called "a high priest for ever after the order of Melchizedek" (6:20). Melchizedek was a priest-king who met with Abraham in Genesis 14:17-20. His priesthood is presented in Hebrews as superior to the Aaronic priesthood and as foreshadowing the priesthood of Christ. Thus, the priesthood of Christ, carried on by the bishops and presbyters (priests) of the Orthodox Church, supersedes the priesthood of the Levites.

[13]See Barrois, The Face of Christ in the Old Testament, 89-101.

[14]John R.W. Stott, Understanding the Bible (Regal Books, 1972) 29.

CHAPTER 4

[1]William Barclay, Introducing the Bible (Abingdon Press, 1972) 71.

[2]Miller, 187.

[3]From the Hymns of the Resurrection recited after the communion of the people.

[4]In the Septuagint, the wisdom literature is presented as a collection of "poetical" writings.

[5]Miller, 86.

[6]Barrois, The Face of Christ in the Old Testament, 103.

[7]See chapter 1, 16-8.

[8]Miller, 125-6, summarizing the views of the prophet Nahum.

[9]The Cost of Discipleship is the title of a book by Dietrich Bonhoeffer (Macmillan, 1963).

[10]See Veselin Kesich, The First Day of the New Creation: The Resurrection and the Christian Faith (SVS Press, 1982) 28f.

[11]Miller, 152.

[12]Works of Love is the title of a book by Sören Kierkegaard (Harper Torchbooks, 1964).

[13]Miller, 152-3.

[14]R.J. Zwi Werblowsky, "Judaism, or the Religion of Israel," in The Concise Encyclopedia of Living Faiths, ed. R.C. Zaehner (Beacon Press, 1959) 33-4.

CHAPTER 5

[1]F.F. Bruce, "Bible," in The New Bible Dictionary, eds. J.D. Douglas, et al. (Wm. B. Eerdmans, 1973) 150.

[2]Ibid., 151.

[3]A good number of contemporary biblical scholars believe that 2 Peter and Jude were written in the late first or early second century. See Charles M. Laymon, gen. ed., *The Interpreter's One-Volume Commentary on the Bible* (Abingdon Press, 1971) 931, 942.

[4]Bruce, "Bible," 150.

[5]F.F. Bruce, "The Fourfold Gospel," in *A New Testament Commentary* (Zondervan, 1973) 93.

[6]The Church was especially provoked by the Marcionite heresy of the mid-second century. Marcion, a crypto-gnostic, denied the canonicity of the entire Old Testament and of most of the books now included in the New Testament. He acknowledged only the authority of an abridged version of the Gospel according to St. Luke and of ten of St. Paul's epistles. See Veselin Kesich, *The Gospel Image of Christ: The Church and Modern Criticism* (SVS Press, 1972) 69-72.

[7]See Eusebius of Caesarea, *Ecclesiastical History* (Baker Book House, 1974) 110-1.

[8]*The New Oxford Annotated Bible with the Apocrypha*, "The New Testament," 1170.

[9]Kesich, *The Gospel Image of Christ*, 41.

[10]Ibid., 38. The word "evangelist" is apparently derived from the Greek verb *euangelizomai*, which means "to announce good tidings" (see ibid., 37).

[11]Ibid., 39.

[12]Irenaeus, "An Exposition of the Faith," in *Early Church Fathers*, tr. and ed. C.C. Richardson (Macmillan, 1976) 370.

[13]Kesich, *The Gospel Image of Christ*, 39.

[14]Ibid., 40.

[15]Ibid., 41-2. The Greek word *synopsis*, by the way, means "to see together."

[16]Bruce, "The Fourfold Gospel," 96.

[17]According to Papias, bishop of Hieropolis in Phrygia during the early first century, "Matthew compiled the *logia* [that is, the 'oracles' or sayings of Christ] in the Hebrew (Aramaic) speech, and everyone translated them as best he could" (quoted in ibid., 97). This collection of the sayings of Jesus may have been the source ("Q") used by Matthew and Luke in the construction of their gospels.

[18]Kesich, *The Gospel Image of Christ*, 46.

[19]See *The Lost Books of the Bible and the Forgotten Books of Eden* (Collins & World, 1974).

[20]The Idumaeans were descendants of the ancient Edomites, the offspring of Jacob's brother Esau. They were Semites, but not Jews. Herod's grandfather had converted to Judaism for political reasons, and the Jews never regarded the Idumaean dynasty as a legitimate continuation of the ancient Hebrew monarchy.

[21]The dating of Christ's birth which is commonly followed was worked out by a monk in the early Middle Ages on the basis of astronomical calculations. His calculations, however, were off by some five or six years.

[22]Nicholas Cabasilas, quoted by Mother Mary and Archimandrite Kallistos Ware in *The Festal Menaion* (Faber & Faber, 1977) 60.

[23]Ibid., 61.

[24]According to the Jewish marriage laws of that time, "betrothal could be dissolved only by a formal act in which the man gave the woman a certificate of divorce" (*Harper Study Bible*, footnote on p. 1438).

[25]Mary and Ware, *The Festal Menaion*, 60.

[26]Ibid.

[27]The Massacre of the Innocents is remembered by the Church every year on December 29.

[28]Mary and Ware, *The Festal Menaion*, 273.

[29]See *The Jerome Biblical Commentary*, vol. 2: "The New Testament," 66, 129.

[30]See above in chapter 3, 85-7.

[31]*Jerome Biblical Commentary*, vol. 2: "The New Testament," 129.

[32]*The Interpreter's One-Volume Commentary on the Bible*, 646.

[33]Mary and Ware, *The Festal Menaion*, 56.

[34]Ibid., 57-8.

[35]Ibid., 58.

[36]See above in chapter 3, 62-6.

[37]D. Gurthrie, et al., eds., *The New Bible Commentary: Revised* (Wm. B. Eerdmans, 1971) 820.

[38]For two interesting Orthodox interpretations of the meaning of the temptation of Christ, see Paul Evdokimov, *The Struggle with God* (Paulist Press, 1966) 111-30; and Veselin Kesich, *The Passion of Christ* (SVS Press, 1965) 8-12.

[39]St. John Chrysostom, *Homilies on the Gospel of Saint Matthew* (Wm. B. Eerdmans, 1975) 80-1.

[40]Satan misapplies the quotation from Psalm 91:11-12, for the psalmist was neither speaking of the Messiah nor encouraging people to put God to the test.

[41]John Chrysostom, *Homilies on the Gospel of Saint Matthew*, 82.

[42]As noted above, Matthew, Mark and Luke, it would appear, were not concerned with the exact chronology and geographical scope of Christ's ministry. Their purpose, we must recall, was not to produce a scientific biography of the Lord, but to preserve the essence of the gospel of Christ as proclaimed by the apostles and to pass that gospel on to the world.

[43]The New Testament speaks also of other apostles besides the original twelve, for example, St. Paul and St. James. But these were added to the apostolic leadership of the early Church after the ascension of Christ.

[44]Kesich, *The Gospel Image of Christ*, 105.

[45]Caesarea Philippi was located to the north of Galilee on the southern slopes of Mount Hermon.

[46]See above in chapter 4, 112-6.

[47]Kesich, *The Gospel Image of Christ*, 100-2.

[48]The scribal law was ultimately written down, and it became the basis for the *Talmud*. The Talmud, which was completed c. 650 A.D., is the second of the holy books of the Jews, the first being the Hebrew Bible (the Old Testament).

[49]Kesich, *The Gospel Image of Christ*, 78, 83-7.

[50]Georges Barrois, *Scripture Readings in Orthodox Worship* (SVS Press, 1977) 166.

[51]Mary and Ware, *The Festal Menaion*, 62.

[52]Ibid., 62-3.

[53]Barrois, *Scripture Readings in Orthodox Worship*, 166.

[54]See Prof. Kesich's discussion of the Olivet discourse in *The Passion of Christ*, 41-51.

[55]Ibid., 52-5.

[56]There seems to be a conflict between the synoptics and the Gospel of St. John on the exact date of Passover during the year of Christ's death. See Kesich, *The Gospel Image of Christ*, 56-60.

[57]Kesich, *The Passion of Christ*, 57-8.

[58]A somewhat different interpretation is offered by C.F.D. Moule, who sees the main point of this usage in the contrast between the "one" and the "many"— the many serves "to emphasize the remarkable fruitfulness of the one act of self-surrender" (quoted in Kesich, *The First Day of the New Creation*, 62).

[59]Kesich, *The Passion of Christ*, 57.

[60]Ibid., 63.

[61]Ibid., 63-4.

[62]Ibid., 66.

[63]Ibid., 76.

[64]*The Harper Study Bible*, footnote on p. 788.

[65]Kesich, *The First Day of the New Creation*, 57-8.

[66]Ibid., 66.

[67]For an excellent study of these appearances, see ibid., 87ff.

[68]On Christ's ascension, see ibid., 155ff.

[69]"Pentecost" is the Greek name for the Jewish Feast of Weeks (*Shabuoth*), a harvest festival held on the fiftieth day after Passover to commemorate the revelation of God's law to Moses on Mount Sinai.

[70]See Kesich, *The Gospel Image of Christ*, 93-7; and also see above, 115-6.

[71]See Kesich, *The Passion of Christ*, 3-20; and also see above, 113-5.

CHAPTER 6

[1]In the gospel book which is kept on the altar in Orthodox Churches, the Gospel of St. John appears first. For the Orthodox Church, the most theological and mystical of the gospels is first, not fourth.

[2]See William Barclay, *The Gospel of John*, 2d ed., vol. 1 (Westminster Press, 1956) xxxi-xl; and Neil, 403.

[3]*The Jerome Biblical Commentary*, vol. 2: "The New Testament," 414-5.

[4]Eusebius, *Ecclesiastical History*, 104f.

[5]Barclay, *The Gospel of John*, vol. 1, xix-xxi.

[6]Oscar Cullmann, *The New Testament: An Introduction for the General Reader* (Westminster Press, 1968) 44.

[7]*The New Oxford Annotated Bible with the Apocrypha*, "The New Testament," 1286.

[8]*The Jerome Biblical Commentary*, vol. 2: "The New Testament," 417.

[9]Kesich, *The Gospel Image of Christ*, 57.

[10]Stott, *Understanding the Bible*, 121, 130.

[11]Kesich, *The Gospel Image of Christ*, 56.

[12]Cullmann, 46-7; and Kesich, *The Gospel Image of Christ*, 59.

[13]Ibid., 59-60.

[14]Neil, 404.

[15]*The Harper Study Bible*, footnote on p. 1584.

[16]See Barclay, *The Gospel of John*, vol. 1, xx-xxi.

[17]See Hans Jonas, *The Gnostic Religion*, 2d ed., revised (Beacon Press, 1963).

[18]Gnosticism did not disappear after the third century; its worldview continues to exist in the twentieth century in Spiritualism, Rosicrucianism, Freemasonry, Scientology, Christian Science, the Unity School of Christianity, and so on.

[19]See above, 112-6.

[20]See above, 140-1 and 154.

[21]*The Harper Study Bible*, footnote on p. 1587.

[22]Barclay, *The Gospel of John*, vol. 1, 86.

[23]Lazor, *Baptism*, 11.

[24]Ibid., 12.

[25]Mark Zivkovich, "You're Only Born Twice," *Upbeat* (December, 1976) 4-5.

[26]See Thomas Hopko, *The Spirit of God* (Morehouse-Barlow Co., 1976).

[27]See above, 73.

[28]See above, 141.

[29]See above, 48-50.

[30]See Barclay, *The Gospel of John*, vol. 1, 39-43.

[31]See Barclay's illuminating discussion of Middle Eastern pastoral practices in ibid., 63-72.

[32]Ibid., 67.

[33]See Kesich, *The First Day of the New Creation*, 16-7, 19, 76.

[34]See Kesich, *The Gospel Image of Christ*, 107; and Kesich, *The First Day of the New Creation*, 180.

[35]*The Harper Study Bible*, footnote on p. 1613.

[36]Kesich, *The First Day of the New Creation*, 55.

[37]On the meaning of the empty tomb, see ibid., 71ff.

[38]See ibid., 166f.

[39]See St. Athanasius, *On the Incarnation* (SVS Press, 1953) 93 and *passim*.

CHAPTER 7

[1]According to tradition, St. Peter was crucified upside down by his own choice, so that his death would show itself to be less significant than that of Christ. St. Paul, as a Roman citizen, was given the "privilege" of being beheaded rather than crucified.

[2]See above, 163-4.

[3]See, for example, C.H. Dodd, *The Meaning of Paul for Today* (Cambridge University Press, 1920).

[4]*The Jerome Biblical Commentary*, vol. 2: "The New Testament," 805.

[5]This verse is quoted from Ronald Knox's translation of the *Holy Bible* (Sheed and Ward, 1950).

[6]See above in chapter 2, ms30-7, 38-44 . . .

[7]See John Meyendorff, *Byzantine Theology: Historical Trends and Doctrinal Themes* (Fordham University Press, 1976) 143-6.

[8]Ibid.

[9]See above in chapter 2, ms38 . . .

[10]F.F. Bruce, *The Message of the New Testament* (Wm. B. Eerdmans, 1973) 39.

[11]See above, 154-5.

[12]From their own cultic mystery religions, the pagan cultures of the early Christian era were familiar with the theme of the dying and rising god. It was not the "mysticism" of Christianity that repelled the pagan world, but rather the "Jewishness" of the "Jesus cult." There is a good discussion of the relationship between the mystery cults and Christianity in Kesich, *The First Day of the New Creation*, 38.

[13]See Lossky, *The Mystical Theology of the Eastern Church*, chapter 7.

[14]Kesich, *The First Day of the New Creation*, 155, 167.

[15]See Athanasius' *On the Incarnation*.

[16]C.S. Lewis, *Mere Christianity* (Macmillan, 1971) 56-61.

[17]J.G. Davies, "Christianity: The Early Church," in *The Concise Encyclopedia of Living Faiths*, 56.

[18]Ibid.

[19]Hopko, *Bible and Church History*, 114.

[20]Lossky, *The Mystical Theology of the Eastern Church*, 167-8.

[21]Knox translation.

[22]In the first-century Church, no distinction was made between baptism and chrismation.

[23]*The Harper Study Bible*, footnote on p. 1705.

[24]See above in chapter 2, ms31-4 . . .

[25]Lossky, *The Mystical Theology of the Eastern Church*, 179.

[26]Ibid., 172-3.

[27]Ibid., 196.

[28]See the views of St. Gregory of Nyssa, St. Irenaeus, St. Gregory of Nazianzen, St. Basil the Great and St. Cyril of Jerusalem in Henry Bettenson, ed., *The Early Christian Fathers* (Oxford University Press, 1963) 98-9; and *The Later Christian Fathers* (Oxford University Press, 1974) 35, 60-2, 101-2 and 145-6.

[29]It should be emphasized that "good works," from an Orthodox point of view, are possible only within the domain of a specifically Christian faith. In the words of St. Seraphim of Sarov (1759-1833), works "not done in the name of Christ, can neither procure us a reward in the life of the age to come, nor win us the grace of God in this present life" (quoted in Lossky, *The Mystical Theology of the Eastern Church*, 196-7). And according to Lossky, "there is for the Christian no such thing as an autonomous good: a work is good in so far as it furthers our union with God, in so far as it makes grace *ours*" (ibid., 197; see Rm 14:23).

[30]For Martin Luther (1483-1546) and classical Reformation Protestantism, the essential message of the gospel is that we are saved by faith alone, and not by works. See H.J. Grimm, *The Reformation Era* (Macmillan, 1965).

[31]Lossky, *The Mystical Theology of the Eastern Church*, 197.

[32]Translation from the *New English Bible* (Cambridge University Press, 1971).

[33]Knox translation.

[34]Knox translation.

[35]Quoted from *The New International Version* (Zondervan, 1978).

[36]Knox translation.

[37]Vladimir Lossky, *In the Image and Likeness of God* (SVS Press, 1974) 97-110.

[38]See above in chapter 4, 109-18.

[39]As for those who have never heard the gospel, they will be judged in the light of their consciences (Rm 2:14-16). In Paul's view, however, very few (if any) ever live up to the light of their own consciences (see Rm 1:18-2:16, 3:9-18). See also Kesich, *The First Day of the New Creation*, footnote on p. 149.

[40]First Corinthians 15 is treated excellently throughout Prof. Kesich's *The First Day of the New Creation*, especially 129ff.

[41]Neil, 462.

CHAPTER 8

[1]The Letter to the Hebrews, although not written by Paul, has always been grouped with the Pauline epistles, for in the early centuries of the Christian era, it was believed to be either a work of St. Paul's or at least a development of his thought by one of his close disciples. See above, 200.

[2]Bruce, *The Message of the New Testament*, 89.

[3]See above, 200-1, 221.

[4]John R.W. Stott, *Basic Introduction to the New Testament* (Inter-Varsity Press, 1973) 105.

[5]See above in chapter 6, 163-4.

[6]Cullmann, 102.

[7]The Letter of James is also important in the Church because it contains statements forming the scriptural foundation for the sacraments of holy unction and confession (Jm 5:13-18).

[8]Cullman, 107; Neil, 519.

[9]Cullmann (114-6) holds that 2 Peter may have been written as late as 150 A.D.

[10]Many scholars believe that 1, 2 and 3 John were written not by St. John the apostle but by one of his close associates known as "John the Elder." See Neil, 526.

[11]Stott, *Basic Introduction to the New Testament*, 128-9.

[12]Neil, 527.

[13]Cullmann, 111-3.

[14]*The Harper Study Bible*, 1857.

CHAPTER 9

[1]*The Harper Study Bible*, 1861.

[2]According to Cullmann, "the apocalyptic literature is abundant. We can cite the Book of Enoch, the Assumption of Moses, the Apocalypse of Baruch, the Testaments of the Twelve Patriarchs. Traces of this literary genre are also found in the Old Testament, especially in the books of Ezekiel and Daniel. Those contained in the Dead Sea Scrolls (Qumran) partially belong to this genre" (footnote on p. 119).

[3]*The Harper Study Bible*, 1862.

[4]Hopko, *Bible and Church History*, 62.

[5]Neil, 537.

[6]Hopko, *Bible and Church History*, 62.

[7]Ibid.

[8]Stott, *Basic Introduction to the New Testament*, 159.

[9]From the Anaphora of the Liturgy of St. John Chrysostom.

[10]Hopko, *Doctrine*, 50.

[11]*The Jerome Biblical Commentary*, vol. 2: "The New Testament," 475.

[12]*The Harper Study Bible*, footnote on p. 1871.

[13]*The Jerome Biblical Commentary*, vol. 2: "The New Testament," 478.

[14]The Holy Spirit is the "living water" spoken of in Revelation 7:17 and John 4:7-15 and 7:37-39.

[15]Hopko, *Bible and Church History*, 64-5.

[16]This verse is used in the petitions of the Litany of Supplication in Orthodox services.

[17]Jacques Ellul, *The Political Illusion* (Random House, Vintage Books, 1972).

[18]If "Nero Caesar" is written in Hebrew, and if the letters are read as numbers, as is possible with the letters of the Hebrew alphabet, and then if the numbers are added up, the total is 666. For John, Domitian was just another Nero—a mad and vicious persecutor of the Church of Christ.

[19]Hopko, *Bible and Church History*, 64.

[20]*The Harper Study Bible*, footnote on p. 1884.

[21]*The Great Divorce* is the title of a book by C.S. Lewis (Macmillan, 1976).

Selected Bibliography

Study Bibles

The following editions of the Bible contain chapter introductions, explanatory footnotes, detailed annotations and other aids for those wishing to study the Scriptures in depth and detail.

The Harper Study Bible. Zondervan Publishing House, 1965. Presented from an Evangelical Protestant point of view, but excellently done. The text (RSV) does not contain the deuterocanonical books of the Old Testament.

The New Oxford Annotated Bible with the Aprocrypha. Oxford University Press, 1977. The only English-language Bible that contains all of the Old Testament books recognized as canonical by the Orthodox Church. The text is the RSV, and the supplementary study aids represent the best of contemporary Protestant, Roman Catholic and Orthodox biblical scholarship. Strongly recommended.

The New Scofield Reference Bible. Oxford University Press, 1967. The King James Version, without the Old Testament deuterocanonical books, and annotated from a Fundamentalist Protestant point of view.

The Oxford Study Edition of the New English Bible with the Apocrypha. Oxford University Press, 1976. Represents the viewpoint of contemporary mainstream Protestant scholarship. Useful.

One-Volume Bible Commentaries

Raymond E. Brown, et al., eds. *The Jerome Biblical Commentary.* Prentice-Hall, 1968.

D. Gurthrie, et al., eds. *The New Bible Commentary: Revised.* William B. Eerdmans Publishing Co., 1971.

Charles M. Laymon, gen. ed. *The Interpreter's One-Volume Commentary on the Bible.* Abingdon Press, 1971.

William Neil. *Harper's Bible Commentary.* Harper & Row, 1975.

General Reference Materials

David and Pat Alexander, eds. *Eerdmans' Handbook to the Bible.* Wm.B. Eerdmans, 1973.

G.A. Buttrick, et al., eds. *The Interpreter's Dictionary of the Bible: An Illustrated Encyclopedia.* 4 vols. and supplement. Abingdon Press, 1962.

J.D. Douglas, et al., eds. *The New Bible Dictionary.* Wm.B. Eerdmans, 1973.

James Strong. *Strong's Exhaustive Concordance of the Bible with Greek and Hebrew Dictionary.* Crusade Bible Publishers, no date.

Burton H. Throckmorton, ed. *Gospel Parallels: A Synopsis of the First Three Gospels.* Thomas Nelson & Sons, 1972.

W.E. Vine. *An Expository Dictionary of New Testament Words with their Precise Meanings for English Readers.* Fleming H. Revell, 1966.

Books of Interest by Non-Orthodox Authors

William Barclay. *Introducing the Bible.* Abingdon Press, 1972.

F.F. Bruce. *The Message of the New Testament.* Wm.B. Eerdmans, 1973.

Oscar Cullmann. *The New Testament: An Introduction for the General Reader.* Westminster Press, 1968.

Robert M. Grant. *A Short History of the Interpretation of the Bible.* Revised edition. Macmillan, 1972.

Ignatius Hunt. *Understanding the Bible.* Sheed and Ward, 1962.

George Martin. *Reading Scripture as the Word of God: Practical Approaches and Attitudes.* Word of Life, 1975.

Adam W. Miller. *Introduction to the Old Testament.* Pillar Books, 1976.

John R.W. Stott. *Basic Introduction to the New Testament.* Inter-Varsity Press, 1973.

_____. *Understanding the Bible.* Regal Books, 1972.

Books of Interest by Orthodox Authors

Georges A. Barrois. *The Face of Christ in the Old Testament.* SVS Press, 1974.

_____. *Scripture Readings in Orthodox Worship.* SVS Press, 1977.

Nicholas Cabasilas. *The Life in Christ.* SVS Press, 1974.

Anthony M. Coniaris. *No Man Ever Spoke as this Man: The Great I Am's of Jesus.* Light and Life Publishing Co., 1969.

Georges Florovsky. *Bible, Church, Tradition: An Eastern Orthodox View.* Nordland Publishing Co., 1972.

Thomas Hopko. *The Orthodox Faith.* 4 vols. Orthodox Church in America, Department of Religious Education, 1971-1976.

_____. *The Spirit of God.* Morehouse-Barlow Co., 1976.

Veselin Kesich. *The First Day of the New Creation: The Resurrection and the Christian Faith.* SVS Press, 1982.

_____. *The Gospel Image of Christ: The Church and Modern Criticism.* SVS Press, 1972.

_____. *The Passion of Christ.* SVS Press, 1965.

Vladimir Lossky. *In the Image and Likeness of God.* SVS Press, 1974.

_____. *The Mystical Theology of the Eastern Church.* SVS Press, 1976.

John Meyendorff. *Byzantine Theology: Historical Trends and Doctrinal Themes.* Fordham University Press, 1974.

Timothy (Fr. Kallistos) Ware. *The Orthodox Church.* Penguin Books, 1972.

_____. *The Orthodox Way.* SVS Press, 1979.